THE MEN WE LOVED

Male Friendship and Nationalism
in Israeli Culture

Danny Kaplan

Berghahn Books
New York • Oxford

First published in 2006 by

Berghahn Books

www.berghahnbooks.com

© 2006 Danny Kaplan

Library of Congress Cataloging-in-Publication Data

Kaplan, Danny.
    The men we loved : male friendship and nationalism in Israeli culture /
    Danny Kaplan.
        p. cm.
    Includes bibliographical references and index.
    ISBN 1-84545-192-9 -- ISBN 1-84545-193-7 (pbk.)
        1. Men—Israel--Psychology. 2. Male friendship—Israel. 3. National-
    ism—Israel. I. Title.

HQ1090.7.I75K36 2006
302.3'4081095694--dc22

                                                                    2006044471

British Library Cataloguing in Publication Data

A catalogue record for this book is available from the British Library.

Printed in the United States on acid-free paper

ISBN 1-84545-192-9 hardback
ISBN 1-84545-193-7 paperback

To Itzik, the joy of my life

CONTENTS

ACKNOWLEDGEMENTS

In a book that is dedicated to reflections on friendship it can get particularly challenging to reflect on all the friends that supported me during this process.

This book is first and foremost the product of inspiring conversations with a range of Israeli men who shared with me their stories and thoughts about their personal friendships. Although I couldn't present their stories in full, I hope that I have been able to bring across some of the profound feelings that they have experienced in their male bonds.

My deepest thanks go to Niza Yanay, who guided me in the most insightful and caring way during my doctorate research at Ben Gurion University of the Negev. Her continuing support during various stages of the writing processes and beyond has been a tremendous source of encouragement. I am also indebted to Eyal Ben-Ari for his enduring guidance and advice.

A long list of friends and colleagues have inspired me with lively discussions or made fruitful comments on various parts of this work. I thank Gideon Aran, Dan Bar-On, Nitza Berkovitch, Yishai Tobin, Yoram Bilu, Chen Bram, Ariela Friedman, Yehuda Goodman, Yuval Harari, Sarit Helman, Hanna Herzog, Ruthellen Josselson, Orly Lubin, Oren Meyers, Tamar Rapoport, Liora Sion, Sasha Weitman, Vered Vinitzky-Seroussi, and Yuval Yonay. I had the benefit of exploring and corroborating some of the ideas put forward in this book with eager students during research seminars on friendship and courses on masculinity held at Hebrew University, Bar Ilan University and the Academic College of Tel Aviv-Yafo.

I am grateful to Meira Weiss, Michael Kimmel, Kate Ferguson, Josh Gamson, Emmanuel Sivan, Haim Hazan, and Miguel Val de Almeida for the advice and encouragement in the process of making this book come true. Marion Berghahn at Berghahn Books has been singularly supportive in the publishing procedure. I am indebted to her and the production team for their skilled editing. I thank Eyal Siles for his involvement in some of the early interviewing and Lilach Nahaloni for her committed work in transcribing the interview recordings. Special thanks to my brother Gal Kaplan for continuingly assisting me in polishing and style editing the manuscript.

My close companions Hagit Bachar, Hami Verbin, Yohay Hakak, and Elly Teman have stood by me like a bridge in times of troubled water. My parents have also been a constant source of support. Finally, I thank my beloved partner Itzik Nahum for giving me everything that a man could ask for in friendship.

Financial support for writing this book was provided by the the Koret Foundation and the Lady Davis Postdoctoral program at Hebrew University, the Horowitz Research Institute on Society and Economy at Tel Aviv University, and the Dafna Izraeli grant for research on gender at Bar-Ilan University. Selected parts of chapter 4 have appeared in "Folk Models of Dyadic Male Bonds in Israeli Culture," *The Sociological Quarterly* 47, forthcoming. Parts of Chapter 5 have been published in "Public Intimacy: Dynamics of Seduction in Homosocial Interactions," *Symbolic Interaction* 28, no. 4: 571–595. Some of the ideas discussed in chapter 6 and 7 appeared in an abridged version in "Fraternal Friendship and Commemorative Desire" *Social Analysis* 50, no.1: 127–146. I thank Adi Nes for permission to use his artwork for the cover design

PROLOGUE

In this book I explore emotions associated with male friendship. I argue that some of these emotions can only be experienced through a sense of loss, and that by entering the public discourse they transform into rituals of passionate commemoration, suggesting a dynamics of collective necrophilia. I perceive this transformation of face-to-face emotions of friendship into a collective mode of desire to be a core aspect of the imagined community, especially in its national form. I situate this claim in contemporary Israeli culture. As an accentuated case of a society going through an enduring political and military national struggle, the Israeli case offers a magnified instance of what may be a profoundly broader male-to-male (homosocial) phenomenon, a phenomenon of commemorative desire. My analysis unfolds step by step, proceeding through stories of men's friendships in typical sites of male interactions, such as school, recreational activities, the workplace, and the military, and concluding with collective, national practices.

The story behind this book is twofold. Originally, what set me out on this study was an incidental expression I came across while reading a book on IDF (Israeli Defense Force) veterans. In an interview with psychologist Amia Lieblich (1989: 57), one of the soldiers, Eitan, born in a religious Kibbutz, recounted the social ties that developed among the men in his infantry unit, after completing their training stage:

> At this stage you become very close to others in the unit. You have more time to sit and chat. You get to know them better and you love them more. This is the famous love among soldiers, which is as much a mystery as love of women.

The question of combat fraternity has intrigued me for a host of reasons. My own experiences in a field-unit on the Israeli border as a soldier and officer (although not in a combat role) left me with something of a void in place of the bonds that such a close-knit situation is alleged to forge between men. Feeling somewhat detached from the dominant social circles of my military unit, I assumed that being gay limited my own experiences in such matters. In fact, only a few of the men I served with remained in contact with each other after terminating their military service. Yet I kept hearing stories of such deep friendships, or at least I thought I did. I felt that when it came to male love, my earlier work on military and masculinity based on interviews with gay and bisexual soldiers (Kaplan 2003a) only scratched the tip of the iceberg.

Returning to Eitan's wording, I sought to understand more of the meaning of this "mysterious" bond. What "famous love" was he referring to? And what does "getting to know them better" imply? I sensed that his phrasing implicitly addressed the renowned biblical verse of King David's lament for Jonathan: "I am distressed for you, my brother Jonathan; very pleasant have you been to me; your love to me was wonderful, passing the love of women" (2 Samuel 1:26).[1] How does such a verse become entwined in the story of a contemporary Jewish-Israeli man?

These questions are not limited to military culture. I felt that there are broader issues at stake related to Israeli society, the sociology of male emotions, and nationalism. As part of my PhD dissertation I set out to explore friendship and fraternity through interviews with heterosexual men. Between 1999 and 2000 I conducted thirty in-depth interviews with a range of Israeli men, discussing their male friendships in various settings and at various stages throughout their lives. This corpus formed my initial group of informants (See appendixes 1 and 2).

Little did I know then that on the very same day that I completed my last interview, 27 September 2000, a Palestinian roadside bomb would be set off against an Israeli patrol in the Gaza Strip; followed the next day by Ariel Sharon's visit to the Temple Mount in Jerusalem, it would mark the start of the second Palestinian Uprising (*Intifada Al-Aqsa*), one of the bloodiest wars in the history of the Jewish-Arab conflict. At the time I was studying toward my PhD at Ben Gurion University in Beer Sheva but most of my social life took place in and around Jerusalem, which was at the heart of the conflict. Although my work has nothing to do with everyday politics, and does not address the Israeli-Palestinian conflict directly, it is inevitably colored by the impact of the events. The themes of solidarity, sacrifice, and death, which were already present implicitly in some of the informants' accounts the previous year, gradually shifted to the forefront of my analysis. Fortunately, only a few of the men I interviewed had experienced the death of a close friend. But this made these men's implicit allusion to these themes all the more significant for me. My study gradually expanded to ethnographic observations based on media coverage of current events, analysis of popular cultural artifacts, and some participant observations in public commemoration ceremonies. While still focusing on friendship and male fraternity, I became more interested in how the two were related to national discourse.

Combining the personal with the political, I explore in this book how private friendships draw on national discourse and, vice versa, how national discourse draws on the emotions of friendship. Employing a phenomenological and ethnomethodological perspective, I analyze the relations between *haverut*, the Hebrew word for various patterns of friendship and sociability, and *re'ut*, a more literary term that specifically connotes heroic, male friendship. Throughout this book I go back to the themes surrounding King David's elegy, which has become a cornerstone of commemoration of fallen soldiers in the Western Tradition, and in Israel in particular. I explore diverse manifestations and displacements of the "wondrous love" between men in Israeli men's lived experience and discuss its implications for nationalism. My case study is both very narrow and very broad. As an ethnographic study focusing on emotions it does not entail a holistic exploration of Israeli localized culture as a whole, but rather a holistic exploration of a *localized emotion* within that given culture. I attempt to explore how a particular set of concepts, values and feelings associated with the idea and practices of male friendship are shaped in the Israeli national context.

Chapter 1 briefly sketches several simplified signposts in the traditions of fraternal friendship in Western thought. It draws a distinction between two leading ideological frameworks for friendship, liberalism, and nationalism, set in the modern distinction between private and public life.

Chapter 2 discusses how Zionist culture provides an exemplary case of the national-ideological framing of fraternal friendship. Fraternal friendship is associated with the Hebrew word *re'ut*, originally a general term for friendship which has narrowed in meaning and now signifies predominantly combat fraternity. Perceiving the modern pioneers and soldiers as successors to the biblical tradition of heroism, Zionist pedagogy reinterpreted and inculcated biblical epics of comradeship into the fabric of the modern Israeli state.

The subsequent chapters turn to explore how friendship is constructed in concrete lived experience, first in everyday life and then in national spaces perceived as sacred. Each chapter presents a meeting point between canonical representations of friendships and their interpretations in narratives and practices of contemporary Israeli men, moving gradually toward culturally more rigid dimensions. In chapter 3 I follow the narratives of long-lasting close friendships as they unfold in different life stages, looking at alternative perceptions of *origin* through which the formation and maintenance of friendships are made sense of. A central account of male friendships focuses on shared activities. This leads to a broader, cultural construct of shared past in line with a familial rhetoric of friendship. Other accounts stress a sudden and immediate "click" relating to a sense of a shared destiny, and reflecting a romantic rhetoric.

Moving to issues of male relatedness and intimacy, chapter 4 delineates an explicit folk-model employed by the interviewees to make sense of the emotions involved in their bonds and discerns two different styles of sharing. The first one revolves around the image of the *hevreman*, endorsing "cool sociability" set in physical action, in line with common gender distinctions; the second revolves around "intellectual sociability," stressing "soul talk" and ideological or psychologistic discourse.

The next chapters address more covert terrain in the discourse and practice of friendship, unraveling how the common rhetoric is haunted and overshadowed by ambiguous emotions, emotions that are at times constrained and at times sanctioned and legitimized by the hegemonic male discourse. Chapter 5 explores homosocial humor set in the context of the group joking relationship and "public intimacy." The men employ a lingo of eccentric and ambivalent speech and bodily gestures that teases the participants and forms a dynamics of seduction. The semipublic spaces of these interactions displace homoerotic desire under the guise of instrumental activity.

Finally, chapters 6 and chapter 7 address the cultural context of *re'ut*, male friendship set in sacred spaces associated with mythic epics of heroic male bonding. Chapter 6 describes three structural features of a hegemonic script for male bonding set in military action: (1) the traumatizing setting that induces the bond; (2) emotional moments of "crying together" that symbolically form a conjugal pact; (3) the maintenance of the pact over time, based on a semi- "post-traumatic" solidarity. Although military friendships rarely develop into intensive, everyday relationships, they are often perceived as strong, enduring, and everlasting.

Chapter 7 explores ways through which male relatedness is made sense of in light of the spectral ideal of death. Instances of anxiety and loss on the verge of death bring the men closer together. Whereas other homosocial circumstances present diverse and often displaced expressions of male affection, circumstances of loss and sites of commemoration present a unique instance where desire between men is publicly declared and legitimized. The rituals of *re'ut* employed in the commemoration of the fallen men serve a double function. First, they mask a national ideology that demands self-sacrifice and martyrdom. Second, they produce a symbolic stance of collective necrophilia, an erotic gazing upon the dead, transforming a repudiated personal sentiment into a national genre of relatedness.

In the discussion I wrap up the main arguments of this book. The interrelations between male fraternity and commemoration provide a crucial link between individual friendship and national solidarity. Rituals of commemoration are not only gendered, they are also eroticized. The act of declaring the lost and yet eternal friendship symbolizes a passionate 'blood pact' between men. At the political level, this passion serves to explain how the imagined ties of the national can take precedence over the blood ties of kinship and matrimony. I interpret fraternal friendship as an emotional-ideological space of both identification and desire whereby the citizen brother becomes, via national commemoration, the desired brother.

Notes

1. All English translations of the Bible have been taken from *The New Oxford Annotated Bible* by Herbert May and Bruce Metzger (1973). However, the term 'wonderful' is inaccurate and should have been translated from the Hebrew as 'wondrous' or 'mysterious.'

PART I
FRIENDSHIP AND IDEOLOGY

Friendship is often viewed as a relatively free-floating social form, when compared to kinship and contractual (hetero)sexual ties. Many studies take as their point of departure the premise that friendship is a "pure" relationship in terms of its voluntary nature, its moral qualities, and its disconnectedness from collectivities with clear interests, boundaries, and power (Eisenstadt 1974: 141). For instance, Cora Du Bois (1974: 16) notes that "friendships are voluntary and gratuitous acts rather than exclusively items of social behavior" involving variable "gratifications" that "may be phrased as intimacy, social conformity, protection, social prestige" and more. Although there is great variation in the manner in which societies distinguish between different kinds of friends, bonds of friendship are often perceived as "voluntary-preferential" in character, lacking the prescribed status of age and sex that define kinship and marriage relationships.

This book follows a different approach, one that views friendship as a social relationship nested in political constraints. Precisely because of its ill-defined quality, friendship is highly dependent on normative indoctrination, which often remains implicit and goes unacknowledged. As an array of emotions, interactions, and expectations friendship is shaped by collective knowledge and ideals shared by members of the social group. As such it is implicated both in lived experience as well as in ideological form. As individuals make sense of their activities in a fundamentally "prereflective" way, ideologies often take the form of tacit knowledge (Fine and Sandstrom 1993; Rogers 1981). I focus on ideological aspects of friendship associated with hegemonic masculinity, a form of male social ascendancy, constructed in relation to various subordinated masculinities as well as in relation to women. Hegemonic masculinity is achieved in a play of social forces extending beyond contests of brute power into the organization of private life and cultural processes (Connell 1987: 183-184).

It produces cultural representations that dominate the very conceptual categories through which men interpret their emotional experiences, including the experience of friendship.

Throughout the ages, various ideologies and schools have attempted to tackle the concept of friendship, almost exclusively in its male form, and to explicitly define or appropriate it. Although I avoid a theoretical exposition, the present work focuses on the interrelations between male friendship and one such ideology, loosely defined as nationalism. The Zionist-Israeli context presents an exemplary case of the ideological labeling that a national framework provides for friendship.

Chapter One

THE CASE OF FRATERNAL FRIENDSHIP

Friendship and the Political in Western Thought

As a topic of scholarly inquiry friendship draws on various discourses in the social sciences and humanities. It incorporates political science and sociological debates on nationalism, liberalism, and socialism and their treatment of *solidarity* and *comradeship*; it involves military, organizational, and behavioral studies on small-group *cohesion* or *fraternities*; it draws on social psychological and developmental research on dyadic *attachment* and *intimacy*; and, finally, on psychoanalytic scholarship and postmodern, queer-theory analysis of *eroticism* and *sexuality*. These discourses are often disconnected and cut off from each other. Dorothy Hammond and Alta Jablow (1987: 243) point out that friendship is interstitial in the social structure of most Western cultures, compared with examples of institutionalized friendships in some other societies. For instance, in the North American context a plethora of books, in genres ranging from pop-psychology to theology have struggled with the meanings of friendship.[1] As noted by Terri Apter and Ruthellen Josselson (1998: 31), the very term "friend" may be used for quite different purposes and take many shapes, ranging from "intimate confidante" to a "tennis partner." Analyzing various patterns of male friendship in non-Western societies, Robert Brain (1976: 105-106) argues that friendship has lost both emotional expression and ceremonial patterning in contemporary Western cultures.

A central tradition of friendship that has influenced modern Western thought is that of the Hellenistic world. Greek thought provided the roots for a central assumption underlying much of modern political understanding: individual, specific friendships could serve as an exemplary analogy for discussing larger social phenomena such as political ties. Plato's discussion of *philia* and *eros*, and most significantly, Aristotle's definitions of friendship types, make the bonds of friendship situated in individual emotional experience into a prerequisite of a just political order. In *Nichomachean Ethics*, one of the earliest explicit formulations of friendship influencing subsequent Western thinking, Aristotle defined three types of primary friendships: first, the higher friendship based on virtue, a bond between two men "who are alike in excellence or virtue," advancing the happiness of each other as an end in itself, a perfect, altruistic relationship (Aristotle 1962: 1156b6-7); second, useful friendship grounded in utility, where the partners feel affection not for one another per se but in terms of their usefulness to each other; third, friendship grounded on pleasure, guided by emotions existing typically among young people, who easily replace one bond after another for the sake of gratification. Aristotle also introduced the notion of civic friendship, the binding force of the community, noting that "friendship also seems to hold states together" (Aristotle 1962: 1155a22). Aristotle's thinking initiated a wide-ranging debate on the relation between an ethic of civic friendship and the notion of personal or primary friendship. Without going deeply into these long-debated issues, a common interpretation of civic friendship identifies it as an extension of primary friendship of the virtuous kind. In a just society citizens experience a form of friendship with each other, doing things for their fellow citizens both individually and as a citizen body, on the basis of shared values, goals, and a sense of justice (Schwarzenbach 1996: 7). By contributing to the utmost actualization of individual citizens, primary friendship generates and sustains the highest good of all, that of the city (Stern-Gillet 1995: 4). Civic friendship, in its turn, is altruistic in the sense that good citizens wish to do what is good for the sake of each other (Scollmeier 1994: 83).

Turning to the modern era, two central processes associated with modernity shaped contemporary ideologies regarding friendship. The first process which has received the majority of scholarly attention, is the rise of individualism. The process of industrialization sharpened the polarization between the growing public realm of the market, the modern state, and the bureaucratic organization on the one hand, and the emerging private realm of intimacy and emotionality on the other hand, embodied in cultural sites such as the nuclear family, primary groups, romantic love, and friendships (Oliker 1998; Silver 1997). Reinforced by ideas of the Enlightenment, an emerging ethos of "personal life" shaped what historian Lawrence Stone has referred to as "affective individualism," a new mentalité that sanctioned the expression of autonomy, self-expression, and introspection as well as the manifestation of sentiment toward intimate others (Stone 1977: 18; quoted in Oliker 1998: 24).

From this perspective, friendship has gradually become more and more detached from the political, public sphere. Philippe Aries (1979; overviewed in Kumar 1997) claimed that families in the premodern European society inhabited a space that was simultaneously private and public, mixing servants and masters, friends and kinship, intimates and strangers. The burdens—social, economic and emotional—were shared "in a sea of sociability." Aspirations for love, companionship, consolation, nurture, and protection were not restricted to the immediate family, as in the modern sensibility. Along these lines, Alan Bray and Michel Rey (1999) emphasized the notion of "the friend" in sixteenth- and seventeenth-century England as a patron, a benefactor, someone to rely on in a potentially hostile world. In such a world bodily intimacy between friends was foremost a form of symbolic capital and a signal of comforting security, reminiscent of the ritualized friendships of ancient Greece.

In contrast, based on the novel eighteenth-century social thought of the Enlightenment, Allan Silver discusses how friendship in modernity dissolved traditional ties based on "necessitudo" or "clan brotherhood"—obligatory bonds defined by "custom, corporate group, station and estate" (Silver 1997: 55). New ideas of civil society based on universal sympathy formed a new kind of friendship relationship freed from the instrumental and calculative orientations that characterized the public realm. It was to be dissociated from impersonal negotiations, explicit contract, rational exchange, and the labor market and to inhabit a distinctive domain of the private life. Friendship became the purest and most widely available instance of the private and the personal—a relation that draws on subjective definitions, ungoverned by the structural definitions that bear on family and kinship. It was the ideal arena for modern notions of personal agency and freedom, based on liberal ideology and morality (Silver 1997; 1990). Under this paradigm friendship represents an epitome of the "pure relationship" that has gradually developed in the late modern age, a voluntary commitment based on intensified intimacy and a tendency towards symmetry, as outlined by Anthony Giddens (1991).

Much of this theorizing on friendship lacks a gendered perspective. As is so often the case in traditional scholarship, it extrapolates from predominantly male experiences to general ideas of friendship. Traditional androcentric (male-oriented) scholarship uses the term "man" not to discuss distinctive considerations of men *qua* men, but as a generic word for human. In doing so, it misdirects attention away from the study of masculinity as a specifically male experience situated in varying social, cultural, and historical formulations. A male-focused theory of relatedness requires a cultural study of gender (Brod 1987: 264).[2] Recently, with the proliferation of research on masculinity a growing body of studies has referred explicitly to male friendship, though mostly in an unsystematic manner (Gutmann 1997: 393).[3] Taking into account gender differences entails anchoring of male relatedness in the sociological division of gender between public and private life, as formulated by feminist thought (Arendt 1958; Rosaldo 1974). The bulk of feminist scholarship identifies male activity with the public realm, and associates the private or "domestic" realm with feminine spaces, typically focusing on issues of family and intimacy (Weintraub 1997). As industrialization moved men more and more to the public sphere, it offered them fewer opportunities to cultivate the kinds of intimate relationships associated with the private sphere. Men's tasks in life, together with society's ideals of hegemonic masculinity, turned them away from emotionality (Oliker 1998: 29-30). As a master cultural category in Western sensibility, the very concept of emotions was to be associated not only with subjectivity, self-expression, and individuality, but also with the notion of the feminine (Lutz 1986: 299).

While the process of industrialization and the ensuing cult of individualism have shaped much of our current understanding of friendship, modernity is associated with yet another process that in turn engenders a totally different kind of ideological labeling for friendship: the ideology of nationalism. National ideology, more than any other, shaped global history throughout the nineteenth and twentieth centuries. Numerous theories address various conditions in modernity that enabled the expansion of nation-states across the globe, such as the decline of religion as a political power and the increase of social mobility for the masses (Gellner 1983), the development of large bureaucracies with strong surveillance mechanisms (Giddens 1987), or the greater ability of elites to manipulate opposition by inventing traditions (Hobsbawm 1982).[4] Among other things, the rise of modern nationalism is related to notions of civil solidarity based on an old-new idea of fraternity, a fraternity associated with an ethic of masculinity and self-sacrifice. Carol Pateman (1989: 49) discusses the ways that male fraternity acts as a binding force between the individual and the modern social order. Adherence to passions of nationality and male solidarity stems directly from a masculine identity that relies on values of self-sacrifice at the expense of liberalist notions of individual self-interest. As noted by Eyal Ben-Ari (1998: 112), ideals of male expendability contribute to the continuity of the nation-state by encouraging men to act according to a code of conduct that advances collective interests through overcoming inhibitions.

A detailed historical account presenting some of these ideas as they unfolded in Western Europe is provided in the seminal work of George Mosse (1975; 1985; 1990; 1993; 1996). Mosse explores the interrelations between modern symbols and practices of nationalism and the development of pervasive values and ideals of masculinity. Since the nineteenth century national ideology has celebrated masculine stereotypes of willpower, self-control, honor, and the courage to die on one's sword as part of its self-image. Such ideals of masculinity were no longer limited to personal virtue but were invoked as a symbol of national generation and as basic to the self-definition of the modern society.

The birth of modern nationalism is very much associated with the emergence of citizens' armies of volunteers and conscripts in France, England, and Prussia. The French Revolution glorified the soldiers' contribution and their death in war. The new soldiers experienced a new kind of community held together by common danger and a common goal—a community of brotherhood (Mosse 1993: 14-15). Interestingly, this process transformed the meaning of *soldiering* from that of paid work (its literal meaning in late Latin, stemming from the Roman coin *solidus*) to its symbolic opposite: a collective civic act of *solidarity* (stemming from the Latin *solidum,* meaning the whole sum and applied in Roman law for a legal unit, such as a family, that accepts liability for the acts of each of its integrants). As noted by David Morgan (1994: 174), the image of combat heroism was similarly transformed from a quality of the individual warrior to an asset of group activity, of the so-called brothers in arms.

A related form of political male activity that was instrumental in national struggles throughout Europe was participation in nationalist fraternities or secret societies. Especially following the collapse of Napoleon's rule and the establishment of the Holy Alliance, grassroots secret societies of conspirators led national agitation. They were often modeled after non-political fraternities such as the Freemasons, incorporating initiation ceremonies, oaths, and gatherings in lodges. The societies recruited among the middle class and represented the cause of liberalism against the reactionary governments. They were able to force concessions from the aristocracy whenever they managed to garner the support of military officers who were popular enough with the troops to incite rebellion (Annan 1967).

In Germany, additional socialization agents that were significant in spreading national consciousness were the gymnastic movement, student fraternities, and youth movements. As horizontal, voluntary organizations with pedagogic objectives, they afforded content and meaning to the emerging sense of "fatherland" through advocating physical, social, and spiritual activities. They sanctioned moral behavior characterized by both individual freedom and group spirit, subscribing to a distinctly male code of conduct in line with classical Greek aesthetics of male beauty, health, and virtue (Mosse 1975: 128). The hundreds of gymnastic organizations established in the German-speaking states pursued the political unification of a German nation and believed their members to be the masculine elite that could fulfill such a vision (Caplan 2003: 177).

The new politics of nineteenth-century German nationalism were preceded by a cultural era often referred to as the "century of friendship" (Oosterhuis and Kennedy 1991: 8). It is associated with the romantic movement among some middle-class men, influenced by the Protestant school of pietism and the literary intellectual circles of *Sturm und Drang.* As part of their resistance to the rational ethics of the Enlightenment, the Romantics emphasized deep, inner emotions expressed through a sacred bond between kindred spirits. They venerated the expression of passionate feelings, whether in religious belief, intimate friendship, or communal bonds. In particular, they sanctioned suffering, violence, and even death and suicide as highly authentic emotional ideals (Greenfeld 1992: 341-342). Eventually, these romanticist values colored the subsequent German nationalism and paved the way to the glorification of war in terms of fraternity and comradeship. Especially leading up to the First World War, such notions were idealized through the misogynist concept of the

Männerbund, an elite community of men united in emotional attachment who form the core of the nation-state, safeguarding such exalted goals of male friendship as moral strength, self-sacrifice, and spirit. In contrast to earlier ideals of friendship, the idea of comradeship based on the war experience presented a community of men united in the service of the higher cause of nationalism (Mosse 1985; Oosterhuis and Kennedy 1991: 187, 243).

All in all, how can one settle these opposing ideologies and frameworks underlying men's friendships? To begin with, how can we formulate and reconcile primary friendships and civic friendships? Are they not contradictory forms of interaction in modern society? Second, given the dominant modernistic view of friendship as a private emotion, what are we to make of fraternal friendships? Should we consider them a remnant of premodern public sociability? If that is the case, how have they become so dominant in modern national discourse? Furthermore, do men's social networks, business relations, exchanges of ideas, and political and military commitments represent instrumental interests lacking in expressive, affective attributes? Then again, what is instrumental about sacrificing oneself for one's country?

Such are the questions and contradictions raised by juxtapositioning men's relatedness between the ideology of the "pure relationship" on the one hand, and that of fraternal friendship on the other hand. In his book *The Politics of Friendship*, Jacques Derrida (1997) delineates many of the intricacies of Western thought pertaining to friendship, fraternity, and the political. He discusses references to friendship in the work of a wide variety of philosophers, from Aristotle, Plato, Cicero, Montaigne, Kant, and Hegel to Nietzsche, Schmitt, Blanchot, and Bataille. Fraternal friendship holds a hegemonic place in the philosophical canon, a phallogocentric domination excluding both feminine friendships and heterosexual friendships. The figure of "the brother" is eventually the core structure of the civil regime. It plays an organizing role in the definition of justice, morality, and democracy. Political issues of sovereignty, power, and representation are marked by the privilege granted to brotherhood. By looking at some of the prevalent features of this hegemonic concept of friendship, especially the tension between camaraderie and enmity, Derrida interrogates the relation between friendship and the very idea of the political. Typical to his unique method of deconstruction, he examines and reexamines the ways in which politics and friendship are homogeneous, contradictory, or both.

Male friendship in Western thought has been characterized ever since Aristotle by mutuality and symmetry. In contrast to the two other traditional relationships in the patriarchal social order, kinship and matrimony, friendship invokes a notion of equality between the two parties. Whereas parent-child and male-female relations are grounded in fundamental difference, male-male relations are grounded in fundamental similarity, and are professedly based on the egalitarian idea of fraternity. Yet Derrida underscores a consistent polarity within friendship, between a political-economical relationship on one hand and an "ultimate," noneconomical and asymmetrical relationship on the other. At the very heart of fraternal friendship lies this opposition between what is systematically conceptualized as a manifest, public, testimonial, and political bond but at the same time is also secretive, private, illegible, apolitical, and mostly not conceptualized (Derrida 1997: 277).

Derrida's discussion of friendship is beyond the scope of this book. I will draw only briefly on some explicit themes from his writing in the final parts of my discussion. Yet his overall involvement in the topic of friendship stimulated me in thinking and rethinking how the political, or ideological, in friendship is bound with the emotional (a term that he did not explicitly address). His work encouraged me to look for spaces in men's lived experiences of friendship that are simultaneously emotional and ideological. Broadly speaking, such an approach coalesces with the postmodern social constructionist perspective of emotions, situating emotions both in cultural-historical context and in symbolic systems of shared knowledge, produced within discursive practices (Yanay 1996: 24). Inspired by Derrida's contemplations, I read fraternal friendship as an "emotional-ideological space"—a collective system of often contradictory, shared emotions, motivated by the productive quality of hegemonic power relations to both constrain and sanction particular discourses and practices of friendship.

Male Homosociality

Lacking sufficiently focused and theoretical studies on friendship and masculinity, there is considerable inconsistency in discussing the issues involved, especially in terms of men's emotions. A key concept for exploring the emotional-ideological spaces of men's friendship is that of homosociality, that is, the social interactions between men that emerge in exclusive same-sex cultural sites and institutions. Over the last two decades, sociohistorical studies have begun to focus on male culture as such, predominantly within the Anglophone world. For instance, exploring men's socialization in North America, Michael Kimmel (1996: 62) describes the "homosocial life, a world of 'rude freedom' outside the conventional boundaries of civilization and away from wives" that inspired the rush to the "Wild West" during the nineteenth century. Elisabeth Pleck and Joseph Pleck (1980: 13) argue that these exclusive, homosocial settings in the battlefield, pubs, fraternities, and the workplace not only created a differentiated male subculture but also encouraged men to forge intimate ties, based on love and affection between equals. Anthony Rotundo (1989) investigated letters, diaries, and oral histories of middle-class men in

New England in the nineteenth century. He concluded that their friendship patterns were similar in their social acceptability, daily content, and physical manifestation to female relationships. The primary difference he observed is that male relationships were bound by the life-course and did not continue into married life, as did their female equivalents; hence, only in their youth were men able to establish strong intimate relationships with other men verging on romance, emotions that later diminished with the onset of career and marriage commitments.

These studies of nineteenth-century male culture suggest a far less stringent distinction between intimate friendship and sociability than is perceived in twentieth-century culture, at least in the Anglo-American context (Hansen 1992: 54). Writings by nineteenth-century European men and their American literary successors were dominated by representations of male friendships as intimate and romanticized, verging on the explicitly sexual. This trend may have been most manifest in the German culture were romantic ideals of emotional and spiritual friendships were open to physical sensuality (Oosterhuis and Kennedy 1991: 10-11). The German word for friend, *Freund*, was often used to mean lover, and *Freundshaft* referred to "erotic-affectional relations, either hetero- or homosexual" (Katz 1992: 450). Michel Foucault argues that since the seventeenth century European institutions such as the military, schools, and the universities have minimized and controlled male affectional relations. This in turn created new pressures in subsequent centuries on sexual acts between men. According to Foucault, "[t]he disappearance of friendship as a social relation and the declaration of homosexuality as a social/political/medical problem are the same process" (Foucault 1997: 171). Allan Bray's brilliant analysis of seventeenth-century friendship in English society presents a similar process (Bray and Rey 1999).

Perhaps the most illuminating theoretical formulation of this trend has been put forward by Eve Sedgwick, based on her innovative queer theory approach. In an analysis of selected English novels of the eighteenth and nineteenth centuries, Sedgwick introduced the phrase "male homosocial desire" to explore the continuum between the homosocial and the homoerotic. She argues that in men's relationships with other men in contemporary Western culture, emotional and sexual expression is often suppressed in the interest of maintaining power. This break between the homosocial and the homoerotic is far less accentuated in female bonding, in non-European cultures, and in premodern Europe. The repressed erotic component of male desire accounts for "correspondences and similarities between the most sanctioned forms of male bonding and the most reprobate expressions of homosexuality" (Sedgwick 1985: 22).

Male homosociality plays a pivotal role in the productive quality of power relations that serve to sanctify masculine identity. Judith Butler (1990) underscored the *proscriptive* basis of gender identity. Instead of viewing gender identity as a pre-assigned set of internal traits, or even as a descriptive formulation based on the social construction of human experience, it is to be understood as a construed relationship among sex, gender, sexual practice, and desire that relates to a dominant normative structure, also known as "compulsory heterosexuality" (Rich 1980).[5] Yet inherent in a proscriptive regulation of male identity, and in its differentiation from the female, is not only a compulsory heterosexuality, but also a *manifested homosociality*, a sociocultural relationship between men aimed at preserving male interests. Based on Claude Lévi-Strauss's (1969) structural analysis of kinship and social exchange, Luce Irrigray (1985a: 101-103) discusses how sociocultural exchange occurs exclusively among men, introducing the notion of a phallocentric economy.[6] Following Irrigray, Butler unravels how the masculine identity is established through an overt act of differentiation between patrilineal clans. The "differentiating" moment of social exchange appears to be a bond between men. The phallocentric economy depends on a "difference" that is never manifested but always presupposed. The relations among patrilineal clans are based on a repressed sexuality, a relationship between men that is about the bonds of men, but takes place through the heterosexual exchange of women (Butler 1990: 38-41).

Michael Kimmel (1994) framed the homosocial aspect of male identity in both social and psychoanalytic terms, and from a male-oriented perspective. As the central developmental task for men is understood to be the achievement of a secure identity as a man, this task becomes a homosocial enactment. Men feel they are under the constant scrutiny and gaze of other men. Male peers or figures of authority evaluate the individual's performance, approve of him, and grant him acceptance into the realm of manhood. Hence, men boast of their accomplishments to one another—from sexual conquest to wealth and power. Instances of heroic conquest of women carry a recurrent homosocial evaluation. This enactment is fraught with the risk of failure and with intense competition. The overriding emotion is one of fear. In the classic Freudian model the fear of the father's power pushes the young boy away from his desire for his mother and towards identification with his father, but this identification involves a repudiation of the potential desire toward the father, and transforms into a flight from intimacy with other men—a repudiation that is never fully successful and hence constantly reenacted in every homosocial relationship. The real fear is not fear of woman but of being ashamed or humiliated in front of other men (Kimmel 1994).[7]

Male friendships therefore extend on a continuum from the homosocial to the homoerotic, a continuum whose visibility in modern Western cultures is radically disrupted (Sedgwick 1985: 1). The term 'homoerotic' should be carefully distinguished from the homosexual. Typically, the homoerotic potential in male relatedness is excluded and disavowed by redefining it as homosexual, and is thus prevented from being negotiated in men's everyday experience. The dividing line, in the context of the present focus on emotions, is that homosexual feelings denote a conscious knowledge of an emotion that is "essentially" there but may not be discussed or performed; it is, in Oscar Wilde's words, the "love that dare not speak its name."[8] In contrast, the homoerotic within homosocial desire represents only a cultural marker, a displacement of ambivalent emotions; it is a love that "never was," a repudiated love that cannot be grieved (Butler 1997: 138). How do these notions figure in the present case of fraternal friendship?

The prevalent framing of friendship in modernity as a social relation between individuals, a formulation that is shaped by liberal thought, precludes an alternative, collective framing that is shaped by national ideology. It also overlooks the ambivalent interplay between these two contradictory levels of the male-to-male experience—the personal, seemingly apolitical level that is considered private, secret, and illegible on the one hand, and the collective, political level that is public, manifest, and testimonial on the other. The homoerotic within the homosocial is a displaced marker that plays on the rupture between these two levels of cultural representation. The purpose of the present work is to explore this interplay in the national context. Recently, anthropologists and cultural historians have joined political sociologists in an attempt to understand the success and spread of nationalism in the modern era. For example, Benedict Anderson's (1991) seminal work *Imagined Communities* offers new ways for exploring the origin and expansion of nationalism from a cultural-psychological perspective. One of the attributes of nationalism that Anderson raises as an initial point of his inquiry is the role of fraternity in inducing self-sacrifice, facilitated by top-to-bottom national rituals of commemoration. The nation, he remarks, is "always conceived as a deep horizontal comradeship" (Anderson 1991: 7). However, he fails to analyze more explicitly the passionate attachments that underlie people's "imagining" of their nation or their willingness to die for its sake (Scheff 1994: 278; Smith 1998: 140). Despite the growing interest in the study of nationalism from a gendered perspective (e.g., Enloe 1989; Mosse 1996; Yuval-Davis 1997; Yuval-Davis and Anthias 1989), to date there has been little microanalysis of how the gendered nature of nationalism is mediated by practices and emotions associated with male bonding. The present work offers a preliminary study of how men negotiate national identity through the specific prism of fraternal friendship.

Notes

1. Some random examples are Pogrebin's (1987) wide-ranging and easy-to-read book on friendship in America, Miller's semi-autobiographical midlife quest into men's friendships (1983), and Sokolowski's (2002) article on friendship from a moral/Christian perspective.

2. For instance, Brod (1987) notes that Freud's canonical outline and the ensuing psychodynamic theories which seemingly address men's development distinctively, tend to do so in a universal and ahistorical way. They use the Oedipal myth not as part of a cultural male mythology of a hero and his quest, not as an exploration of male rites of passage, but as a model for generic human development. Instead, a male-focused theory of relatedness entails an exploration of male transitions across the life cycle, acknowledging practices that shape and define these transformations in various cultures. Such is, for instance, David Gilmore's (1990) comparative study on the cultural making of manhood.

3. Gutmann (1997) surveyed major anthropological studies of male enclaves. Some additional rich ethnographic studies that address male relatedness, though not as their prime focus, are the study of erotics among the Sambia in Papua New Guinea (Herdt and Stoller 1990), the study of significant others as "convoys" across the lifespan in modern Japan (Plath 1980), a study of animal theft as a basis of male friendship in a Cretan village (Herzfeld 1985), and the study of male café sociability among Portuguese villagers (Val de Almeida 1996).

4. For a detailed, critical review of the modernist approach see Anthony Smith (1998).

5. By Butler's reading, 'identity' is a normative ideal, an effect of regulatory discursive practice of gender formation and division. The coherence and continuation of the person are not logical analytic features of personhood, but socially instituted and maintained norms of intelligibility (Butler 1990). In particular, Butler challenged the heterosexual/homosexual binary that differentiates between (emotional) identification and (sexual) desire. The normative understanding allows for either (heterosexual) identification with one's own gender and sexual desire for the opposite gender, or (homosexual) identification with the opposite gender and sexual desire for one's own. Yet identifications are multiple and contestatory. Individuals may desire most strongly those individuals who reflect a fantasy of recovering a primary object of a lost love (Butler 1993).

6. Claude Lévi-Strauss (1969: 115) stated that "the total relationship of exchange which constitutes marriage is not established between a man and a women, but between two groups of men, and the woman figures only as one of the objects in the exchange, not as one of the partners." Luce Irrigray (1985b) argues that this patrilineal society is regulated by a "hidden law of homosexuality," whereby the phallus symbolizes masculine desire and therefore remains invisible and forbidden, so as not to expose the true functioning of society. This prohibition is the core of the phallocentric paradigm, creating an absence which assures a presence, the phallic presence.

7. What Kimmel (1994) offered here is the missing piece in the puzzle of desire and identification, noted by Judith Butler in note 5 above: If the pre-Oedipal boy identifies with the mother, and sees his father through her eyes, it is with a combination of awe, emulation, and desire. Repudiating mother and identifying with father only partially answers his dilemma. What is he to do with that homoerotic desire, the desire he felt seeing father the way his mother saw his father? He must repress it, since homoerotic desire is cast as a feminine desire. By Kimmel's reading homophobia is the effort to suppress that desire.

8. A phrase from a poem written by Wilde's lover, Alfred Douglas ("Bosie"). The prosecution in his trial demanded that Wilde explain the phrase; he responded that it refers to the "great affection of an elder for a younger man as there was between David and Jonathan, such as Plato made the very basis of his philosophy, and such as you find in the sonnets of Michelangelo and Shakespeare. It is that deep, spiritual affection that is as pure as it is perfect" (Beckson 1998: 382).

Chapter Two

RE'UT: *FRIENDSHIP IN ZIONIST IDEOLOGY*

Introduction: *Re'ut* and *Haverut*

Zionist-Israeli culture offers an exemplary, indeed extreme case for the emotional-ideological labeling that a national framework provides for friendship. In a television talk show in 2004 celebrating the fifty-sixth anniversary of Israel's independence, one of the participants, Shaikeh Levi, an entertainer and former member of the legendary Israeli comedy group Ha-Gashash Ha-Hiver talked about the things that bothered him in current Israeli society.[1] The one thing that made him feel happy and proud about this country was the bonds of friendship. This friendship that people share with one another, he said, was something unique that couldn't be found in any other country in the world. How does friendship acquire such singularity in Israeli consciousness?

In contemporary Israeli Hebrew, *re'ut*, similar to its synonyms *yedidut* and *haverut*, signifies friendship. However, the three terms differ in their connotations. *Haverut*, the most widely used term for friendship, encompasses diverse meanings of sociability. It may refer both to the interpersonal and supportive sphere of a chum, a pal, an intimate friend, or a buddy, and to a fellow, a comrade, or a member in the organizational and collective domain. In current Hebrew usage it has also become the distinct term to signify an unmarried romantic partner, that is, boy/girlfriend, which is then distinguished from other types of friends by adding the definite article *ha-haver* (and *ha-haverah* for girlfriend).

Unlike *haverut*, *yedidut* invokes only the interpersonal sphere of friendship. In earlier phases of modern Hebrew it was used to imply an intimate and potentially sexual-romantic companionship, and at any rate a relationship that is more than just a friend.[2] In recent years *yadid* has transformed to denote a person who is more than an acquaintance (*makar*) but is not as significant overtime as a close friend or a romantic friend. That *ha-haver* has taken over a role once held by *yadid* may reflect the changes in dating customs in modern-secular Israeli society. In contrast to traditional Jewish prohibitions on dating before marriage, the growing acknowledgment of steady heterosexual ties (and recently of homosexual ties) beyond the preliminary dating stage and prior to the commitment stage of the marriage partnership, has necessitated a more definite term for boy/girlfriend. The result is an even greater extension of meanings for the term *haverut* in current Israeli Hebrew.

In contrast to the myriad meanings of *haverut*, the connotations of *re'ut* have narrowed. To begin with, *re'ut* stands higher in the linguistic register than its synonyms; it is more commonplace in literary form than in oral language. Aside from that, it seems to have partly transformed in meaning. In its traditional usage in Jewish sources *re'ut* carries, similar to *haverut*, a range of connotations. Its meanings extend from the interpersonal sphere to the collective sphere of fraternal or civil relations, in biblical phrases such as *ve-ahavta le-re'acha ka-mocha* ("you shall love your neighbor as yourself," Leviticus 19:18).[3] In contrast, in contemporary Israeli culture *re'ut* is associated with a specific context of friendship. First, it has become more gendered. The terms *haver* and *yadid* easily acquire the feminine form—*havera* and *yedida*, respectively—and are used indiscriminately for same-gender and opposite-gender friendships (although the so-called platonic opposite-gender friendships nevertheless evoke explicit sexual tensions, which same gender bonds do not). In contrast, *re'ut* is used exclusively for same-gender bonds, and predominantly for male-to-male relations under the form *re'a*. The feminine form *re'ah*, denoting women's friendships, appears very seldom in biblical Hebrew and is no longer in usage in modern Hebrew. A derivative form, *ra'aya*, is used in biblical Hebrew to refer to a beloved woman (from a male perspective) and in modern Hebrew as a synonym for wife.

Second, in addition to becoming more gendered than *haverut*, *re'ut* carries a specific association with the military and with joint experiences of hardship more generally. One of the interviewees in the present study, Avi, a 38-year-old tax clerk, made this clear distinction:[4] " . . . people who passed through difficult times together, that's *re'ut* . . . men go through these things mostly in the army, mostly because of that, because that's where you go through all the processes of cohesion and all that stuff . . . if it's not in a military context no one will say *re'ut*, they would always call it *haverut*." What more, having also interviewed men who served in combat units and went through actual combat, I was surprised that for many of them *re'ut* was detached from their personal experience of friendship with fellow soldiers, and associated instead with military tactics and doctrines. General N., who held a senior position in the Air Force, explained that *re'ut* in the battlefield involved "this kind of dynamics of mutual defense and mutual help that is not necessarily on a personal basis . . . it is part of the code of combat . . . it has more to do with the combat doctrine."

It seems that within the military itself *re'ut* has gradually become a form of professional conduct that has little to do with interpersonal sentiments.

In some instances it may even *contradict* the very idea of friendship. One of my contact persons informed me of how, during a recent duty in the military reserve, he noted a conversation between two regular soldiers, an NCO (non-commissioned officer) and his subordinate, regarding the refusal of the latter to cooperate with a fellow soldier. Attempting to persuade the soldier that he should overcome his reservations, the NCO explained that friendship is an individual preference that shouldn't interfere with his work, and that this was exactly the meaning of *re'ut*, namely the duty to work together within the military. The NCO's interpretation places *re'ut* and *haverut* on two opposing poles within the continuum of emotions related to friendship—an interpretation far removed from the primary, biblical meaning of *re'ut* as friendship per se.

To recapitulate, the myriad forms and terms designating male friendship, from the prized quality of an exclusive intimate relationship to a duty-based mode of conduct, reflects the evasive character of homosocial emotions that are culturally constructed, idolized, legitimized, and yet constrained. In its current usage among Zionist constituents of Israeli society re'ut has transformed to connote a specific coloring of homosocial male bonding associated with heroism and military commitments. How did this change come about?

The Institutionalization of Fraternity in Zionist History

Zionist thought developed predominantly in Eastern and Central Europe in the late nineteenth century, influenced by surrounding national movements and the growing threat of anti-Semitism. In this sense, its conceptualization of male fraternity developed along the Western traditions described in chapter 1. Yet given Zionism's self-perception as the direct successor of the biblical people of Israel, it is interesting to follow the specific shape that male bonding has taken among the old-new Jewish nation.

As in most national movements, the majority of Zionist pioneers endorsed a secular lifestyle. In terms of the emergent political culture, however, the pre-state and early-state Jewish community in Israel could be best envisioned as a "civil religion" (Liebman and Don-Yehiya 1983). Instead of tradition being rejected, various Jewish symbols and customs penetrated throughout the political culture and institutions, and were reinterpreted and assigned new values that met contemporary needs. Ratifying and legitimizing Zionist identity entailed a link to a consensual tradition in which country, people, and military power replaced God and religious practices. In particular, Zionist ideology has glorified war for the sake of the people and the homeland by assimilating Jewish heritage of biblical times, tapping a shared sense of common history to reinforce a sense of common destiny. Settlers and soldiers were deemed successors to the tradition of courage, revealed in the biblical period, that had vanished in the two thousand years of Diaspora.[5] The Zionist revolution entailed not only the return of the Jewish people to their old-new homeland, but also an emancipation of the Jewish man. The new image of the Jewish man was to be rid of associations with its Diaspora predecessor that spelled a dislocated, "sheep-like," passive-feminine existence; these were to be replaced with images of physical labor, prowess, and harshness. Zionist masculinity was reconstructed as a masculinity of the body, realized through settlement of the land, and a masculinity of self-defense, accomplished through military power (Biale 1992). In an attempt to reject the Talmudic-Diaspora Jewish value system of colonized, unmanly ethics of survival, Zionist ideology interjected a nineteenth-century romantic value system of manhood as the courage to die on one's sword (Boyarin 1997a: 324).

It is not coincidental that the previous chapter on the roots of fraternal friendship in Europe drew heavily on examples from the German case. These were also the roots of some early Zionist thinkers and activists who were raised in the German-speaking Jewish world at the turn of the twentieth century. In 1886 a handful of German-Jewish students in Breslau established their own exclusive student fraternity, and by the turn of the century nine such fraternities had established a national German association of Jewish students. As a second generation of Jews assimilated into German culture and committed to a secular-liberal worldview, they went one step further in an attempt to publicly embrace German nationalism. Inspired by the German gymnastic movement, they endorsed a new Jewish identity based on "physical strength and agility that will increase Jewish self-confidence and self-respect" (Caplan 2003: 182). The Jewish fraternities employed rituals that were trademarks of general German fraternities, such as songs, duels, and paramilitary symbols.

Whereas such German-Jewish fraternities remained relatively small, parallel organizations of Zionist conviction adopted a corresponding mindset throughout the Jewish world of Central and Eastern Europe. Indeed, Theodor Herzl and Max Nordau, the two leading figures of the Zionist movement, were both affected by a blend of Jewish emancipation and the German masculine value system. They endorsed ideas of enlightenment and liberalism on the one hand, and ideas of nationalism colored by German ideals on the other (Mosse 1993). During his student years in Vienna, Herzl joined a German student fraternity, only to be driven out of the group because of its growing anti-Semitism (Elon 1975). Boyarin (1997b: 285, 290) analyzed how Herzl was preoccupied in his writing with German codes of male honor such as dueling. Nordau explicitly endorsed a new type of "muscle Judaism" and advocated the creation of "deep-chested, powerfully built and keen-eyed men" (Mosse 1993: 164). Influenced by the German gymnastic movement, he viewed the fit and able body as a key to the regeneration of the Jewish national spirit. Echoing the Greek Revival ideals of manliness, Nordau relished a biblical ideal of strong men who could compete on equal terms with "Greek" rivals. Along these lines, he founded the Zionist gymnastic society Bar-Kochba with branches in many Jewish communities (Mosse 1993: 166, 168).

Herzl and Nordau founded so-called Political Zionism. Yet the movement that shaped Zionist activity on the ground is the school known as Practical Zionism, which originated chiefly in Eastern Europe. In the wake of growing anti-Semitism and pogroms in Russia, Practical Zionism advocated actual immigration to Palestine, rural settlement throughout the land, and educational work.[6] While the first wave of immigrants held relatively traditional Jewish values, a second wave of immigrants (the second *aliyah*) subscribed to European revolutionary socialist ideology adapted to the Zionist cause. They sanctified agricultural manual labor together with settlement activity. The historical circumstances of this new generation of immigrants, detached from their families, as well as their ideological inclination to embrace a new Jewish identity, bolstered the significance of the intimate peer-group as a replacement of the traditional family structure and a source of social support. Along these lines, some immigrants established a type of intimate agricultural commune, the *kevutza* (group), a precursor of subsequent Kibbutz settlements. Emphasizing strong communal ties and small-group solidarity, the Kibbutz pioneers cherished comradeship as the idealized form of intimate relationships.[7]

The communal ideology was reinforced by the gradual development of a national ethos advocating military power. In 1907 a handful of second-wave immigrants founded the first local paramilitary organization, called Bar-Giora (named after Simeon Bar Giora, the Jewish military leader in the war against Rome, 66–70 C.E.). The organization, soon renamed Ha-Shomer (the Watchman Guild), and served to provide hired guardsmen for the Jewish settlements, especially in the lower Galilee, in order to protect them from encroachment and damage to crops and property by neighboring Arabs. Its founders had had prior involvement in self-defense organizations in Russia in response to the pogroms. Although never exceeding a hundred members, the organization considered itself to be the nucleus of a future Jewish army.[8] *Ha-Shomer* constituted a secret society, much along the lines of ritualized male fraternities elsewhere. Members were initiated to the group in a nocturnal ceremony shrouded in mystery and swore total secrecy and loyalty to the organization. They promoted the image of the strong, confident, and fearsome "guard on his horse" as a concrete embodiment of the heroic "New Jew" along the lines of the "muscle Judaism" advocated by Nordau (Almog 1997: 168, 219).

The Zionist ideals of manhood and male bonding crystallized with the "1948 generation" of the *sabra*—the Israeli-born males who reached the prime of their youth in the 1940s and fought for the establishment of the Israeli state in 1948.[9] The *sabra* represented everything that the old Jew lacked: youth, strength, health, physical labor, and deep-rootedness (Rubinshtein 1977). The most conspicuous representatives of the *sabra* ethos were the Kibbutz-born youth, given the leading role of Kibbutz society in the political culture (Almog 1997).

Values of fraternity achieved their clearest formulation in the Palmach. The Palmach forces founded in 1941 were the elite semi-infantry units of the Haganah organization (literally, "The Defense"), the largest Jewish underground militia in the *yishuv* established in 1920 by the socialist leadership. As argued by Moshe Shamir (Shamir, Guri, and Shacham 1994: 27), a prominent author associated with the Palmach circle, the Palmach reflected the amalgamation of three symbols—a continuation of the pioneering movements, the significance of self-defense, and the spirit of volunteering: it was "one of the magnificent manifestations in our times of the ideal of giving over that of taking." Because many joined the Palmach troops on the basis of local networks of friends, they did not require a long term of explicit military indoctrination in order to subscribe to the norms of comradeship associated with soldiery. For these men, the decree to fight for the sake of friends may have been a rather concrete matter. Given the dominance of Kibbutz members in the Palmach body, communal ideals of collectivity and group solidarity may have implicitly reinforced the values of male bonding in Palmach circles, and as a result, in subsequent Israeli military culture.

Taken together, Kibbutz socialization and Palmach culture epitomize the masculine values of the *sabra*, among them the stress on group sociability. Although the salience of male bonding in the specific generational context of the *sabra* is not unique, and echoes the need for a sense of belonging to a specific circle that characterizes youth peer groups elsewhere, it is afforded cultural distinctiveness by its connection to "Zionist religion" and Jewish tradition (Almog 1997: 451), as well as by its association with communal ideology.

In 1948, following the outbreak of the War of Independence, the newly established Israeli government founded the IDF (Israeli Defense Forces) based on the infrastructure of the Haganah, which was officially dismantled, as were the other Jewish militias. The IDF presents yet another significant signpost in institutionalizing fraternal ideals in Israeli culture. The promotion of brotherhood and mutual affection as a mode of small unit cohesion and combat effectiveness has become a marked characteristic of the IDF (Henderson 1985: 38; Kellet 1982: 259). Eventually, re'ut came to be defined explicitly as an official part of the IDF's Code of Ethics, as it was recently reformulated by philosopher Asa Kasher (1996: 233): "Re'ut between IDF soldiers is combat fraternity, their constant devotion to each other, their willingness to provide valuable help, come to the rescue and even risk their lives for their fellow men."

The Inculcation of *Re'ut*

The bottom line of it is that when he [a soldier] talks of the State of Israel he isn't talking about the State of Israel but about his [military] company. What links him to this country is not a tradition or Jewish identity but the feeling of being one of the boys.

— *A platoon commander cited in Ben-Ari (1998: 100).*

The actual term *re'ut* apparently attained cultural salience only with the 1948 generation, based on the growing literary representation of the *sabra*. Between 1943 and 1945 Moshe Shamir and his literary peer group published four volumes of an anthology consisting of stories, songs and drawings created by young *sabra* artists under the title *Yalkut Ha-re'im* (The friends' collection)(Shamir and Tanai 1943/1992). In retrospect Shamir analyzed the choice of the term *re'im* as a natural continuation of the literary trends of the period. Their literary predecessor Avraham Schlonsky had founded a publishing house by the name of *Yachdav* and a cultural performance club, *Tzavta*; both names are synonyms for 'together.' All these terms mark the collectivistic values underlying the pioneering spirit of the time, shaped by the surrounding socialist climate shared by this peer group (Shamir and Tanai 1943/1992: 10). *Yalkut* means both a 'collection' and a 'rucksack,' hence creating another association between *re'ut*, Palmach group culture, and the rucksack carried in scouting activities in the youth movements and the paramilitary units (Almog 1997: 22). Haim Guri, the most prominent poet of the 1948 generation to have participated in the War of Independence as a Palmach officer, described his war experiences in many poems that often addressed the themes of *re'ut* directly. His first book of poetry, "Flowers of Flame" (Guri 1949), attained immediate popularity during the war. Before long his songs were cited and adopted in collective rituals and ceremonies that celebrated independence and victory yet still addressed the horrors of battle, all the while emphasizing male bonding. Some of Guri's poems were composed as popular songs, most pronouncedly the song *Ha-re'ut* (The friendship) (Guri 1950/2000: 147-148). Guri's popularity practically renders him the "cultural copywriter" of *re'ut* in Israeli culture.[10]

Despite these rich cultural representations, explicit discussion of the concept of *re'ut* has for the most part remained absent from Israeli literature and subsequent scholarship. Indeed, the common character of male friendship depicted by Guri and his contemporaries is of a silent, numb emotion, not to be expressed through any explicit, colorful gestures. In his popular song *Ha-re'ut* Guri writes: "*re'ut*—we carried you without words, gray, stubborn and silent" (Guri 1950/2000: 147). The cultural representations of *re'ut* channeled male bonding to the realm of the *unspoken*. This presents a difficult methodological challenge for a study that attempts to examine a concept and an emotion that is both culturally *salient* and *silent* at one and the same time.

In exploring the ideology underlying the concept of *re'ut* I focus on three dimensions: the idea, the cultural narrative and the performative measures that cultivated *re'ut*. None of these aspects are unique to the Zionist movement. As discussed earlier, they draw on European attributes associating male fraternity with the participation in the national struggle. In terms of the general idea, Zionism aimed to bestow on the new Israeli men the equal status of "brother" citizens.[11] Based on the already existing tradition of solidarity between Jewish members, along the lines of the Talmudic phrase "All Israel are sureties one for another" (*Massechet Shevu'oth* 39a),[12] this familial or tribal solidarity was to be transformed into a political culture that eventually reflected the juxtapositioning of a tribal ethos with statism.[13] The violent nature of the Arab-Jewish conflict implied that the endurance and maintenance of the Jewish community in *Eretz Yisrael* required an act of sacrifice. Similar to other national movements, Zionist mythology alluded to the blood of the fallen men as a means to reinforce the national collective, symbolizing the pact between the Jewish people, the nation and the land (Albaum-Dror 1996: 131). It produced a martyrological ethos that interwove the secular mourning for fallen soldiers with a consciousness of historic continuity, whereby the entity above the individual became the nation, instead of God (Sivan 1991). Hence, death by *kidush ha-moledet* (sanctifying the homeland) replaced the long-standing tradition of *kidush ha-shem*—sanctifying and sacrificing one's life in the name of God—a tradition that goes back to the Talmudic period and is associated initially with Rabbi Akiva (Fishbane 1994: 60).

The point is that sacrifice is not simply understood as a deed for the sake of the Israeli people as a nation or the land of Israel as its territory, but more specifically in terms of male solidarity and camaraderie. In a public address in 1946, Itzhak Sadeh, the first commander of the Palmach, provided one of the more explicit accounts of *re'ut*, beginning with the following definition:

> *Re'ut ha-lochamim* [combat comradeship] is probably the peak of friendship. Without it nothing can be fulfilled, because *hagshama* [fulfillment] always demands the common effort of people, understanding of the objective, mental preparation.

Sadeh draws an association between *re'ut* and *hagshama*, another key symbol in Zionist ideology loaded with rich semantic meaning.[14] Oz Almog (1997: 110) describes *hagshama* (literally, fulfillment or actualization) as a cultural code that captures at one and the same time the idea of individual self-fulfillment and a commitment to the collective dream of Zionist enterprise, especially in terms of agricultural settlement. From an abstract idea *hagshama* has turned into a synonym for the concrete act of pioneering through joining a settlement, "leaving to *hagshama.*" The double layer of semantic fields embedded in this term—covering both an individual self-fulfillment and a collective ideal—echoes another key symbol of Israeli culture, *gibush* (literally, crystallization). As explicated by Tamar Katriel (1991), at the individual level *gibush* can be applied to the intrapsychic domain to connote identity crystallization and personal maturity. But it has another meaning, referring also to the group cohesiveness originating in the communal ideals of socialist Zionism. In this sense, it implies an undifferentiated collectivity based on joint endeavors, cooperation, shared sentiments, and above all a sense of togetherness. It seems that a close relation exists between *hagshama*—the local Zionist ideal of collective and self-fulfillment—and *gibush,* the desired social mechanism through which *hagshama* is produced. I suggest that together, these two ideological, social, and psychological values result in a central emotional product of Zionist ideology, namely *re'ut.* Under this reading, *re'ut* is a national-emotional ideal, reflecting both self-realization and group cohesion, and set most pronouncedly in the ideals of settlement and military activity.

Of all my interviewees and informants, General N. was the most outspoken in responding to my question about the relationship between *re'ut* and ideology:

> Friendship or *re'ut* between groups of people can and should be an independent quality, but with the specific character it acquired in Israel . . . as a society still under construction, required to create an atmosphere of self-sacrifice and volunteering and commitment. . . . I don't know which came first, whether the ideology brought about friendship or perhaps the friendship brought about the ideology. I do know that the setting and the conditions produced [in addition] to standard human needs [for friendship] also this extra need for social cohesion (*gibush*) . . .

General N. summarized concisely some of the key tenets of the Zionist idea of *re'ut.* He stressed the political circumstances of Israeli society that necessitated social cohesion, and how these circumstances shape a certain ideology of friendship. Furthermore, he acknowledged that people's individuals need for friendship cannot be distinguished from this ideological framework. He also added that this link is probably more intense in Israel than in some other countries, such as in the established nation-states of Europe.

As for the narrative of *re'ut,* the story of male bonding was ready-made in the Bible, awaiting easy reinterpretation and reincorporation in line with the framing of nationalism as a civil religion. The unique formulation of *re'ut* emerges in the story of David and Jonathan (described in fragments from 1 Samuel 18:1 to 2 Samuel 1:27). David, a shepherd boy from the tribe of Judea, volunteers to fight for King Saul. Jonathan, son of King Saul, falls in love with David upon his return from the battlefield. King Saul becomes jealous of David's success and tries to kill him. David runs away, and Jonathan protects him from Saul, swears loyalty to David, and in so doing acknowledges the accession of David to the throne at his expense. The story emphasizes two central themes—a bond between two men operating as an exclusive pair, and sacrificial heroism. After Jonathan and Saul were killed in a battle the Israelites lost to the Philistines at Mount Gilbo'a, David (who immediately became the King of Judea) made a lament that has become an epitome of male courage and sacrifice.

It begins with the words "Thy glory, O Israel, is slain upon the high places! How are the mighty fallen!" (2 Samuel 1: 19). Of special significance is a specific verse that David addresses directly to his dead friend Jonathan: "I am distressed for you, my brother Jonathan; very pleasant have you been to me; your love to me was wonderful [also mysterious], passing the love of women" (2 Samuel 1:26). It is easy to read into this narrative hegemonic emotional values of masculinity, values that are common to many masculine-national ideologies. These center on courage, devotion, and unyielding adherence to goals (*dvekut ba-matara*), and on the ability to withstand physical and emotional pressure. But the choice of this specific narrative emphasizes one asset above all others, a mysterious loyalty to a friend up to a point of total sacrifice.

The story of David and Jonathan has become a cornerstone of heroic friendship in the Western tradition. Robert Brain (1976) opened his extensive anthropological overview of male friendship with a comparison of David and Jonathan's story to ritualized forms of friendship in Western and non-Western societies. Despite some attempts to read into the story evidence for a sexual liaison between the two men, it seems that the main intention of the story was to extol the transcendence of male friendship over the carnal love of a woman. Letty Pogrebin (1987: 273) notes that although Michal, David's wife and the daughter of Saul, also comes to David's rescue in various episodes in the biblical story, it is only the devotion and love of Jonathan that is acknowledged. David Halperin (1990: 83) suggests that Jonathan's devotion is emphasized perhaps precisely because it is more miraculous and therefore provides a better way to frame the passing of the kingship from the house of Saul to the house of David as a result of God's will. Halperin argues that by shifting the emphasis from conjugal love to a much more startling and less expected kind of friendship—that of male love—the biblical narrator sanctifies David's right to kingship. By this reading, Jonathan's love for David was startling not because of any sexual component, but because it was stronger and more militant than a heterosexual bond could have been; it portrays a true sacrifice.[15] Just as the biblical source intended to portray this sacrifice as a sign of God's power and was not interested in the personal-psychological aspects of the act of friendship, so too the Zionist reinterpretation uses the narrative to legitimize national goals. It sketches men's relatedness not as an interpersonal emotion but as a *national* emotional space.

The Zionist enterprise employed more than just an idea and a narrative of male bonding. It produced performative means to inculcate its convictions. Diverse pedagogic agents were—and still are—involved in reinforcing the hegemonic perception of *re'ut*. Institutions such as the school system, youth movements, media, and the military employ a range of measures such as songs, slogans, rituals, and tales to bring about the metanarrative. In many secular schools, as I recall from my own childhood experience as well, David's elegy is one of the few verses that students are required to memorize by heart during the compulsory Bible classes. In subsequent chapters I describe various exemplary poems, phrases, and rituals that demonstrate this indoctrination of *re'ut* among Israeli men.

The military relies on such cultivation of *re'ut* in society in order to generate its own organizational need for cohesion, as argued by the former head of the military's psychology unit, Reuven Gal (1986: 153): "The prevalence of cohesion in the IDF's units is not just the result of military organization. Above all, it reflects the nature of educational and social values in Israel. Israel is basically a group-oriented society. . . . Youngsters are socialized from their early years to develop a strong sense of friendships that will continue throughout their lives with a deep sense of commitment." The military, in its turn, contributes to the maintenance of male bonding in society at large, mainly through its reserve system. Sarit Helman (1999) analyzes how a sense of community and solidarity is formed in Israeli society though the participation of its hegemonic male constituents in the reserve system, contributing to the extension of face-to-face emotional interactions to an imagined collective solidarity among the larger male community.

The successful inculcation of *re'ut* as ideology entails serious constraints on its semantic field. Now that it has been officially incorporated into the IDF Code of Ethics (Kasher 1996: 233), it seems that *re'ut* has no longer anything to do with emotions. This is at least what one may draw from Kasher's argument that "you can't command love . . . you can't put in the code of ethics anything related to emotions"—an argument he raised in the context of an attempt to justify what some considered to be his political decision to initially omit "love of country" from the new Code (Ha'aretz 2001). It follows by this logic, then, that unlike love of country or other cultural emotions that are part and parcel of the Zionist cause, *re'ut* is no longer a voluntary, albeit ideologically based, emotion, having become an organizationally prescribed code of conduct, a military directive, and nothing more.

This transformation of *re'ut* from a fuzzy ideal of friendship and solidarity to a nationally acknowledged and at times even organizationally well-defined code of soldiery vividly illustrates how *re'ut* in Israeli society has narrowed in meaning, precisely because of the attempt to capitalize on its significance for the national cause. If the macrohistory of fraternity sketched in chapter 1 demonstrated how professional soldiery in premodern Europe transformed into modern national solidarity, the present inquiry into fraternity in the localized Israeli context suggests that this solidarity can just as easily be trimmed down to soldiery. Obviously, both processes present only a superficial picture of the relations between friendship and nationalism, when one attempts to reduce them both to the rhetorical level of ideology. Yet ideology goes into much deeper, unacknowledged emotional spaces of friendship, as these unfold both in everyday life and in instances of combat and commemoration that acquire national sacredness. These two spheres of friendship deserve further elaboration. They require a broader, phenomenological and ethnographic study of themes underlying *re'ut* as an emotional-ideological space, an inquiry that is undertaken in the next chapters.

Notes

1. The male trio Ha-Gashash Ha-Hiver (the "pale scout") was the most popular comedy group in Israeli entertainment between the 1960s and the 1990s. Their comedy shows, sketches, songs, and films, depicted everyday life situations that emphasized a variety of social and ethnic stereotypes of Israeli-Jewish men. Many idioms from their sketches, written by leading Israeli playwrights, entered the common Hebrew language, mostly thanks to their artistic combination of high Hebrew with a variety of ethnic, lower-class, and idiosyncratic argots.
2. Some have suggested that in early Zionist terminology a male gentile with whom one had a close relationship would also be referred to as *yadid* (Dekel 2001).
3. The common English translation of the term *re'ah* in the above phrase to 'neighbor' is somewhat misleading. In line with Christian traditions it favors an interpretation of the biblical verse as preaching for universal love to fellow men (Maghen 1999). In contrast, retaining the original meaning of "love your *friend* as yourself" would emphasize an ethic of preferential love to one's favorite people.
4. See Appendix 2 for biographical details of interviewees and major themes of their friendship narratives. Translations from the Hebrew of the narratives, poems, and other cultural texts are my own.
5. For instance, former Israeli President Chaim Herzog wrote a book on the heritage of Israeli heroes, noting that he did not include any heroes between *Bar-Kochva* and the modern period, because "lacking a country of their own the Jews went through almost 2000 years without the appearance of a worthy military hero amongst them" (Herzog 1991: 10).
6. The great majority of Jewish immigrants to Palestine between 1880 and 1929 (some 170,000 people) came from Russia and other Eastern European countries. German and Austrian Jews were to come en masse only during the immigration of the 1930s in response to Hitler's rise to power.
7. Baker and Hertz (1981) analyzed the structure of intimacy in a study of Kibbutz friendships. The characteristics of early Kibbutz life were conducive to the maintenance of a group intimacy: small size, homogenous membership, common cultural origin, frequent face-to-face interaction, physical proximity, and an explicit communal ideology.
8. For brief information on early Zionist immigration, settlement, and organizations in Palestine see Internet sources: http://www.jafi.org.il/education/100/ and http://www.jewishvirtuallibrary.org/jsource/Immigration/Second_Aliyah.html (accessed 5 December 2005)

9. The term *Sabra* derives from the Arabic name for a type of cactus fruit imported to the region in earlier centuries. New Jewish immigrants to Palestine used it as a nickname for the first generation of settlers. It later came to connote a person who is rough and prickly on the outside, yet sweet and tender within (Almog 1997: 15).

10. In this respect Guri's association with *re'ut* resembles the common association of Walt Whitman with "adhesiveness" or comradely love in American culture in the aftermath of the Civil War (Deitcher 2001).

11. It should be noted that from its very inception, political Zionism endorsed full civil rights for women. At the same time, Herzl's Zionist vision was preoccupied with liberating Jewish men and left little leeway for women in the political sphere (see Bunzl 1997; Gluzman 1997).

12. English translation by Epstein (1935: 238).

13. For an overview of Zionist military socialization as a rite of passage to a semireligious statism see Kaplan (2000; following Liebman and Don-Yehiya 1983). Based on a different, political-science framework, yet describing a similar trend, Shafir and Peled (1998) have characterized alternative discourses of citizenship in the Israeli political collective, identifying the dominant perceptions as a mixture of an "ethno-nationalist" and a "republican" ethos.

14. By "key symbol" I refer to Sherry Ortner's (1973: 1338) analysis of the cultural symbols in a given culture that embody systems of meaning central to that society and crucial to its distinctive organization.

15. Halperin (1990) underscores the ideological intentions of the biblical narrator by comparing two different versions of the story. A specific theory in biblical studies considers the books of Samuel to be a result of an amalgamation of two historical sources: an earlier source that was favorable to a relatively secular concept of Israeli kingship, and a later source that attempted to subordinate the kingship to the authority of priesthood conceived as a vehicle of God's will. In the text associated with the earlier source there is hardly any mention of the friendship between David and Jonathan. David rises to a position of prominence in Saul's court largely on his own merits, and nothing is said about his eventually becoming a king until after Saul and Jonathan both die in battle. In contrast, the text associated with the later source attempts to emphasize the passing of the kingship from the house of Saul to the house of David through divine intervention. This source attempts to portray David as possessing a charismatic appeal, a sanctity that conspires to advance his fortunes. This is achieved through a dramatic twist in which Jonathan, King Saul's own son, deserts the royal court to be with David, the very man who is to usurp him. While in the early source it is Michal, Saul's daughter, who falls in love with David, marries him, and later protects him from the murder attempt of King Saul, it seems that the later source found this tradition of conjugal love to be insufficiently remarkable, and transferred the role previously played by Saul's daughter to his son, Jonathan.

Part II

Friendship in Everyday Life

The study of friendship from an ethnographic perspective is strewn with methodological obstacles. Friendship develops over time. It is made from both small, minute instances of concrete interactions as well as from attitudes and generalizations abstracted from a long series of such interactions. In addition, many aspects of friendship bonds are perceived as private. They offer little leeway for traditional participant observation without affecting the interactions in drastic ways. The researcher is often confronted with yet another quality of friendship ties: their banality. One way or another, almost everyone is involved in such bonds, can say something about them, and what he or she have to say often seems plain and predictable. Probing emotional themes underlying friendship is even more difficult, especially with regard to men, who often avoid lengthy discussions of their emotional inner lives (Coltrane 1994). Academic writing on the general qualities of friendship does not provide much to go on either. On the contrary, since many of the more systematic discussions of friendship reside in the decontextualized frameworks of social psychology, the findings often seemed trivial or irrelevant in terms of the present perspective.

The common, contemporary notion that friendship ties are "voluntary" and "preferential" is reflected in the way that friendship in everyday life straddles diverse patterns of relationships set in various life periods and social institutions, with seemingly little cultural modeling. As noted earlier, this fluidity is reflected in the wide range of contexts associated with the standard, general term for friendship in Hebrew, *haverut*, whose meaning range from solidarity, to support, to intimacy, and up to romantic bonds. Given the general approach underlying this book—that friendship is nested in cultural and political constraints—how can one associate the fluid patterning of everyday friendship with underlying emotional-ideological spaces? These are the kinds of dilemmas that accompanied me in dealing with male friendship in everyday life. Broadly speaking, I have chosen to analyze men's experiences of *haverut* through three different methodological approaches: general narratives of friendship, folk-models of male sharing, and homosocial interactions in semipublic circumstances.

Chapter Three

HISTORY AND DESTINY: FRIENDSHIP NARRATIVES

Introduction: Friendship in the Narrated Experience

As a first step in unraveling male friendship in everyday life I follow the origin and maintenance of close friendships from a narrative perspective (see Appendix 1 for further elaboration on narrative methodology). I describe some of the stories in detail in order to provide a feel for the material and present recurrent themes that emerge. I return to these themes in subsequent chapters to elaborate on them from a variety of theoretical approaches.

General studies of friendship within the social sciences follow two main modes of inquiry. The first derives from a structural distinction going back all the way back to Aristotle, attempting to differentiate between types of friends. The dominant typology in contemporary research distinguishes between casual, close, and best friend (e.g., Gurdin 1996; Nardi 1999; Wright 1982). A second mode of inquiry has to do with processes of friendship formation and maintenance, explored from a range of psychological and sociological frameworks.[1] The narrative perspective used here is similar to this latter inquiry in that it follows the development of friendship along the life-course, but it employs a more holistic analysis of the structure of the plot and the sequencing of events, enabling an examination of coherence and internal contradictions in the meanings assigned to friendship across the narrative, as it unfolds from the retrospective point of view of the interviewee. Based on the theoretical distinction between narrative truth and historical truth (Spence 1982), narrative analysis draws on the tensions between the life-history and the life-story (Rosenthal 1993; Lieblich, Tuval-Mashiach, and Zilber 1998). Interviews that are particularly constructive in this sense are those that present a condensed account of a given friendship, describing its formation and maintenance over time, as part of the initial "free narrative" of the interviewee (Rosenthal 1993: 60). Consider the following extract regarding a best friendship relayed by Yaron, a single PhD student aged thirty-two. In his initial free narrative Yaron describes his friendship with Alon, which started in kindergarten, broke off following their geographical separation, and resumed to become an intense bond only toward the end of high school. The renewed bond revolved around shared activities in school and was strong enough to sustain subsequent geographical distances in the military, and later in adulthood:

> We met for the first time at kindergarten . . . I think that even back then it was at least on the level of close friends, if not best friends . . . we would visit each other's homes, and we'd meet beyond kindergarten hours. After that, in elementary school we went to different schools, so the relationship was cut off . . . suddenly we met again in high school . . . and more or less around twelfth grade we began to see each other, in various circumstances. We were both runners in school. We participated in school championships and in races. We were in the same advanced math class, so we sat together. And so the bond grew stronger again, especially while studying for the matriculation exams. And more or less after the school period was over, he remained the friend with whom I kept in touch, and it only grew stronger . . . and [today] we don't need to meet frequently in order to maintain a good bond. It's well enough if we speak once or twice a month . . . he lives now with his girlfriend in Tel Aviv, so we meet much less. But in that sense, it's like, it's defined beyond anything else as this kind of friendship: I'm his best friend and he's my best friend. And that's the basis for the whole thing.

In this initial sequence about his "best friend," Yaron alluded to the circumstances of their encounters, the quality and intensity of their bond, their mutual activities, and the maintenance of their relationship over a long period of time. A glance at most of the narratives would confirm that people indeed relate to their friendships in terms of these issues studied analytically in the general scholarly literature.

However, restricting the narrated experience of friendship to these banal and superficial factors tells us little about collective systems of meanings shared by the interviewees and attached to their experiences. Consider the basic concept of a "best friend" often examined in the social-psychological literature. Its place is far more evasive in actual lived experience. Yaron had indeed a very strong sense of a best friend, one he considered as such from as early as kindergarten and up to his present adult life, a rather rare phenomena. But most interviewees did not present one initial long-lasting story of close friendship and preferred to discuss a few close friendships instead, varying across different periods in their lives. Posing an explicit question, "What makes him your closest (or best) friend?" would either prompt the interviewee to respond in accordance with this notion, or, the contrary, stimulate him to refute the concept altogether. Some stressed how close friendship is dependent on a host of circumstances, such as the technical availability and possibilities for getting together, the sharing of mutual interests, and the participation in the same specific activities. A good example in this vein is the case of Raviv, whose free narrative centered on one single friendship with his naval co-officer, Milles. Nevertheless, Raviv declined to define Milles as his "best friend," explaining that in contrast to the constant striving and preoccupation with heterosexual ties, men do not preoccupy themselves in thinking about their male friends, they just "go along with them":

> There's no such thing as best friend. It's like asking whom do you love, or what's the food you love best. . . I can tell you that sometimes I feel much closer to Milles than to Hanan [another male friend]. And Adi— whom I dated over the last three months and spent way more time with her than with either of them—she's still not as close to me as the two of them . . . when you're with a friend you don't say: "Hey, can he be my friend?" No, you simply go along with it. But when I'm in a romantic relationship I keep thinking if it feels good or not.

Note that although Milles rejected the notion of "best friend," he viewed his two male friends as closer than a woman he was currently dating. This in itself is revealing. It demonstrates that the men may sense their relationships as close even when they are reluctant to consider this closeness in clear-cut, well-defined terms.

The present focus on male friendship offers another important point of departure from most generalized frameworks for friendship. Most friendship studies tend to focus on dyadic relationships, neglecting the importance of a group bond. In Hebrew the common term for a group that is bound by friendship ties is *havurah* (stemming from the same root as *haverut*, *h-v-r*). This term is distinguished from the general term for group (*kevutza*), and in Zionist context this *havurah* is colored with connotations of male homosociality, a topic I address in subsequent chapters. In terms of the free narratives among my core sample of men, five men chose in their initial story to focus on a group of men, *havurah*, as their close, intimate associates. In some cases this intimate group accompanied them for many years and formed the focal point of their male relationships. In addition, a few men related to a threesome, combining the discussion of each friend separately with the story of the three as a group.

Origins

Following stories of friendship is a useful way to delineate basic *narrative building blocks*. These are cultural constructs that people employ, often implicitly, to make sense of how or why a friendship has formed, developed, or ended. In so doing I focus on the concept of *origin*. Within the prevalent social-psychological literature on friendship the concept of origin is reduced to environmental or personal factors that induce familiarity and facilitate the formation of a friendship, such as physical proximity (the propinquity effect), similarity, and reciprocal liking (Berscheid and Reis 1998). In their effort to generalize such frameworks tend to disregard the cultural and organizational context that shapes the meaning of friendship at different stages across the life-course. Men pass recognizable, collective signposts that help them frame the origin, maintenance, or ending of specific bonds. In the typical Israeli case, major such signposts are: childhood environment, the local neighborhood, school, youth movements, military service, higher education, the workplace, and hobby-related activities. As dominant social institutions for Israeli men, these spheres are key socializing sites for forming friendships. Simply put, these are the places where Israeli men meet, spend time together in mutual activities, and go through difficult and joyful times together.

In what follows I briefly describe a few such signposts, particularly of childhood and adolescence origin, and contrast them with friendships originating in the military and in settings of higher education. Many interviewees referred to long-lasting close relationships originating in childhood or adolescence and lasting till adulthood. Indeed, in my core sample of thirty interviews, friendships from the childhood neighborhood setting, or, as was more often the case, from elementary or high school, formed the main narration. The phrase "childhood friends" (*havrey yaldut*) is more likely than other descriptors of origin to be employed as a self-standing idiom in Israeli discourse on friendship, and to serve as a basis for comparing other types of friendship bonds. This was also a predominant pattern in various narrative interviews on friendship conducted by Israeli students in my research seminars.

I will present four stories of childhood friendships told by Ehud, Gadi, Nachshon, and Meir. Ehud, aged twenty-six, described his two close friends since elementary school, who with him formed a "threesome":

> Tzur is one of my closest and best friends . . . together with Rotem, we formed this kind of threesome, me, Tzur and Rotem. . . . This last Saturday the three of us hung out together at Tzur's, chatting, as we like to do . . . good food and good conversation . . . it's amazing that the bond did not [break] . . . it's only getting stronger, I mean these guys are simply my brothers, just like that, I always laugh about it, I tell them when our kids will play together, my kids will beat up Tzur's kids and Rotem's kids will go and tell on them.

How did they meet? Ehud arrived in a new town and a new school in fourth grade. He was to join a class that had already been studying subjects he was unfamiliar with, such as Arabic. He recounted how the teacher told him to approach Tzur, the best pupil in Arabic, who could help him out with his studies: "I recall that I approached him, introduced myself and said what the teacher said about studying Arabic and so on.

He said something like 'OK, come to my house.' At his home we mostly ate, his mother was the greatest cook, still is, and so we mostly ate and played. I didn't get to study Arabic with him, ever since, but I gained a terrific friend."

Another account of childhood friendship is presented by Gadi, aged forty-eight, who focused on a long-lasting friendship among a *havurah* that formed during his childhood in a *ma'abara* and has been forming a significant part of his adult life ever since.[2] Gadi reconstructed a touching, almost nostalgic account of this youthful bond, giving a taste of the sights, sounds, and even smells of his social life in the 1950s. I present short passages selected from his vivid story:

> I think *the* story is a group of childhood friends . . . from the *ma'abara* . . . in fact the same friends from elementary school, almost all from the same class . . . we've remained in continual and stable contact for something like forty-five years. . . . I think everything we did—we did together. There was no television then. . . . We'd occupy an entire row at the cinema, all the guys an entire row. At a slightly [older] age we'd go to parties, dancing, and some dating . . . also a lot of sports activity, football, basketball. . . . On Saturday mornings we'd go to the beach and back, easily twelve kilometers. Then we'd eat. At noon, on Saturdays when there was a football match going on, we'd go and see *Ha-Poel* [the football club] play. . . . In winter the road from the *ma'abara* to school would turn into a lake. And the thing to do was to build rafts from wood, to float and to try pushing each another off the raft.

The circumstances that draw two friends together are sometimes reinforced by a sense of uniqueness in terms of their personality or activities. Nachshon, aged forty-seven, described his lifelong friendship with Gershon from preschool to the present, emphasizing the peculiar traits and hobbies that gave his friend an "anti-basketball" image among their peers and placed him on a par with Nachshon's own inclinations. The two of them hung out together and kept going as a steady pair throughout their childhood, attending the same classes, sitting next to each other in high school, and sticking together in the youth movement:

> During preschool we lived next door to each other . . . and you never know whether it's kids who decide to become friends or if the parents decide . . . and because we lived in the same neighborhood and went to the same class, and perhaps here too, he was small and chubby . . . they forced him to play the violin from an early age, so in terms of popularity, re basketball, he was on the side of the violin . . . so you understand where he's at. And when we used to go on treks in the Boy Scouts he was the guy who would barely make it to the top of the hill . . . and I'm with him, I'm his friend.

Finally, perhaps the most elaborate and intense account of a childhood friendship extending all the way to early adulthood is Meir's relationship with Baruch. They were cousins of similar age, and passed a lot of time together "from the cradle," spending long hours and days together during school holidays and vacations when Baruch's family would come to a visit. Over time their attempts to maintain a close relationship were met with new constraints and possibilities posed by subsequent social institutions in their lives. In adolescence, the wider peer group started to play a greater role in their bond. Despite having to attend different schools, Meir and Baruch managed to keep their bond intact, combining it with a small group of friends that they shared, a group that lasted throughout high school till early adulthood:

> This bond extended throughout all aspects of our lives, that is, I recall now that even in junior high when people started to go to parties, somehow we ended up at the same parties . . . even though it's quite rare at this age, when it goes by schools. . . . Around ninth grade a group of friends formed around me, some of my neighborhood buddies, him and two friends of his, and together we became a closed circle among ourselves. And this thing went on for many years, up to our mid twenties . . . we'd go to parties, picnics and social events, we'd meet at our homes.

Moving on to the military is likely to impose new constraints on the maintenance of bonds from high school. It is rare that two close friends can serve in the same unit and positions in the military. Yet his was the case for Nachshon and Gershon, who applied some family connections with military officials so that they could join the same unit and the same training course in the first stages of military service: "And it carried on to the military . . . as soon as we arrived in boot camp together we obviously chose beds next to each other and helped one another in everything." But even when they serve in different units, as is most often the case, most Israeli men manage to keep their childhood bonds intact. Depending on the nature of their military service, soldiers get to return home either on a daily basis or on weekends, so their social life in the civil sphere does not necessarily dwindle. In Meir's case, the period of military service, together with a formation of steady relationships with girlfriends and the crystallization of their circle of high school friends, was the perfect stage for maintaining his exclusive and close bond with his cousin-friend Baruch: "That period was perhaps the climax of our closeness. Although I enlisted three months before he did, we were always amused by the fact that just as he was boarding the airplane for a trip abroad, I was told to board the trucks [to boot camp]. But very soon we both served close to home. It was a period of blooming social life. [We spent] lots of evenings playing games and so on, with all our friends."

Finally, Gadi's story is one of the more exemplary cases of how the various geographical separations of a group of childhood friends—not only during high school and the military, but also following a range of changes in their adult lives, marriages, career choices, and individual relocations across the (relatively small) country—did not spoil their long-lasting bond. He claimed that all the personal events that each of them went through, whether happy or sad, only served to reinforce their bond, noting that this very fact was perhaps "*the* story within their story." To conclude, the extent to which childhood or adolescence friendships were maintained beyond the military varied enormously from one interviewee to another. Yet it is clear that for many Israeli men, relationships originating in childhood or early adolescence form the basis of a life-long companionship.

I turn to friendships originating in the military. In many cases, accounts of such bonds did not differ from those originating earlier. But for some interviewees, especially those serving in combat units, military bonds held a special place in their narrated experience. Their most distinguishing feature was that they evolved in the harsh setting of military life, which effectively forces men to be close to each other and creates a "test of friendship," as Modi, who served in the Golani infantry brigade put it: "learning what friendship means during this period, how people react, what it's like to be close to a person in enforced circumstances, where you don't choose people but you can still learn." Modi gives the following, typical example of his military bonding with Diego, with whom he shared the same tent: "We met at the battalion . . . we were something like a year and a half together, a relatively long time, living in the same tent and leading the same life. We both served as operational sergeants. . . and we had close relations in terms of exchanging shifts and helping each other out. I recall very well that if I or he were especially tired we had no problem remaining an entire extra shift . . . and later the relationship simply faded, but it was a very, very close relationship."

Raviv offered a detailed account of how such a connection formed during his career service in the navy:

> I met Milles at the navy officer's course. . . and then we found ourselves in a similar situation when we were stationed for training in Europe, because we were both . . . of the same status, younger than everyone else, and his girlfriend had just left him in similar circumstances to an incident I had a year earlier . . . it was traumatic for him too, not as bad I think, but he also found himself in a country where no one speaks the language, people are cold and not friendly, there are no books, no films, and the only people you can communicate with are colleagues, either your commanders, or your subordinates, and all your friends are far away. . . . It started out with weekends when we would go and do stuff together . . . and it continued with deep conversations . . . maybe it was a matter of choice or lack of choice, and we fell into this situation of being together and going through experiences together, and that's how it developed.

Although serving overseas is a rare situation for IDF soldiers, Raviv's story serves to highlight several of the structural-emotional aspects that tend to underlie the emergence of close bonds in the military in general. The recruit is transferred to a new, foreign surrounding, with special cultural codes, stripped of his earlier lifestyle and secluded from easy means of communication with the outside world.[3] Furthermore, he is detached from his earlier circle of friends and becomes involved in a highly hierarchical work environment that discourages the formation of voluntary interpersonal relations. What seems to connect him to other men is a similar experience of hardship and trauma, although in Raviv's case their mutual trauma was not directly induced by military activity but by a painful separation from their girlfriends (partly due to their conditions of service). The seclusion and the binding trauma brought them together, almost unwillingly, and from that point onward their bond developed, reinforced by their joint experiences.

Despite the emotional significance of some military bonds, it was rather surprising that many interviewees recounted how these relationships nevertheless faded out after their service ended, or else were restricted to scarce reunions. That a bond may dissolve following changes in environment and life events is not surprising. But in the case of the military, it poses a tension between an intensive bond on the one hand and its subsequent breakup on the other, especially when compared to bonds originating in childhood or high school that have often survived geographical and circumstantial constraints. In this sense, military friendships pose a puzzling contradiction: they do not form a central part in the actual narratives of the majority of my informants; yet as noted in the introduction on *re'ut*, they form the dominant image for male bonding in Israeli culture. These contradicting dynamics will be explored in much greater depth in chapter 6.

Close friendships originating in adulthood presented much more diverse circumstances and social settings. They were less salient in the interviewees' free narratives, and were usually chosen as secondary stories. The more structured accounts centered on bonds created in college. They often revolved around shared preferences in studies, in social activities, and in "adventuring," most notably with regards to parties, women, and, as in the following account by Amnon, a playwright, also drugs: "An important part of our friendship was a period of 'tripping' together on LSD . . . these LSD trips were some of the strongest experiences in my life. And we took it together . . . we had a lot of shared adventures with women, which also strengthened our friendship. And one time it was tested, when he even forgave me for sleeping with his girlfriend."

Some of these friendship narratives were colored by an intense and often wild atmosphere associated with college life, perhaps against the background of the humdrum routines of studying activities. At any rate, college bonds often formed a basis for relationships lasting well beyond the college period, although not as much as friendships originating in adolescence. However, these accounts did not usually take a large part in the narratives, and college ties were not significant in terms of culture-specific constructs for making sense of friendship, compared to childhood and military origins. In this respect, for most Israeli men, including those of middle-class and higher-education background studied here, the college period does not seem to be a formative signpost in the development of male friendships, in contradiction to its image in many other Western societies.

Shared Activities: From Adventures to Folklore

Here I turn to discuss the concept of origin from a different angle. Instead of focusing on signposts across the life-course where the friendship has been formed, I delineate common themes emerging from the narratives that are used by the interviewees as building blocks for making sense of how their bonds were formed. A central account of male friendships focuses on shared activities. This is a recurrent finding in the literature on male friendship, especially when compared with women's friendships (Rubin 1986). The content of these activities may vary along the course of life, and is shaped by surrounding social circumstances and institutions. It can range from playing games, to seeking adventures, to the invention of whole worlds. In childhood and early adolescence shared activities evidently focus on games and sports and it is interesting to note how these can extend into adult male interactions. For instance, the cornerstone of Meir's friendship with Baruch from infancy to adolescence was the pleasure they shared in playing games in which they invented their own rules: "We both didn't know how to play chess. And we would take the board and sit together for hours at a time, inventing rules and playing with one another and enjoying very much being together." Over time, indistinct playing activities transform into more focused and specific activities of shared interests—in other words, they develop into hobbies. Roman described the development of his friendship with Aron early in highschool and beyond. They lived in the same neighborhood and met at a youth sports club for flying model airplanes: "And why did we become friends? . . . maybe similar interests . . . So we'd go flying planes together, and we used to go out to play pool, and go to restaurants, and later we'd teach courses together [in flying model airplanes] for children."

The kinds of games that men choose to play together are often connected with adventure seeking. In some cases, adventures involving mischief and risk taking seemed to form the highlight of the friendship, especially in childhood and adolescence. Roman relayed how: "we would do lots of crap, like even stealing. Early in the morning, on our way out to fly the model planes, the delivery guy would leave some milk and bread rolls next to the grocery store. Nobody was there so we'd take some food with us for the day."

When adventures are not easily in sight, they can be easily imagined. Returning to Meir's story, his bond with Baruch centered on the invention of imaginary worlds. Inspired by popular mystery and spy books, they wrote some stories of their own and then played out some of the scripts themselves:

> It started in third grade. We wrote adventure books, "The Brave Sailors in the Mystery of the Unobtainable Magnetic Substance," seriously . . . and they would encounter all these criminal gangs and needed to solve the world's problems, a sort of mixture of James Bond with all sorts of thriller movies we'd seen . . . now the amazing thing about it is how it developed into all sorts of things. When we grew older we decided that we could spot spies who were trying to jeopardize national security. We decided that whoever drove a Citroen car in the neighborhood, I remember this in detail, was a spy . . . and we needed to follow them.

Roman's specialized hobby of flying model planes with his friend Aron developed into a joint endeavor for improving the models, and gradually grew into a full-blown adult occupation of building devices and fantasizing about patents. Their sport practically turned in to an amateur start-up for inventing patents: "We'd fantasize about all sorts of ideas for patents and perhaps try to build some. . . . During school we'd be together at night building MRPV [mini remotely-piloted vehicle]. And we invented patents. For example, did you hear of this shaving handle with the cream inside of it? It was taken from us . . . I recall it was mainly during the nights, at four or five in the morning . . . we'd work on these ideas. We had tools and lathes and we worked endlessly. Nothing came out of it, money-wise I mean." Roman and his friend would share ideas, consult each other, and plan how to invent their patents. His story reveals not only how their relationship centered on activities, but also how these activities formed the focal point of their conversations and communication. This pattern has been repeatedly reported in the psychological gender literature on male relatedness, arguing that men tend to discuss and talk about external, instrumental issues, often refraining from talking about the relationship itself (Real 1997). At the same time, as the men move from playing games and seeking adventures to inventing worlds together, they share a rich imaginary world, a world of their own. As such their bond may form a deep emotional space with direct bearing on a sense of intimacy, a topic addressed in subsequent chapters.

Shared activities are not only a prominent factor in the actual male bonding but also a major adhesive force for *reconstructing* these bonds in the narrative. A retelling of the shared activities, especially those involving exploits and adventures, carries various attributes. First, as in any narrative reconstruction, dramatic events form vivid narrative moments that interviewees are more likely to recollect. Especially when dealing with the reconstruction of relationships, they form relational moments, the "what" of the interaction, which is easier to verbalize than underlying emotional processes that remain behind the scenes (Josselson 1992: 26). More than that, the easy accessibility of such adventurous moments renders them central not only to the individual reconstruction of the friendship, but also to the continuing negotiation of the relationship between two or more friends. As an event that they allude to again and again, it serves to reenact their bond. Avi mentioned a key thrilling event he had shared with his friend and colleague during their joint work as administrators under the Israeli Civil Administration in Gaza during the first *Intifada*:

> There was this incident . . . at the time it seemed a bit scary but today when we recall it we always laugh about it . . . we had to drive toward the police station . . . I was in the leading vehicle and he was driving in a jeep behind me. There was a gap between us, I took a turnoff, and his engine suddenly quit . . . [they] left the Jeep and went on foot to the station, it wasn't more than 150–200 meters . . . I doubled back and saw that the vehicle was abandoned with the keys inside. I began to dread that they had been kidnapped, and I called him over the radio and eventually saw him reach the station. I keep teasing him about it and saying, 'you should have at least taken the keys with you!' He panicked, he didn't think of it . . . to this day we still laugh about it.

The frightening adventure became a joyful recollection that reinforced their bond, something they could return to, relate to, and as a result, incorporate within their bond as a means to relate to each other. Hence, the significance of the mutual recollection of shared activities is that it becomes the cornerstone for another kind of 'doing': *Telling*. Referring to special things or events that they shared together in the past by telling them again and again in the present provides a reenactment of the 'doing.' Instead of talking about the bond itself, as an entity of its own, they simply tell it. Adventures become a productive mode for relational exchange, a symbolic commodity for the ongoing interaction. Telling adventures becomes part of what the relationship is about. It is especially central to male homosociality in the context of the group, the *havura*. Consider the following example from Gadi's story, recounting an episode of a wrestling game among the group of boys that ended with potentially fatal consequences, only to become a "hilarious" and "funny" story whenever the group members came together in the years to come:

> And you can repeat the same story twenty times, and it's always hilarious again. For instance, the story of how Yoav, Shimi and Moshe—who were always together, an inseparable lot—would go and hit each other, playfully, like wrestling . . . [and one time Yoav], well I guess he got hit hard or simply got mad . . . and Shimi received a serious blow. It was in Yoav's house. Each time I picture this it makes me laugh again. He got punched and lost consciousness. They didn't quite understand what happened. They didn't think at all, laid him down on the bed, covered him up and left, Yoav and the other guy. And then

when evening came Shimi's mother started yelling from her porch, "Shimi! Do you know where Shimi is?" And Yoav said, "I don't know.". . . only two hours later did Shimi finally wake up, couldn't remember what had happened . . . when Yoav describes it's much funnier than when I do.

Garry Fine (1988: 46) notes the significance of pranks in preadolescent friendships. Pranks hold sufficient cultural significance that tellings of them are considered worthy of repetition. Talking about the prank may be equal in significance to actually carrying it out. In this sense the dynamics of adult male friendships resemble those of childhood bonds. The shared activity becomes part of the collective narrative that can be reenacted in the public sphere. It serves an adhesive function in creating a sense of belonging. As a result, the concrete experiences of doing things together— such as game playing, inventing worlds, taking risks—are transformed by the dynamics of telling and retelling into the broader realm of *folklore*. It is this folklore that creates a sense of specific identity for a given friendship, whether of a dyad or a group.

Shared Past: A Familial Rhetoric

On a larger scale, the accumulation of shared activities over a period of time builds up to a broader narrative formulation of how a given bond has lasted and is maintained through the notion of a *shared past*. Having gone by many signposts in life, spending time together in mutual activities, sharing times of difficulty and of joy—all these bring about a sense of a shared past. This concept was suggested to me by Yaron, when reflecting on the endurance of his long-lasting friendship with Alon: "In this respect there are all sorts of friendships that you could define them as friendships based on a kind of shared past. And they often fade out, and this happened to me with other friends too. Everyone goes his own way. But we made it, I mean, the bond is strong. And we don't need to meet that frequently to keep it up."

How does a shared past give meaning to an ongoing friendship? How does it serve to maintain and contain the bond, especially when the friends do not meet so often? A few cultural-emotional constructs are in play here. A recurrent term used by the men to illustrate the strengths of a given bond is the phrase *ben-bait* (literally, "son of the house"). It denotes someone who is part of the family: he is well known to the family of his friend, may visit them often and stay at their house on a regular basis. Symbolically, he is treated as a son by the friend's parents. In some cases, this is a concrete, historical account of how the friendship has evolved. Nachshon summed up the familial aspect of his friendship with Gershon, formed at early childhood:

Here's a thing of childhood, of living in each other's homes . . . he would come to my house and have dinner, for years and years. So it's a neighborhood bond, familial bond, I don't know what to call it. It's not a strong friendship, a deep spiritual bond, it's simply family, an additional family . . . it's this calm, safe, taken for granted thing you're supposed to have with your brother. You were just born together, you'll also die together. I'll never be cut off from him. Why? Because! Because we're together from kindergarten.

For Nachshon, a familial bond signified the fact that while this was a simple relationship, lacking in deep emotional investment, it promised to be safe, secure and stable. Nonetheless, irrespective of the actual historical origin of the friendship, whether from childhood and the family house or from later in life, to attribute the term *ben-bait* to a current relationship is to afford it the related familial qualities. It triggers an immediate association between the status of *ben-bait* and that of a lifelong relationship, as Benny put it, when asked about the maintenance of the bond with his close friend from the military: "It's really for life. He's also *ben-bait* in my home . . . I am in his. The bond is very [strong], we know each other's families." Shmuel Eisenstadt (1974) pointed out that despite its core characteristic as voluntary, friendship holds an ambivalent relationship with kinship. Although the two relationships appear to be symbolically and organizationally distinct, they share many ideals. Talking about friends in terms of kinship is, indeed, a very common analogy people make when discussing friendship (Nardi 1999; Rubin 1985). The core quality of the familial bond is its totality, especially in terms of altruism and sacrifice. Members of kin are perceived to be ready to do everything for one another, and this analogy is used to describe the emotions behind the male bonds. Ehud described his feelings toward Tzur and Rotem as: "familial, I mean, it's really a family, it's really like they're my brothers, people I am ready to do anything for their sake and they are willing to do for me, that's really how it is."

The familial rhetoric goes hand in hand with the term "brother," a recurrent term in almost all the narratives. Brotherhood represents familiarity, empathy, and closeness. It is repeatedly used in collective discourse of friendship in both the Jewish and the Israeli-Zionist context, with clear connotations of national sentiments, as a means to signify closeness between nonrelated individuals. Its usage in personal discourse of friendship functions in a similar vein. It conveys a total, unbound relationship that can reinforce close-knit ties between unrelated kin, not only between the two friend "brothers," but also between the "brother-in-law" and the father. Yoram described how his enduring bond with his childhood friend Rani was reinforced by Rani's strong connection with Yoram's father. Not only did they treat Rani as a "a son of the house," but they viewed him as a son-in-law, or, rather, as a daughter-in-law, as the following anecdote suggests: "My parents call him "Rina," as if he's my girlfriend . . . he's good friends with my dad. Sometimes he comes to my house and I'm not there, so he sits and talks with my dad . . . [when his girlfriend left him] he was so heartbroken, we talked together, me, my dad and him, and he spilled his guts, it was late at night, I went to bed. And he went on and talked with my dad, telling him he wrote her a letter . . . "

Another usage of the term brother draws a comparison between a long lasting friendship and the notion of an *extra* brother. Gadi's case of childhood *havurah* is the most illustrative in this respect. Being an only child, he wondered whether his group of lifelong friends formed a kind of substitute on his part for a sense of a family, and especially for brothers. As a result, he reflected on whether the closest of his friends from the group symbolized this sense of a brother: "Perhaps in my case, it formed some kind of substitute for being an only child. In my family I didn't have any brothers to play with and to feel close to. So naturally, I'll say in the clearest way . . . Yoav was an especially close brother. Yes, definitely, a feeling of brothers."

The familial rhetoric advances the notion of friends that accompany one in life. Similar to the family, they become part of the emotional home that people carry with themselves wherever they go. Tamir, aged thirty-four, offered a concise account of how Israeli men typically gather their group of friends from various stations in their lives, predominantly from high school, terming this core group that would always accompany him as "the band": "We're a group. Over time each person brought in his own friends, so that we gathered [friends] over the course of life, you meet people at junior high, at high school, in the military . . . I think that the band, my band anyways is based on the childhood friends, who studied together at school . . . and then they dispersed, went to different combat units . . . and this is maybe the intimate circle that accompanied me along the years, always accompanied me, always will."

Along these lines, Hezi, a married engineer, summed up the place of the friends that have gathered in his life, each representing his personal development at different life stages. Referring to his various sports hobbies, these friends have become, in his words: "The axis of my pleasures in life . . . they were all in some way together with me in everything I did along the way. That is, each of my friends has taken part in some of my pleasures, whether in the sea, in the air, under water. They more or less flowed with me."

David Plath (1980: 224–225) analyzed the continuing role of the individual's primary group across the lifespan in modern Japan as a "convoy" of significant others. Although the Israeli accounts are perhaps less manifest, this accumulation of friends in the course of life invokes a similar image of the relational self as a wagon traveling on the roads of life, picking up companions at various stations as it goes along. As with the notion of the family, the image of convoy suggests a strong sense of stability. Hezi offered another image of how this primary group of friends represented an addition of extra legs to the family table, hence assisting in securing and stabilizing the table: "I'm stable also thanks to my good friends . . . that is, my wife is the most stable thing in my life, but there are additional legs around me. When I look at it, I am one leg, and my wife is one leg, and it's stable enough to stand on two legs, but if you have another five legs around you're much more stable."

Judd Ne'eman, an academic and screen writer representative of the "state generation" (see Appendix 1), described to me his lifelong companionship with a group of men, a *havurah*, that crystallized initially during his military service. For decades he has continued to meet regularly with some of these friends and additional ones that came along. Together they formed a sense of a primary group that often met on weekends and sat together for a *haflah* (Arabic for festive meal), as he recounted: "One of the houses became a house of gathering, and over a long period, every Friday night, the *havurah* would gather there, plus all the peripheral people, and that's how it developed; that was the mechanism, you could say. . . coming at Fridays, bringing the food and wine, and sitting down, like at a *haflah*." He proceeded to note that even as the group has grown larger over the years, and as everyone's social networks has expanded, whenever they would meet at large social or family events "then there's always a table for us. Sometimes it's the last table to remain, and so we sit and talk and talk. Suddenly we lose ourselves and it's like time has stopped in its tracks." In other words, similar to the role of the table in festive events of the extended family (or the *hamula*, another term derived from Arabic) the *havura* weekend meetings become an extension, and, to a certain extent, a replacement of the family. The table, then, becomes an emotional symbol not only of stability but also of the need for the rehabilitation of family experiences, as Judd concluded, echoing Gadi's earlier idea of friendship as substitute for family: "It was the healing experience for old familial wounds, a better familial relationship. . . in the sense that I would come to one of these homes . . . and feel more comfortable than coming to my parents . . . it was a sort of substitute."

Having established some of the notions, metaphors, and emotional needs behind the familial rhetoric of male friendship, we can turn to how it draws on the narrative building block of a shared past. In many of the examples above a sense of shared past is grounded firmly in the men's actual life-history of a continuing strong bond. But in some instances the narrated account of a given bond seems to adhere to the cultural construct of shared past more than the actual life experiences seem to entail. These cases underscore the significance of shared past as a narrative building block of long-lasting friendships. I draw here on the possible tensions between the historical circumstances through which the experience has formed and the way it is constructed in the retrospective explanation given by the interviewee (Rosenthal 1993; Spence 1982). This gap can shed light on personal and cultural systems of meanings through which friendship is made sense of.

Let us examine two such examples. Tamir tried to make sense of the circumstances that have made Ilan, the "leader of the band" as he termed him, his closest friend. Noting that Ilan was a childhood friend, he could only dimly recall how the two of them had taken part in street quarrels and engaged in fights: "He was a friend from childhood who would beat me up when I was small . . . I met him in street fights . . . I can't recall what it was about, beatings, fighting, I don't know, water bombs, it's childhood fights." He also recalled how the school memories he shared with Ilan formed part of their continuing relationship. Just a day prior to our interview he had happened to pass with Ilan by their elementary school when: "suddenly we stood there at the grounds . . . at the spot where each morning we attended the morning call, we stood there, each in his own place, [recalling] 'here's where the sixth graders stood'. . . and 'do you remember Benny who had to stay behind for two years at the Special Ed class, and today he's about to become a brigadier in the army?'. . . We were just having these laughs about our childhood."

But these mutual memories in themselves did not necessarily form the actual basis for their ongoing friendship. In fact, in terms of Tamir's life-history what drew him closer to Ilan were the sheer circumstances of their military service. Like most of his circle of friends, Tamir served in a combat unit. The particular circumstances of Ilan's military service on an 'open' base made him more accessible and enabled Tamir to "ring him up" and get together with him "whenever I'd come on leave [and] there was no one [else] around." Technically, the knowledge that they shared a past together was only secondary to the circumstances that turned their acquaintanceship into a more close-knit ongoing friendship in adulthood. It is only now, having formed a close friendship, that they would go back and track their "roots" together.

A similar point can be made in the case of Yaron. In his introductory account noted at the beginning of this chapter, of his best-friendship with Alon originating in kindergarten, Yaron explained their bond as based on a sense of shared past. After kindergarten the bond had broken due to their geographical separation, but it was resumed and developed into an intense relationship toward the end of high school. The renewed bond had become strong enough to overcome the partial separation forced by the military, and from then onward they met and continue to meet regularly. But if we look more closely at the actual, concrete life-history that has brought Yaron and Alon back together, we note that on their renewed meeting in high school their bond did not resume immediately: "But we didn't become friends (*haverim*) right away. That is, we were in good contact, casual friends (*yedidim*). We'd say 'hello' to each other. And more or less around twelfth grade we began to see each other, in diverse settings." Indeed, it took another few years for the circumstances of similar interests in sports and similar study preferences in math to lead to the proximity that reinforced their friendship until they finally got really close when studying together for the matriculation exams. For all practical purposes, their high school bond was a new kind of friendship that had less to do with their early childhood history and more with the typical activities of high school life. But it seems that for Yaron, their shared kindergarten past dwelled in the background and gave a sense of meaning to this bond. It is here that the notion of a shared past is no less a cultural construct than it is a life experience: a lingering sense of a past gives a certain primordial, almost mythic meaning to an existing relationship. For many other interviewees, who unlike Yaron could hardly even recall concrete friendship experiences from their past history with a given friend, the very notion of such a shared past is a way to explain the present and reinforces their sense of security in a given bond. It is a cultural building block that has an emotional role in fortifying the relationship.

In sum, the cultural building block of shared past affords meaning to an ongoing friendship. Irrespective of the historical circumstances that have caused the men to reinforce their bond, the attribution of the bond as based on a shared past is what often makes it meaningful in the present. As shared activities are transformed into folklore, this folklore in turn transforms the present friendship back into a sense of a meaningful past. This is where the effect of collective memory, on the most localized scale, can be seen at its best. It is not the concrete past experiences themselves that are meaningful; rather, what is significant is that these experiences create a justification to form a *tradition*, a tradition of friendship based on localized mythology. The historical experiences are a "black box"; they form a lingering sense of a past that in turn gives some magical meaning to a present relationship. In many ways, friendship *is* such a tradition: the dynamic of telling and retelling, constructing and reconstructing past experiences serves to recreate new joint experiences and reinvent the friendship. The friendship can be viewed as an "invention of tradition," yet not as a top-bottom approach administered by the authorities, as this notion has been originally invoked by Eric Hobsbawm (1982) in the context of nation-building, but as a concept at the micro level of how individuals make sense of their significant interpersonal interactions.

Shared Destiny: A Romantic Rhetoric

The following account by Amnon suggests that in addition to a sense of shared past there are other ways to make sense of a friendship. Amnon began his story of a long-lasting friendship with Binyamin by describing how they met in officer's school and then after the five-month-long course, went their separate ways. Many years had past before they met and resumed the bond, having accidentally found out that they lived in the same city, and then became the closest of friends: "And somehow in that period of five months some kind of bond had formed that I think didn't fulfill itself . . . we did not meet again until by chance we found out that we live in the same city. And then the bond resumed. . . . For twelve years we've been meeting every week. I've often asked myself this question, how this bond has managed to last so many years . . . there's this strange thing of an unfulfilled *re'ut*." It is interesting to note how Amnon formulated the relation between the two phases of the relationship: "In the army, there was this intuition that there's a potential, and this potential revealed itself during these later years." Rather than basing the ongoing bond, as many others would, on the construct of a *shared past*, he held the earlier one to have been an *unfulfilled* bond, a promising potential that was fulfilled only years later, making it possible for them to resume the bond immediately. This formulation deserves further attention, for instead of imagining a past it seems to imagine a future.

Most of the narratives considered so far describe a gradually emerging bond in a given setting whereby some mutual interest brought two (or more) friends together. But in a few stories the onset of the friendship is described as a sudden encounter between two men, referred to as an immediate "click." It involved a situation when one of the friends, or both, arrived in a new social setting, most notably in the military, although these accounts are not limited to the military context. As these stories offer an interesting reading, I present in some detail three such significant accounts, told as free narratives. The first striking case is that of Nachshon:

> The story began quite strangely and accidentally. It started in boot camp . . . in the middle of all the insane activity at boot camp, in an incredible, miraculous, inexplicable way similarly to how people sometimes describe love at first sight with someone, exactly along these lines. One day I saw this small, pale man that wasn't even in my company, he was in the second company, and yet something in that glance, something had started us talking. During basic training we hardly had any contact except for some glances here and there, we noticed each other and chatted . . . [we knew] we wanted to talk and meet, I don't know what. Then, when we arrived at a military course that lasted for six months at a closed base, and we were both there, the bond started to develop, and it lasted from age eighteen to thirty-three or so, in a very intensive way that I'll describe to you.

In this account, which began his interview, Nachshon described his first encounter with his close friend Michael (who later became a prominent Israeli writer), as well the development and decline of their bond over time. They were in different platoons in the hectic situation of basic training, and "miraculous" circumstances brought them to talk to each other for the first time, a moment described as "love at first sight." The actual "incubation" of their bond, as he later put it, took place when they spent the ensuing six months together in military training. From that point onward they left for different bases, and after their military service moved to live in different areas; yet they maintained an intensive relationship. This dramatic formulation of his friendship with Michael stands in strong contrast to the way in which Nachshon described his earlier lifelong friendship with Gershon, mentioned earlier, in terms of a familial rhetoric. What is the role of Nachshon's initial encounter with Michael in his understanding of their relationship? He suggested that "in retrospect, since we had become such good friends we could recall this initial exchange of glances, this spotting of each other, before our first in-depth conversation." This early spotting conveys a notion of an anticipated future, a shared destiny.

As a means to explain a strong bond, the notion of shared past is enhanced, then, by that of *shared destiny*. I refer to this narrative construct as a "romantic rhetoric," although this term should not be confused with the cultural and historical senses of the romantic, which I discuss in chapter 6. But in terms of a building block in the narrative, the notion of shared destiny can be viewed as a romantic rhetoric of friendship in that it invokes an immediate click, an exclusive, intimate partnership based, among other things, on emotional thrills, that in some instances is colored by romantic terms by the interviewees explicitly, such as love at first sight. Unlike other accounts of male bonding, these accounts are restricted to a relationship between two men only.

Haim presented another extraordinary story of a very strong attachment that developed with Yitzhak, whom he first met when hitching a ride from his military base, where Haim served as a career officer:

> He gave me a lift to Tel Aviv. I was preoccupied with a terrible incident of a solider threatening to commit suicide, and I told him. . . he was fascinated and listened to me the whole ride, and I recall when we arrived . . . he said something like, 'Hearing you tell this is like being in a movie. I enjoyed the ride,' he said. So I told him, 'I'm glad, thanks for listening because I needed to talk to someone . . . and then a week later or so, on the way to the bus, he sees me and says hello . . . now I'd never before seen him stand . . . and he's 191 cm tall. I said hello. So he said, 'Do you remember me?' I said, 'I think so' [he said] 'don't you remember giving me a ride the other day and telling me about so and so?' He remembered simply everything. . . . [he said] 'I'm working here at offices next to the city. There's a café there, why don't we go and have a cup of coffee.' I said, 'Why not.' So we sat there and since that day to this day there hasn't been a day when we didn't speak at least twice, at least.

Although later in his narrative Haim described in detail how their relationship had gradually built up, note how in this initial account he offers a melodramatic formulation of how they bonded immediately, hooking up for coffee and starting a relationship of twelve years, so that "since that day to this day" they had almost never parted. Their relationship did come to an abrupt end a few months prior to our interview upon Yitzhak's sudden death, which I will turn to discuss in part three.

Yet another dramatic story was presented by Hezi, who recounted his "falling in love" with Yoni, a soldier who was transferred to his base and was to work with him in the same position, as a war-room operations sergeant:

> And here I come to talk of Yoni. Yoni is a brother friend. If there's a friend-ship that I can say was like falling in love with a friend, it's Yoni . . . he was stationed at another base of our unit up north . . . I knew him through the phone, by his voice, perhaps once I might have seen him but not more than that. As part of our job we would exchange messages, I knew he was cute, and he knew I was the clown of my base . . . and then he turned up and I saw him and started talking with him. I was supposed to teach him the job for one day, and stay the night [shift] with him. I won't forget this . . . it came to a situation that in between telephone calls and work we constantly talked and got to know each other. The only thing we didn't have in common I think was that he was a vegetarian or something. With time, in a manner of hours, I simply fell in love with him, I loved him. . . . And then night came, we both had beds in the same room, with the table in between. I go to sleep and put my head down and I see him under the table. We began asking each other personal questions . . . we went to bed at around eleven, and sud-denly it was four in the morning, and we were still talking.

Beyond the fact that they all allude to a close friendship, there is little in common between the details of these relationships, and their place in each person's life. Technically, what they seem to a share is a circum-stance of preliminary contact between the two men, sometimes accom-panied with a hint of flirtatious courting, and at any rate forming some kind of anticipation. This preliminary contact is then followed by an intense encounter, a moment of an instant connection from which point onward the friendship immediately becomes an intensive bond. This intense encounter is the striking point where these romantic accounts depart from other accounts of friendship. While in other cases we've seen so far the men drew on shared activities and eventually on a shared past as a retrospective explanation for a given bond, here it seems that they deliberately create together in one intense moment a truly imagined shared past, an exclusive past shared between the two of them, a past constructed as means to build a future, constructed in anticipation for a shared future. This is how Hezi recollected, in great detail, his unique encounter with Yoni:

> I recall we talked about everything. We talked about work in the army, and what it was like for him to serve in the north. Kind of filling in each other's history. When he told me about a certain period, I would tell him about the same period in my life; where we grew up; where we started off; what oth-ers were like. It's like we completed for one another the story of our life, at the interesting level of things for one another. After a few hours of work and plenty of laughs we saw that our mindset was similar, and so suddenly we

were filling in for one another what each had been missing, things that from
that day onward I know about him and he knows about me. In principle we
leveled the line [evened things up] that night.

The term "leveling the line" derives originally from IDF terminology.
It relates to fire drills where soldiers are taught to stay in a straight line
so as not to shoot each other while they advance to shoot at targets. By
"leveling the line" Hezi positioned himself and his friend as equal to one
another so that they could now move on forward together. But in Hezi's
depiction, the future holds much more than simply moving forward together; it holds the promise for a union between the two parts of one soul:
"and so suddenly we were completing for one another what the other had
been missing." Hezi touched on the ultimate description of the "romantic" ideal, which goes back to one of ancient myths described in Plato's
symposium, the merging of the self with its missing piece, the fantasy of
a total union (Plato 1951; Josselson 1992: 75).

Another feature of dyadic bonds that implies a romantic rhetoric is
the attempt to carve out a sense of exclusive intimacy between the two
men. Homosocial relationships are denied easy access to exclusivity. They
do not enjoy the luxury of privacy that adult heterosexual partnerships
do, within the confines of the domestic home. Male confidants need to
actively carve out a special space, both geographically and emotionally,
where their sense of intimacy can be maintained. Some of these spaces
may acquire a specific coloring of male intimacy and become a kind of
emotional *sanctuary*. Hezi related the facts of a casual friendship with
Dudi, whom he had known since kindergarten. In high school their bond
was forged around cutting classes and hanging out on the beach. Later on,
during military service, the harsh experiences each of them went through
reinforced the bond by creating a stronger need to confide in one another.
They would meet on weekend leaves at the same place on the beach, and
this public space became an isolated space where they could develop
a stronger intimacy: "It all centered around that same spot in the sand
under the same beach shed, all those years. The only times I saw Dudi
hurting was there . . . a spot that was somehow another space reserved
for us as close friends where he could almost cry over friends that died
around him in Lebanon, things like that."

These secluded spaces of emotional sanctuary can assist in creating the
semiromantic ambience that some interviewees have alluded to in their
accounts of long-lasting friendships. Nachshon analyzed the "incubation"
of his intensive relationship with Michael, when they both attended a
long, professional course in their military training. They would leave the
base at night and go out to the nearby fields: "We walked around mostly
in the fields outside the base, night by night, and it's there that this foundation and bond was formed. . . . Almost every other day we'd finish
class at ten, eleven at night, it was a very intensive course, and at eleven

we'd go out to the fields and chat. This pattern started out there and went on for fifteen years."

In addition, they maintained their bond during these subsequent years by two means—ongoing letter correspondence and carefully designed meetings once every three weeks for three or four hours at a time, in remote places where they could simply be together alone:

> And mainly, as soon as the army service ended, it became a strong commitment to meet every two to three weeks and to talk, beyond phone conversations. The meetings would always take place in nature, in the hills, on the beach, at a quiet spot with only the two of us . . . we set up this routine of a certain time schedule and we consistently carried it out, for ten years, once every three weeks. . . . We'd sit in the place where there was complete silence, a remote café, a beach, whatever, the Carmel forest . . . the point was that there were no people around, no disturbances. It was a closed circle of two people that the outside world can't invade.

These periodic meetings took place at ritualized moments in time and space, detached from everyday life, representing a shared emotional state unique to the two confidants.

Evidently, maintaining close friendships tends to become more difficult with the changes that occur in men's lives between early and late adulthood. The growing responsibilities and emotional investments in family life and career considerations reduce opportunities for creating secluded spaces to negotiate dyadic friendships. Similar trends have been noted elsewhere. For instance, Anthony Rotundo (1989) studied middle-class men in northern United States in the nineteenth-century, depicting "romantic" ties during youth that tended to diminish with the onset of marriage and career obligations. In the Israeli case, the homosocial enclave afforded by military service in early adulthood and the periodic reserve duty throughout subsequent adult life facilitates the negotiation of intimacy beyond the youth period and provides the men with additional "justification" to leave family and career commitments in order to be with some of their military friends. Such meetings can then take place not only during actual military duty but also through private initiative. But these are mostly group reunions. In this sense Nachshon's account of dyadic reunions with his military friend is rather uncommon.

Perhaps the epitome of an exclusive, private, sanctified space is when the two close friends can travel together for a substantial period of time. Haim described how he and Yitzhak insisted on going together abroad on vacation on their own. Leaving behind the "real" world of spouses, family, and work, they carved for themselves the prefect romantic quest, where they could negotiate their intimacy:

> Every few months we'd find reasons to go abroad . . . when the kids were born she [Haim's wife] couldn't come anymore . . . one time, on the trip

before our last, we drove for twelve hours nonstop. We didn't stop talking . . . except for moments that we said 'enough, let's have ten minutes of quiet,' and then we only waited for these ten minutes to end . . . d'you know what's it like to sit with a man for twelve hours, and before that, it's not like we didn't talk the day before. There wasn't a topic or a person in the world that we didn't analyze, turn around, discuss . . . it was madness.

The actual activities on the trip seem only secondary to the promise of simply being together, going though shared experiences.

In contrast to special trips, there are also many simple ways to form spaces of exclusivity within everyday life. Amnon described the simple way that he and Benjamin created an exclusive space in their weekly timetable, in a way that merged with their familial routines:"Every Saturday morning at eight-thirty we meet, come what may. We do a walk of seven or eight kilometers, come back, eat breakfast together, and so we spend two and a half hours together. Sometimes the women join us, when we get back." Such small rituals enable the men to meet their emotional need to be together on a regular basis.

Part of the idolizing and idealization of these male bonds seems to come from their comparison to the humdrum of family life. In these secluded moments outside everyday life, the experience becomes "romantic," as Hezi, who is also married, put it:

[There are] two circles. In the family circle I'm with the small things, with washing the dishes, with doing laundry. . . . In the greater circle of friends . . . you get the level of communication for actual things, for the fun things that they are meant to be for . . . look, when I glide [hang-gliding] with my friend and we see the sunset above the Sea of Galilee it's a romantic moment, because the situation is like that, but it's not only for that. Most of the things you do with your friends are pleasant; if you do with your friends only unpleasant stuff that's really bad for you.

By this reading, the voluntary nature of the homosocial bond places it on the side of one's significant pleasures in life, relegating family activities to the realm of petty obligations. What more, given the social restrictions on heterosexual adventures outside marriage, the homosocial adventuring provides the men with a taste of "extra-marital" thrills in a safely legitimate setting.

However, homosocial bonds have their own limits. Expressing a strong desire to stay close to his friends, Hezi also noted the clear limitations restricting their relationships: "The geographical distance is really a problem . . . we're much busier, working longer hours. If you have kids than it's the kids. I think that somehow it pushes aside all these things, hoping that a day will come and we could somehow live next to each other, but . . . I can't build a village of my friends." This implausible fantasy of living side by side with one's friends in an imaginary village recurred in different versions with several interviewees. Yehuda, younger and unmarried, went along with such a vision in a much more concrete and unreserved way, expressing an explicit desire to hook up with his best friend Rami, hoping that their career choices would enable them to stay together in the same spot and set up a home together: "Looks like we will be many years together yet. We even plan it. We once said that we'll probably end up buying a big communal house, each of us on a different floor, one day he would cook and the other day I would, and we would share our stuff. We'd come back from work, each would have his own corner but we could also be together."

This vision portrays a desire for *pairing* constructed in the manner of heterosexual marriage. Indeed, the notion of a pair was often explicit in the interviewees' accounts. In some cases it was reflected in their everyday relationships, and not confined to exclusive, secluded spaces. Perry, also unmarried, unfolded the implications of his close-knit and intimate relationship with Shlomi. Being in such close contact with each other, they were sometimes termed "husband and wife": "We simply live one inside the other. . . at the everyday level of life he's so involved in my life . . . from the most silly things, I mean if we go see the [sport] finals together we talk about it for two weeks . . . there's things I can talk about with him and not with her [a close friend], and I can speak with him differently, more freely. . . . They often call us husband and wife."

The Chemistry Metaphor

A recurrent metaphor for the interaction associated with friendship is the chemistry metaphor. This image was the most common way to explain how a strong bond formed or evolved. It captures the notion of strong similarity and complementarity between the two (or more) friends. It also invokes a recurrent image of being "in the same head," i.e., having the same mindset. A related notion is a sense of a flowing communication, a mutual language, through special codes and gestures and up to the point of total telepathy. In more extreme accounts this image is accentuated by the myth of a twinship, whereby the two men share not only the same head but also the same soul. I illustrate the use of this metaphor by focusing predominantly on narratives related to the romantic rhetoric, but many aspects of chemistry served also to explain other narratives, including those that stressed a familial rhetoric.

Whereas chemistry is a rational science, the interviewees use it from precisely an opposite perspective, as an unexplainable, semimagical power that brings the men together, reminiscent, perhaps, of alchemy more than chemistry. Shahar alluded to chemistry in order to stress the irrationality of his bonds: "You don't bond with people because he's this or that, it's just one of those things that happens . . . perhaps not to bond with someone is a rational decision. But with friendship I think the reasons are less rational. The fact is that it happened and the chemistry has formed, you can't say it's because he's this or that."

Chemistry denotes attraction between people. It draws on the age-old question of whether people are attracted to those they perceive as similar to themselves or to opposites (Aristotle 1962: 1155a33). One notion is that personal attraction is a case of similar souls seeking to unite; the other is that personal attraction is a case of two opposites attracting each other like the positive and negative poles of a magnet. N., the senior air force commander, perceived this magnetic field as a case of where each side completes the other: "There are magnets where the underlying motivation is complementing one another, satisfying curiosity about other worlds that other people can contribute to you. So the support and help actually derives from complementing one another."

Yehuda related to the differences between him and his best friend Rami. He perceived himself as more outgoing and talkative, and Rami as more introverted and silent. However, they became more similar as their relationship evolved, with each serving as a mirror for the other and thus getting closer. The apparent contradiction in their personalities created a sense of complementary union. A similar notion of similarity reinforced by differences was raised by Nachshon. He stressed the intellectual and emotional affinity between himself and his friend Michael. Coming from different directions and backgrounds, the fact that they reached exactly the same insights separately and then shared them together served to strengthen their sense of similarity and union.

As an explanatory construct, the chemistry metaphor it is not restricted to the romantic formulations of friendship. Some men also employed it when referring to slowly evolving bonds based on shared past experiences and growing understanding between the friends. But chemistry is an especially constructive way to make sense of an immediate click and strong, quickly evolving interactions. This is how Hezi explained his "falling in love" with Yoni, described earlier: "I simply fell in love with him, I loved him. I saw an honest, pure, true person who laughed at every silly little thing I said and I laughed from at every silly little thing he said, a kind of chemistry that I'd never had with anyone else."

A key image of the chemistry metaphor is the image of being "in the same head," (*be-otto rosh*), i.e., having the same mindset, thinking alike. Another interviewee, Shuki, a computer programmer aged twenty-nine, noted that even though his friendship with Ari has developed over time, a sense of an essential similarity was there from the very beginning, based on a "connection in the head": "The kind of connection we had was from the start a connection in the head, we met and found ourselves engaging in conversations." Shuki's use of the term "head" emphasizes that their chemistry was on an intellectual level. What connected them was their ability to talk "the same language," as well as to "think in the same way; we can understand each other's ideas."

Being "in the same head" also implies a flowing, unrestricted communication. Along these lines, Yoram described his unexplained connection with his newly acquired friend from college, Nir: "We formed this shared language, we were the head trouble-makers in class, we would think alike, I can't explain it but we were simply the same head. I felt with him simply in the same head. We even had the same grades, it's amazing, everything was alike." In this respect, the flowing communication involved in being "in the same head" extends beyond intellectual, linguistic, and social affinity; it can reach a point of telepathy. This is how Hezi described his growing bond with Yoni, which expanded into a threesome with another friend they met in college, Ami: "We had amazing telepathy. Every time I'd call Yoni at work Ami would call too, every time . . . and then we'd have a conference call immediately. That was also the kind of thing we would do in those days."

Sharing "the same head" is one step removed from sharing the same body or soul, which brings us to another key image of chemistry, that of twinship. Twinship is the ideal paradigm for similarity in friendship. Its significance is twofold. First, it underscores extreme familiarity between the friends in terms of sharing the same experiences, going through the same path. Along these lines, Gadi employed the concept of twinship in order to underscore not only his similarity to his best friend from the military, Gidon, but also the fact that Gidon was: "a twin in terms of the path we went through throughout our service, and in meeting after the army. Everywhere, I mean in boot camp, in the platoons . . . we found a connection between us, a connection of closeness, of understanding . . . and it's the same path all over again. We both flunked out of officers' school, went on to be instructors in the same battalion."

At a deeper level, the concept of twins carries within it a notion of closeness that is stronger than brotherhood. Twins are perceived as literally connected as two bodies in one soul, enjoying total understanding, sharing the same preferences and tastes, and communicating with absolute telepathy. This is how Meir described his relationship with Baruch: "So ever since I can begin remembering you could say that we were simply connected in a phenomenal way. It's really more than a brother, because we would think of the same things, love the same things . . . it's how you express your thoughts, in what tone, under what situation. Which movies you enjoy, what parts you like best . . . whether you would prefer this corner in the garden over that corner." Wherever they were, their experiences were alike, so that one could replace the other. Studying in the same programs and attending the same classes in university, "there was no point in us both sitting in classes because if you read the class notes they were the same notes. It was unbelievable how much you could reach almost the same notes, with the same nuances." And over time their bond resulted with in the deepest intimacy: "And with age things only became deeper, there was more a sense of togetherness, of closeness, that reflected in everything that's good and bad, and what you want to talk about, the most hidden secrets etc."

It is here that the chemistry metaphor acquires its full magical, miraculous significance. Talking of his new college friend Nir, Yoram enthusiastically relayed the uncanny coincidence that somehow destined them both to go through the same events in life: "All these three years we did everything together. We even both went through accidents, two weeks apart. I had an accident on my scooter and two weeks later he went through an accident on his motorcycle, exactly the same. People came up to us in class and said 'What's going on?!'. . . I don't know, there's so many things I can't explain."

Twinship invokes and underscores the notion of shared destiny. Far beyond the concept of similarity, the twinship myth invokes the Aristotelian paradigm of friendship: "a single soul dwelling in two bodies" (cited in Josselson 1992: 161). When the two "twins" meet for the first time, realizing they were meant to be one, they need to catch up on their imaginary shared past, each one finding in the other his missing piece, so that they can now unite again and fulfill their shared destiny.

Interim summary: Narrative Building Blocks of Friendship

The present chapter has offered a general glance into Israeli men's narratives of friendship across the life-course. It delineates various narrative building blocks, ways by which informants explain the strengths of long-lasting, close bonds. My intention was to demonstrate that underneath the structural and often banal formulations of friendships, as these are often discussed in the social sciences, some deep cultural meaning systems are in play. Beyond the chronological origins of friendships at different life stages, I have focused on three mutually nonexclusive meta-themes that represent "origin." A central account of male friendships focuses on shared activities, from playing games to telling stories. It demonstrates how concrete experiences are transformed into the broader realm of folklore. This folklore in turn endows the present friendship with a sense of a meaningful past, creating a broad cultural construct of friendship that I have termed shared past. It resonates with a familial rhetoric of friendship along the lines of kinship and involves a continuing reconstruction, or invention, of the friendship's "traditions." It reflects the localized dynamics of collective memory, played out in the smallest of possible collectives—the dyad, the threesome, or intimate group.

An alternative cultural construct of origin employed by the interviewees is that of shared destiny. In some cases it is set in the context of dramatic circumstances that accompany the first encounters between the men, in which case the narrative stresses a sudden and immediate click between them, a semimagical power that brought them together, similar to a romantic rhetoric. It represents a longing for a shared future and is reinforced by carving out secluded, sanctified spaces where the two can enjoy their exclusive bond. The romantic accounts are not a prevalent description of male relationships. Most interviewees did not employ explicit romantic terminology. But their very presence as a building block in some narratives and their indirect presence in others—for instance, through the chemistry metaphor—depict the potential for emotional richness in homosocial relations and deserve further attention, as I will explore in the following chapters.

Notes

1. For instance: studies of interpersonal attraction focusing on the circumstances that contribute to the formation of an acquaintanceship and the processes through which people become friends, whether in terms of environmental factors such as physical proximity and familiarity, or in terms of individual factors such as psychological, social-occupational and ethnic similarity (e.g., Berscheid and Reis 1998; Gurdin 1996: 122); studies of social and historical circumstances that shape the intensity and frequency of the relationship over time (e.g., Lopata 1981; Rotundo 1989); and studies of social penetration (Altman and Taylor 1973) or reciprocity (Rubin 1975) that analyze growing emotional intimacy within the relationship.
2. The *ma'abarot* were temporary camps established by the Israeli government in the 1950s to lodge refugees and new immigrants from an array of Jewishcommunities, especially mizrachi immigrants. Gadi's *ma'abara*, however, consisted of a rather mixed community, including *ashkenazi* immigrants, such as himself.
3. Liora Sion (1997), following Victor Turner (1974: 94–97), has analyzed the ritualized-emotional aspects of the combat training that strips the new recruits of their earlier civilian status and transforms them into full-fledged soldiers.

Chapter Four

Two Styles of Sharing: The *Hevreman* and the Intellectual

Introduction: Is male intimacy a contradiction in terms?

In this chapter I turn to a more *gendered* analysis of Israeli male friendships. I move from general building blocks of friendship in the narrated experience to take a closer look at explicit male rhetoric of sociability and intimate sharing in everyday life, and how this rhetoric draws on local values of hegemonic masculinity. Following academic trends elsewhere, recent years have seen the first fruits of research on ideals and practices of masculinity in Israeli culture. Many studies discuss the special role that the military holds for Israeli masculinity and associated factors such as citizenship, solidarity, emotions, and sexuality. Most of the analyses focus on the dominant, hegemonic values of masculinity (e.g., Ben-Ari 2001; Helman 1999; Lieblich 1989; Sion 1997; Yosef 2001) and some have also explored how marginalized groups negotiate these values (e.g., Kaplan 2003a; Lomsky-Feder and Rapaport 2000; Monterescu 2003; Sasson-Levy 2002). Yet so far, there has been no study of Israeli culture focusing on masculine relatedness—on the intricacies of male-to-male bonding, both inside and outside the military.

Many studies on gender and relatedness in recent decades, predominantly in Anglo-American cultures, suggest that male friendships are relatively lacking in intimacy compared to women's friendships. Scholars have argued that men are less likely to disclose their feelings to other men, are less willing to talk about personal topics, provide less emotional support than women do, and express less physical affection and closeness in their bonds (e.g., Josselson 1992: 232; Miller 1983; Pleck 1975; Rubin 1985; Sherrod 1987). A similar trend has been noted in Israel (e.g., Eshel, Sharabany, and Friedman 1998). Based on Donald Winnicot's (1971) initial psychoanalytic distinction between 'being' and 'doing,' the recurrent view emerging from the literature on same-sex friendship is that men engage in similar interests and mutual activities and are involved in "doing" things together, yet often lack an ability to reach significant intimacy between one another, of "being" together. Lillian Rubin put forward what is perhaps the most compelling argument in this vein. She suggested that men's relationships consist of "bonding without intimacy," a relationship often felt as an intense connection yet lacking in verbal expression and in discussion of feelings (Rubin 1986: 169). Similarly, Amia Lieblich associated Israeli men with 'doing' on the basis of stereotypes of men as performance-oriented through terms such as *bitzuist* ('performer'), preferring to solve difficulties through action and less expressive in the emotional sphere (Lieblich 1983). The dominant assumption in these studies, which were conducted mostly within psychological frameworks, associates intimacy, and the related notions of closeness and sharing, with *disclosure*—i.e., the overt verbal expression of internal emotional experience. Under this view, male friendships are perceived to lack intimacy because men often avoid disclosing and "revealing" their feelings and inner states, especially to other men (Josselson 1992: 230). Some popular psychological literature has reinforced such images to the point of presenting contemporary men as emotionally handicapped (see, for instance, Nardi and Nardi 1992; Real 1997).

Although many of the men I interviewed acknowledged the prevalent stereotypes regarding the dichotomy in men and women's bonds, it would be difficult to place their own friendships under such a narrow view of the "male" type sociability. To begin with, at the semantic level, consider the following definition Raviv formulated for his close friendship with Milles. Reflecting on the activities the two of them shared, he noted: "A good friend is someone you can go through shared experiences with, and this is one more thing I had with Milles." In Hebrew "experience" (*havaya*) is a general term that could refer not only to actions but also to the subjective feelings attached to these actions. It is therefore open to various interpretations and cannot be narrowed down to either "doing" or "being."

Furthermore, in the concluding section of the interview, I asked the informants explicitly for their general definition and understanding of male intimacy. One aspect of intimacy they alluded to was the ability to expose oneself in the presence of friends by telling them of intimate matters. For instance, Shuky responded: "The ability to share things that you don't share with other people . . . For example its hard for me to share my weaknesses, or when I feel bad I don't talk to people about it. But with friends I can share it. So that's intimacy—not being afraid to share parts you are afraid to share with other people." These and similar definitions draw on a core characteristic of intimate friendship discussed both in sociology and in psychology. Allan Silver notes the normative ideal of friendship in modern culture as a relationship bound up with intimacy, understood as "the confident revelation of one's inner self to a trusted other" (Silver 1990: 1477). From a psychological perspective, Ruthellen Josselson discusses intimacy as the penetration of barriers, the capacity to "let down defensive walls that keep us from revealing ourselves" and "simply be who we are" (Josselson 1992: 165). Such definitions reiterate the notion of 'being' and include the capacity of being vulnerable, presenting one's weaknesses without feeling ashamed, and trusting the other to be supportive rather than judgmental.

However, it is important to place such isolated responses in broader context. Shuki's definition associates intimacy with the term "sharing." This was a recurrent term employed by most informants. What does sharing consist of? Beyond explicit definitions, what is more revealing is how the informants relate to intimate sharing in their free narratives when describing their personal bonds and how the distinctions they make draw on shared cultural values.

A closer systematic analysis of the free narratives suggests a consistent distinction between two styles of sharing. Benny, aged twenty-six, provided a good starting point for this distinction. Benny began his interview introducing two friends from his military service in an elite reconnaissance unit:

> I had two really close friends, each of a different sort, Yaroni and Leibo . . . with one it was more fun doing those kinds of soul-to-soul conversations . . . [Leibo] is a kind of psychologist, he actually studied psychology, really . . . And the other one is Yaroni who is a different sort completely. He's very active, full of schemes and jests.

Benny characterized two kinds of friends, each representing a different type of male bonding. Leibo is designated as a psychological-intellectual friend, with whom one can engage in deep conversations. Yaroni is presented as an outgoing, adventurous, and socially active kind of friend, with whom one can engage in jests and teasing activities. Many interviewees echoed these distinctions in describing some of their actual friendships. Their accounts were nested in two alternative, persistent images of Israeli-Zionist masculinity. The first type revolves around *hevreman* sociability; the second, around "intellectual" or ideologically inclined sociability. Furthermore, underlying each prototype is a different understanding of how close friends express emotional support. Eventually, they present two different ways through which the broad notion of "sharing" is made sense of. I substantiate the personal narratives with some canonic representations and historical sources that demonstrate how the men's perceptions subscribe to collective knowledge they share as hegemonic members of contemporary Israeli society.

The *Hevreman:* Cool Sociability

The Yiddish-derived term *hevreman* (literally, 'man of the group') served as a hegemonic behavioral model for the first *sabras*. From its initial usage in the pioneering era at the beginning of the twentieth century, the *hevre-man* was explicitly contrasted with the Jew of the Diaspora, and was consequently perceived as the dominant reflection of the "New Jew" in the Zionist revolution (Almog 1997: 371). In addition to the values of youth, strength, health, physical labor, and deep-rootedness, sociability evolved as another ideal of this new hegemonic masculinity. For instance, a characteristic eulogy for fallen soldiers during the 1948 War of Independence centered on the notion of "being one of the *hevreh*" and a great friend (Sivan 1991: 165).

The writer Yehuda Atlas presented a critical picture of these cultural images, describing the camaraderie of his childhood friendships in the 1950s as based on a phony, superficial sense of sociability in the manner of *"arema shel hevre al ha-deshe"* (pile of guys on the grass).[1] He interpreted this kind of sociability as lacking intimate disclosure: "I don't recall any true conversation, from the heart, between two kids. Talking about matters of the heart was considered softy, nerdy. The only answer to 'How are you?' was 'No problems.'" (cited in Almog 1997: 451). Tamar Katriel (2004) notes that the Israeli directness of style known as *dugri* speech, which has been associated with the *sabra*, represents the tendency to disclose what's on one's mind in a straightforward, spontaneous, and predominantly impolite manner and does not usually involve emotional openness toward the interlocutor. Such trends are consistent with the communal ideology that characterized the early (socialist) Zionism and may have shaped men's relatedness in later generations. Wayne Baker and Rosanna Hertz (1981: 260, 264) argue that kibbutz structure and ideology set restrictions on the capacity for exclusive intimacy between individuals in an effort to foster the spirit of brotherhood. The intimacy of community substitutes for exclusive intimate relations. How are these notions reflected in contemporary perceptions of male bonding?

Benny described his military buddy, Yaroni: "He is a *kibbutznik* from the same region as me, and, I don't know, we thought alike, in terms of girls and stuff. And he was very dominant, Yaroni was the leader of the squad, he's charismatic and brave and he didn't give a fuck about anything." This is the typical portrait of the *hevreman*: kibbutz origin; heterosexual accomplishments; group dominance based on charisma; and bravery that is closely associated with rule breaking.

The *hevreman* is somewhat close in status to the contemporary American concept of a cool guy. The English term 'cool' itself has been assimilated in recent years by Israeli youth and media-oriented discourse from American culture (Rosenthal 2001: 78), referring to the trendy way to react and to relate to people, prescribing a prototypical kind of conduct. This sociability is associated with the homosocial group. Peter Lyman (1987) underscored how the male group bond is governed by a solidarity of shared risk, directed toward the breaking of conventional norms in the interest of group arousal and controlled by a pose of "being cool." Along these lines, the *hevreman* engages in "cool" activities involving risk taking and mischievous deeds. Ehud, aged twenty-six, recollected some of the exploits of his best friend since elementary school, Tzur:

> We walk down the street and suddenly he [Tzur] says to this guy we never met before who was just looking at the shop-window—he calls to him "Aaron!" The guy doesn't understand what the hell's happening. He goes on, "Mother's crying because of you, when will you come home?" And people start gathering around and asking, "What's wrong?" and he says, "He left us for another woman. Aaron, Aaron, we forgive you for everything!" . . . [and people] start attacking poor Aaron—he's not even called Aaron, but it doesn't matter. So it's all this funny stuff that can happen only with Tzur [laughs], what a personality.

The *hevreman* holds a pivotal role in initiating and inspiring activities by being sociable and easy-going (Almog 1997: 371). Much of what he does aims to impress his friends. Perhaps the most common denominator for such social engagement is the manifestation of (hetero)sexual achievements. Consider the following account by Benny:

> When you hang out with Yaroni he goes all the way—marijuana and beyond, easily. He also hits on anything in a skirt. If he doesn't end the night with a good fuck he doesn't call it a night . . . anything that moves, it doesn't matter what she looks like. She could look like a bull—he would make a pass at her just to end the night with a fuck and just for the sake of a laugh with the guys.

Under these norms, the sexual conquest of women is presented only as means to create a source of excitement within the group of friends. This cultural norm is captured in the common Israeli phrase "rush off and tell the guys," cynically describing how, the moment after having sex, Israeli men are eager to return to the guys and boast of their conquest.

Cool sociability is particularly valued in military culture. Whereas Ehud talked with great appreciation of his close friend Tzur throughout his narration, it seems that his merits became most visible during his military service:

> Tzur was a military star during his service. . . . They appointed him to a position that was usually carried out by an officer, and everyone was amazed by him, I mean he's the only one I know that could take this huge radio boom box, like black guys in elevators in the US, and dance to the music in the middle of his office, and when his commander enters and starts yelling at him he grabs him by the hand and starts dancing with him and the commander joins the party. And at the same time he would do the job perfectly . . . [in his unit] they made him this memory book with all kinds of stories, even more amazing and weird.

This example shows that what is especially valued in cool conduct is its success in combining lightheartedness, bordering on disobedience, with professional accomplishment. It's hip to be a rebel only if you can get away with it and still be admired by the system.

In this respect, the *hevreman* acquires the role of a leader of the male group. Gadi describes the leading role that Yoav held and still holds in maintaining and enlivening their longstanding childhood *havurah* by telling stories and jokes: "I can say that this *havurah* . . . usually crystallized around someone . . . I think that he [Yoav] more than anyone else, hosted people, and initiated, and in every reunion he would bring back the fun, the stories and jokes, the humor. . . it's like, if Yoav says 'come' everyone would come." By spicing up the group activities, preserving the fun atmosphere and turning past experiences into jokes, *hevreman* sociability is the key to managing the groups' folklore and the reconstruction of its traditions. If part of what friendships are made of is the ongoing invention of tradition, as discussed in chapter 3, *hevreman* sociability is the central mechanism of this practice.

On the face of it, the connotation of being cool suggests the opposite of intimate sharing and exposure. Cool performance is typically associated with the control of emotions. For instance, in military culture it reflects the ability to act with confidence, poise, and composure under trying circumstances (Ben-Ari 1998: 45). In the context of the homosocial group a cool attitude implies not responding angrily and seriously to practical jokes and acts of aggression between the men. Peter Lyman (1987: 161) analyzed this style as a "procedural" and "rule governed" relationship, as opposed to personal relationships based on intimacy and commitment. But what happens when this style of cool sociability is removed from the group context and experienced in dyadic circumstances?

The "Jack Test": Physical Support

The greater significance of the *hevreman*, in terms of relatedness is his role as a source of physical support, his readiness to help out a friend by being there for him in the right place at the right time. He may be easy-going and carefree, yet is always trustworthy and committed to his friends. A similar image has been noted in Oz Almog's account of *sabra* sociability (Almog 1997: 371). Some interviewees viewed this notion as the crucial test for male friendship. Tamir, a 34-year-old bachelor, described a prototypical scenario for this kind of support, which on the face of it seems to revolve around instrumental help. He called it "the jack test":

> Friendship between men means someone you can trust. . . in terms of help, like if you're moving [house] and need help in moving the refrigerator he'll come and give you a hand. I define it as if you, say, drive in the Arava [desert] highway in the middle of the night and get stranded without a [tire] jack you'll call him and he will get there. They call this the jack test.

I adopted Tamir's jack test scenario and asked subsequent interviewees to comment on this notion as a test case for friendship, asking them in what way it might be a valid analogy for helping their close friends. Some acknowledged this kind of test as the key to close friendship. Gadi, aged forty-eight, argued:

> In times of trial that's what counts. When someone is really in distress. That's exactly the key. . . When someone's daughter was in hospital and you come to visit her nonstop, and take turns sitting with her to fill in for her mother or father. There are no limits . . . It's when you really need the support, the first person that comes to mind, that you can pick up the phone and call him up.

Gadi's example stretches the jack test scenario, with its technical connotations, to a broader space of emotional involvement in the interpersonal sphere. Yet the common feature of both examples is the notion of unlimited support and availability. As one of the characteristics of the *hevreman*, this kind of support draws on a cool or hip demeanor. It may involve the breaking of external norms or rules, not just for the sake of group thrills, as noted earlier, but also for the sake of helping out a friend. Benny describes Yaroni's attitude: "He'll help you in any possible way, even if it meant going supposedly off course."

The crucial question is whether this kind of physical support should be interpreted as merely "instrumental" and lacking an expressive, emotional attribute. Consider another of Ehud's anecdotes about his friend Tzur:

> We were together in basic training, at the same base, but in different companies. One day in the middle of all that hell I suddenly see him, I thought I was dreaming, I was dead thirsty and had had no time to go to drink. And here he was handing me his canteen, and it had cold juice in it, nothing less. It was as if in the middle of a forced march an ice cream van would have stopped by, something on that level.

The simple gesture of being provided with a cold drink was experienced by Ehud as an amazing source of comfort and support, precisely because his close friend knew how to be there for him, in the right place and at the right time. This kind of physical support involves a strong aspect of emotional nourishment.

Benny stressed how the emotional support he received from Yaroni was not achieved through overt verbal communication, but by a sense of their great closeness:

> It was hard to do deep soul-to-soul conversations with him. He didn't like that, he wasn't very open at all; he was a very closed person. We would more or less communicate without talking about things, I would simply

know what was bothering him and he would know what was bothering me. There was this closeness, an immense chemistry . . . Yaroni could say "Cut the bullshit, get a grip on yourself," he wasn't like any other person on the side that you would think "Heck, why is he trying to encourage me right now." No, he knew exactly how to hit the right spots in me because he knew me so well.

In this context, the stress is on a nonexplicit mode of communication and sharing, contrasted with the alternative mode of soul-to-soul conversations. Despite being "closed," Yaroni could feel his friend's needs and relate to them in an intimate way. Benny offered a telling illustration of this kind of intimacy:

I always knew that whenever I had a problem I could come to his bed, with him . . . [While I was on reserve duty] I had nowhere to stay in Tel Aviv . . . and I would finish a day of training late at night and come to Yaroni's apartment. He would get rid of the girl, if he would have one that night—"listen, something's come up, there's some problems and you need to clear out"—and I would go with him to his bed in his little apartment, in his room.

Offering to share one's own bed (in this case at the expense of a girl for the night) can serve as an exemplary case of the underlying sharing involved in this style of support. It is a physical gesture that could be interpreted as providing the primary needs for "holding" and "containment" (Josselson 1992: 29–30). Despite the normative constraints on male-to-male bodily interactions, the men express strong physical closeness, as part of their willingness to engage in an act of unrestrained sharing. It is yet again a symbol of boundless availability for the sake of the friend, and in this sense it is another instance of the "jack test." Cool sharing implies leaving everything (and everyone) else aside, sacrificing personal comforts, and simply being there when one's friend is in need. From the men's perspective, the bed illustration, and the folk scenario of the jack test in general, combine physical or instrumental support with an experience of nourishment, closeness, and intimate exclusivity.

Re'a Le-Ra'ayon: Intellectual Sociability

The intellectual-ideological friend represents the countermodel to the *hevreman*'s hegemonic model for Zionist masculinity. Since the era of the Enlightenment in the mid nineteenth century, and, indeed, before the rise of the national-Zionist identity, Jewish men negotiated a new secular identity of an intellectual man involved in ideological concerns and practicing a cosmopolitan lifestyle. Various historical sources record not only the rich intellectual life of some prominent Jewish intellectuals, but also their deep friendships with male counterparts, and especially with other Jewish men of similar social background and ideological inclinations. A celebrated example that has been studied extensively is the friendship between Sigmund Freud and Wilhelm Fliess (Boyarin 1997b; Erikson 1980).[2] Another notable case involving not only Jewish intellectuals but also a Zionist context is the friendship between Gershom Scholem and Walter Benjamin (Scholem 1981).

Perhaps the clearest image reflecting the differentiation between the two Jewish identities is Max Nordau's contrast between the "coffeehouse Jew" and the "muscle Jew" (Mosse 1996: 152). In a similar vein, the Zionist pioneers tried to differentiate themselves from the image of the culturally educated intellectual, referring to this image derogatorily as a *tarbutnik* ("culturalist"). Yet at the same time, the intellectual and ideological world of the Zionist pioneers paradoxically resembled that of cosmopolitan Jewish culture. For example, in some socialist circles the men endlessly preoccupied themselves with ideology and dogma and their possible implementation in the everyday life of pioneering (Almog 1997: 216–217, 219). In addition, from its very inception Kibbutz life revolved around rich cultural activities set in community centers titled "houses of culture" (*batei tarbut*). Norms of communal consumption created conditions for creative leisure, enabling a specific division of free time for leisure activities (Rosner 1979).

What is interesting is how the distinction between the two types of male relatedness surfaces in contemporary narratives of friendships. Nachshon described his own long-lasting bond with Michael in light of the hegemonic role model of the more outgoing, *hevreh* type of friendship:

> It's not a friendship of going out together to bars, . . . it doesn't have any context of fraternity, of making sacrifices for one another. . . . We were exactly the opposite of *hevreh* people. That is, if there is one thing we have in common it's that we both went through high school and all detached, cut off and alienated from the basketball jocks in the class, ok? . . . [we had in common] the love of books and culture, and the lack of violence and thuggery and sports and all these classic masculine characteristics.

Although Nachshon perceived this intellectual, nonphysical sociability as contrasting with the *hevreman* style, he nevertheless viewed it as a masculine role model, not to be confused with femininity or homosexual masculinity: "It's not feminine . . . it's the need to express masculinity in non-physical terms, ok? . . . I'm allowed to be Jacob and not only Esau, aren't I? That is to say, I could be not only a warrior but also a home dweller, a man of books, a loyal friend, which on the one hand is not homosexual and on the other hand it's not masculinity in its stereotypical, bad sense." By comparing the intellectual/warrior dichotomy to the distinction between Jacob, one of the mythological fathers of Judaism, and his brother Esau, Nachshon ascribed supremacy to the former as an intellectual role model. The intellectual suddenly becomes heroic, gaining legitimacy from the biblical-Hebrew ethos to the same extent that the image of the new Jew as warrior gained its legitimacy from other biblical figures. This interpretation highlights an intellectual style of bonding that is not necessarily held to be less masculine than its counterpart, but is simply an alternative model for making sense of male friendship in the Jewish-Israeli context.

Intellectual sociability revolves around specialized, sophisticated, culturally inclined interests. Shuki described the kinds of activities he shared with his best friend from college: "We studied one year together. We were like intellectual friends. Culturally. We shared the same taste in arts. We listened to things that other people don't listen to . . . So we mainly had talks about how things were done, design. We talk and we go to movies, galleries. Performances of artists. Look at things, or walk through beautiful streets in Tel Aviv and look at interesting houses, and we talk."

Unsurprisingly, the college setting is more prone to encourage a mode of sociability based on stylistic preferences and intellectual exchange than other social settings. In this respect, if the military is a bastion of *hevreman* sociability, then higher education reinforces intellectual ties. What is more significant is that for some men, college friendships were not only instrumental for pursuing specialized, sophisticated interests but also for establishing a new kind of interpersonal affinity, an ability to share ideas, values, and set up a "pact," as Amnon briefly described the origin of a particular bond: "We studied art together. . . we saw ourselves as artists, sharing the same goals, as if we had this artistic pact. And very quickly it developed."

In this sense, intellectual relatedness focuses on the exchange of ideas. When discussing his much closer and longer lasting friendship with Binyamin, Amnon identified in their pact a distinct need for an exclusive interlocutor, a *ben-si'ach*, that could not be met elsewhere: "It provides me with a balance, it satisfies a need that I can not fulfill here at home, a need for a partner, a *ben-si'ach*, that I can't find at home, a partner that I can't find among my colleagues at work either." What is the nature of this discourse? Amnon reflected: "The central thing in our meetings is our conversations . . . it started from concrete questions, like I said, about girls, women, what you do and how, but it also got in many cases to more metaphysical questions, related for instance to developing a political worldview, and a religious worldview. Is there a God, isn't there a God, what history means . . . how politics get determined."

The topics of this dialogue can range from issues concerning their private lives to questions in political, social, and philosophical affairs, forming an undifferentiated link between the personal and the ideological. Rubik Rosenthal (2001: 155) notes that *re'a* (friend) might be loosely related to the word *ra'ayon* (idea) following an etymological association between the ordinary biblical usage of *re'a* as 'friend' and its rare occurrence in the Bible as thoughts in the sense of 'will' or 'desire,' such as in the phrase *banta le-re'î me-rachok* ("thou discernest my thoughts from afar")(Psalms 139:2). This ancient association between *re'a* as a friend, as will, and as the root of 'idea' brings to mind a possibility that one of the underlying intuitive and primordial senses of friendship (in the form of *re'ut*) is a notion of deep yet abstract alliance and understanding between individuals, an exchange of ideas (*ra'ayon*).[3] It suggests that at the heart of one folk image of male friendship is an ideological affinity—an intellectual exchange of ideas.

Feminist-psychological literature acknowledged this kind of "intellectual intercourse" as an important aspect of male relatedness, explained by men's greater need for "abstractness in relationships" compared with women's tendency for more "affective and ineffable realms of connection" (Josselson 1992: 224). According to this view men are more likely than women to be invested emotionally in other people based on the ideas these others convey, with the result that "ideology, for men, is often interchangeable with relatedness" (Josselson 1992: 233). This brings us to the question of the internal meaning assigned to this mode of interaction, particularly in terms of sharing and support. What are the expressive aspects of "intellectual" relatedness? Is it a substitute for ineffable, deep relatedness? Or is it an additional mode for expressing intimacy, another way to demonstrate support?

Sichot Nefesh (Soul Talk): Psychologistic Support

In his introductory distinction between his two good friends, the account that triggered my examination of this folk distinction, Benny noted: "[with Leibo] it was more fun doing those kinds of *sichot nefesh*. . . . He's a kind of psychologist . . . Leibo is the intellectual type, an endlessly babbling brainiac. But you know he's really smart, very smart and has a different perspective on life. . . . It's fun to have conversations with him, he's always interested, you can talk with him over an hour on the phone." *Sichot nefesh* (literally, soul talk) refers to soul-to-soul conversations. Historically, *sichot nefesh* has been associated with an institutionalized mode of communication among the "intimate group" in early Kibbutz life (most notably in the diaries of the *Bitaniya* commune in the 1920s). As analyzed by Tamar Katriel (2004), these gatherings were associated with the ideal of producing a small-scale community dialogue, grounded in the intimate sharing of crucial life experiences and holding the promise of a spiritual connection among the participants.

In contemporary Israeli discourse the notion of soul-to-soul talk is probably more a reflection of the growing dominance of an American psychologisitic rhetoric encouraging interpersonal conversation and communication mediated by the popular media, than it is a reflection of early Zionist ideology. Unlike the *hevreman*, the intellectual friend holds lengthy conversations. He represents the ability to be *articulate* in one's relationships, an ability drawing on psychological self-awareness. The intellectual interaction is associated with the verbal expression of emotions, whereby closeness and intimacy are made sense of in *psychologistic* terms. For instance, Perry employed psychologistic jargon to differentiate between his male friendships, contrasting his best friend Shlomi with a previous high school friend, Amir. Whereas Amir was "fun to be with" for a while, Perry felt that he could not "open up" to him the way he could to women friends and to Shlomi, and that in retrospect, this might have been the reason why he and Amir never became "soul mates."

The intellectual friendship is likened to a relationship with a psychologist. Raviv described one of his close friends, Hanan, as: "the levelheaded, calculated type . . . it's like talking to a psychologist, he knows me really, really well." In some cases the friendship appears to have evolved into a structure very close to a full-blown model of conversation-based therapy sessions, whereby each of the two friends alternately plays the role of the psychologist. Most noteworthy in this respect is Nachshon's account of his meetings with Michael: "And everything that I went through the previous three weeks, regarding myself, friends, girlfriends, my parents . . . it's my life plus how I looked at myself and thought how I could recount it. . . . I've never been to a psychologist, but I suppose it's a similar thing . . . and then during the meeting . . . many times one of us would talk for an hour, an hour and a half, and the other would respond."

In this kind of interaction, the friend serves to mirror, reaffirm, and respond to his partner. It almost seems as if their only point of departure from psychological therapy is that the interaction and support is understood to be mutual: "The need was to get reaffirmation for what you did, for how you developed and what you thought, and for your internal and cultural world from a person you appreciated very much and enjoyed speaking with. . . I would go through the meeting in my thoughts for hours after that . . . it was mutual self-observation." Nachshon concluded that this kind of interaction reflected intimacy, which he defined as: "Looking each other in the eyes and telling everything that weighs on your heart, including very unpleasant moments, your weak and painful points . . . every eyeblink and every self-insight was put on the table." In other words, intimacy in soul talk represents a mode of communication based on a heightened sense of self-awareness, which enables people to psychologize and philosophize about their issues and concerns.

How far are such conversations removed from unmediated, intimate sharing? Ruthellen Josselson (1992: 39) notes that the primordial need for 'holding' may become abstracted in adult life into depersonified relationships, a larger meaning system, such as religious beliefs and ideologies that provide something "to hold on to." The point is that from the informant's perspective, such ideological inclinations transformed into mutual discourse may have the affective outcome of intimate sharing. In some instances, the exchange of abstract ideas may enable the partners to find comfort in their friendship and provide interpersonal reassurance for expressing their vulnerabilities. Consider how the two features, the philosophizing and the holding, are combined in Modi's account of a short-term relationship with a friend from his military service:

> In those moments when I was depressed and desperate from the entire [military] setting . . . in those moments he knew how to give me the answer, he wasn't playing the comedian, he wasn't going through the routines of 'come on have a cup of coffee and tea and cakes.' Our conversations went very deep, into philosophy. He was a conservative, religious guy, and I was your totally secular guy. But our conversations around religion weren't just argumentative, but definitely deep philosophical conversations.

Notice again how this type of support is described in contrast with the routines of another form of sociability, that of playing the comedian or offering coffee and cakes—in other words, the entertaining, cool, *hevreman*, type of support.

In the intellectual style of relatedness support for one's friends is perceived in psychologistic terms and contrasted with physical support. Informants that favored intellectual sociability rejected the "jack test" as a trial for close friendship. Nachshon argued:

> We have two friends whose understanding of friendship is that if I were stranded with a motorcycle in Afula and I'd call him up and say "come!" he would come. For them this is the essence of the word friendship. And for me and Michael it's exactly the opposite . . . we don't need the physical, material proof to maintain our bond. It's like I and M. made a pact not to ask each other anything practical, except for lending an ear.

Similarly, Shuki rejected the Jack test idea, exclaiming: "Well, excuse me, but I'd do the same for you. I mean really, is that a test for friendship? I think it's silly . . . in a situation when I had to turn to someone I didn't turn to my first option, for technical or other reasons. You turn to whoever you can in that moment."

Taken together, the intellectual style presents a linkage between psychologistic discourse, in phrases such as "lending an ear," and an underlying ideological-intellectual affinity, a pact with the close friend who is perceived, not simply as an interlocutor, but as a "partner for discourse," a *ben-si'ach*. This pact echoes the association between *re'a* and *ra'ayon* (friend and idea). In particular, the concept of *sichot nefesh*, soul talk, captures at one and the same time an ideal of mutual consultation over interpersonal concerns and a deep engagement in ideological discourse. Both aspects of the intellectual intercourse are experienced as an intimate dialogue that is dependent on the verbal articulation of emotions and thoughts. This verbal intercourse shapes—indeed, becomes the essence of—the friendship.

Interim Summary: A Folk Model of Male Relatedness

The picture drawn above demonstrates the rich modes through which Israeli men negotiate intimate sharing in their everyday, lived experience, a
richness that has been little discussed in studies on friendship and gender.
Rather than examining male relatedness from the external point of view
of the psychological and sociological literature, I have delineated a "folk
model" of the emotions attached to male friendships, particularly with
regard to intimacy. Folk knowledge is based on *typifications* of lived experience (Rogers 1981) and consists of simple images, metaphors and categories through which people clump their experience in understandable
and repeatable chunks (Rosch 1978). These commonsense distinctions are
made from the point of view of the informants. They are a counterpoint
to scientific models, such as those provided by a psychological theory of
emotions (D'Andrade 1987). Obviously, the two styles of sharing could
be reduced to a distinction between opposing personality types, the first
alluding to a more extrovert and sociable personality and the latter to a
more contemplative one. However, what is interesting from a folk model
perspective is how these accounts are nested in cultural values and in two
alternative, dominant images of modern Jewish masculinity.

The first type, going back to Zionist values of the "New Jew," revolves
around the image of the *hevreman*, engaging in cool, fun activities that
border on mischief. It emphasizes physical support, based on a scenario
of total availability extending from technical, instrumental help to the
emotional support symbolized by sharing one's bed. The emphasis is
on a nonverbal mode of communication, sensing the friend's needs and
relating to them from a stance of closeness. The countermodel is that
of intellectual relatedness, situated historically in the image of modern,
cosmopolitan Judaism as well as in the Zionist preoccupation with ideological concerns. It stresses an intellectual pact based on the exchange of
tastes, opinions, and ideas, suggesting a linguistic association between
re'a (friend) and *ra'ayon* (idea). In terms of mutual support, it draws on
the notion of *sichot nefesh*, whereby the men's closeness is expressed in
psychologistic terms and is dependent on self-awareness and the verbal
articulation of emotions.

The two styles of sharing hinge not only on historical images but also
on institutional settings. *Hevreman* relatedness, even when practiced between two men only, is set against the backdrop of group sociability and
is especially marked in military settings. Intellectual relatedness, on the
other hand, is more typical of bonds that originate from the outset in a
particular contact between two or three men at most, based on mutual
interests. In this respect, it may be promoted in the college environment
or a specialized work setting.

How does this folk distinction bear on the 'being' versus 'doing'
paradigm of gender and intimacy? On the face of it, the model of cool

sociability and of physical support seems to echo a stance of 'doing,' whereas the countermodel of the intellectual and psychologistic support partly resembles the verbal disclosure associated with a stance of 'being.' In this sense, the very differentiation between these two models that emerges in the men's accounts suggests that Israeli men partly assimilate the distinctions in gender relatedness made by the feminist-psychological literature, possibly because these have been reflected in local media that are highly influenced by their American counterparts. In this vein, Karin Walker (1994) argues that the efflorescence of literature and media representations of gender differences in intimacy serve to create a widespread, uniform "cultural ideology" of these differences to such an extent that contemporary men themselves acknowledge these gender stereotypes. In a culture that increasingly encourages the expression of feelings, feminist writing, psychologists, and advocates of "men's liberation" have inculcated a critique of the alleged barriers that keep men from emotional intimacy (Kimmel 2000: 205).

The Israeli model of intellectual relatedness adopts the psychologistic discourse to present a similar critique of the "cool" style of bonding. This model has become more prominent in Israeli culture with the relative shift in the valorization of rural versus urban lifestyle. As the former lifestyle enjoyed cultural dominance during the early years of agricultural settlement, it encouraged *hevreman* style of sharing. But over the years, metropolitan urban lifestyle has become more and more pervasive and culturally esteemed. Since urban life offers greater accessibility to cultural-intellectual resources, it may further encourage the practice of an "intellectual" style of sharing. Along these lines, Oz Almog (2004: 984) has suggested that tendencies toward globalization among the Israeli elite have gradually replaced the *sabra* and its stress on "tough" masculinity with the idiom of the "Yuppie" and the potential for a "sensitive" and educated model of masculinity.

The various images and tropes of friendship discussed here present a normative picture, or rather, an ideal one. They avoid the negative emotions that are part and parcel of friendship, such as competitiveness, envy, and hatred. Beyond the distinction between the two styles of sharing what emerges is a general acknowledgment of a few basic emotions, set in a kind of hierarchical model extending from trust and intimacy up to unconditional love. Trust and mutual confidence are the basic aspects of friendship upon which all the rest may lie. It is the assurance that the friend will be there in good and bad times. It is often conceptualized through test cases, such as the folk scenario of the jack test, but it is just as often expressed in psychologistic terms, in disclosing one's innermost thoughts. Both aspects create a sense of intimate sharing. This sense of trust, in turn, is strengthened by admiration of the other's merits. It is also accompanied by feelings of mutual identification based on both similar and complementary traits. Indeed, it can reach high levels of flowing communication up to the point of seeming telepathy, and a notion of shared destiny and twinship, as discussed in chapter 3.

Finally, what is the place of love in this folk model? Love is the highest emotion in the hierarchy, as Yehuda put it:

> You reach a certain level in the friendship where you can already say that you love him. Loving him means that it's fun to be with him; it means I'll be with him even when it isn't such fun to be with him. . . and that if for a certain period of time we don't see each other, or don't meet up or don't talk—then when we suddenly meet up everything will bloom anew, as if nothing happened. The emotion is strong.

Love is the final indication that the bond is unconditional, lasting over time and unimpaired by circumstances. What is more, feelings of love may surge following a period of separation. These issues draw on deep longings that most interviewees refrained from describing explicitly. Yehuda's poetic formulation of love as "blooming anew" opens up a window to the accompanying unacknowledged emotions of passion and desire, a complex set of emotions that defy a simple folk model and deserve a more subtle exploration, the subject of the following chapters.

Notes

1. An expression from a popular song written by Meir Ariel, "The lawn-legend" (*agadat desheh*) (Pessachson and Eligon 1981: 215).
2. Erik Erikson characterized Freud with relation to his attitude with relation to Fliess as a "sometimes tragic believer in a kind of spiritual friendship" (Erikson 1980: 47).
3. Aphek and Tobin (1988) explored word systems in Hebrew whereby phonological or semantic associations between words sharing a common denominator in their core root (in this case, a double-consonantal root *r-'a*may converge with folk-etymological and even associative, unconscious interrelations, representing the speakers' intuitive use of language.

Chapter Five

PUBLIC INTIMACY AND THE MISCOMMUNICATION OF DESIRE

Introduction: The Homosocial Joking Relationship

"I could say to him 'you son-of-a-bitch!' and he would understand that I loved him." This is how Eli, a 40-year-old air-conditioning technician, described to me the way he communicated his feelings toward his close buddy and a work colleague. Friendship involves a wide spectrum of emotions, from affection, love, and passion to hatred and animosity. But how is it that a curse could be understood to express a sign of love? Are there particular ways by which certain emotions are communicated between men?

The previous chapters explored how male informants explicitly referred to emotions of closeness, intimacy and some aspects of love. So far, feelings associated with desire have been absent from the discussion. At the concluding part of the semi-structured interviews I asked the men to reflect on the place of various emotions in their male bonds. In discussing love (*ahava*) most interviewees distinguished between love for a male friend and love for a woman. Hezi was one of a few men who argued for the similarity of love in both cases, yet still marked a distinction in terms of sexual desire: "There is no difference. That's the point . . . I think there is no difference between my love for my friends and my understanding for my wife, except for the physical things that attract me in one direction and could never in my life attract me in this direction, for instance." It is interesting to observe how Hezi's perceptions unfold in this single sentence. He began with the conviction that there is no difference between his feelings toward men and women in terms of love, yet when unfolding this thought he refrained from directly comparing his love for his fellow friends to that of his wife, by placing "love for my friends" on a par with "understanding" for his wife. What's more, although I had not yet asked him about desire, he felt a need to deny any desire for his friends, by contradicting it with the "physical things" he shares with his wife. This *unfolding* of love to a *negation of desire* is at the heart of the present analysis.

I also asked the men explicitly about the place that desire or passion (the Hebrew term I used was *tshuka*) held in their male bonds. Here, the denial was overboard. They were usually very quick, sharp, and definite in their responses, much more so than to any other question I introduced. They tended to adopt a narrowly defined definition of desire as a sexual, bodily attraction, differentiating between heterosexual and homosexual attraction. This, in turn, enabled them to totally dissociate passion or desire from their male bonds.

But if the analysis is not restricted to the men's explicit reference to desire, there might be a variety of situations in male interactions where desire between the men is *implicitly* communicated, or rather *miscommunicated*. Humor is a mode of communication particularly susceptible to this kind of analysis. It has long been noted that joking behavior deals with emotions and tensions evolving in everyday life circumstances by expressing them indirectly, negotiating feelings that might otherwise endanger the social interaction (Emerson 1969). Many studies of male sociability note the role of humor and play, broadly defined, in men's interactions, including among close friends. In male subcultures such as preadolescent Little League, a vast majority of partners participating in pranks are best friends or close friends (Fine 1988: 47–48). The wide array of joking interactions extends into adult life. Humor and pranks in male subcultures are central strategies for refering to muted conflicts, offering culturally sanctioned safety valves to express potentially dangerous sentiments (Brandes 1980).

The joking relationship is a common theme in canonic representations of the Israeli male *havurah* (group bonding). It is especially salient in the folklore of combat military units, centering on practical jokes and hoaxes (Milshtein and Doron 1994: 122; Sion and Ben-Ari, 2005). Haim Guri's poem "A few words in praise of my friends" (Guri 1981: 228–231) captures many aspects of male friendship in the context of the Palmach units. Guri chose to read the poem to me during our interview. In one passage he refers to one of the Palmach's central trademarks, the *chizbat*, the public ritual of telling tall tales, especially when sitting around the campfire:

> I had friends who knew how to trick people and laugh,
> To tell jokes and recount fables
> In a society of truth speakers
> On winter nights under the tent-sheets and sheds
> And on summer nights under the stars.

This joking culture presents a ritualized language of relatedness, a distinct mode for communicating emotions. In the subsequent verse Guri writes:

> And many of my friends were liars.
> When you asked them how they felt,

Or if they needed anything, they would say—we're 'a hundred percent.'
And their eyes were red and their face covered with a two-week long beard
And they could hardly move.

Guri depicts the men's language as a language of *lying*, conveying the opposite of one's feelings, when it comes to expressing physical and emotional strain. The poem emphasizes how his friends avoided disclosing their emotions, a notion echoing the dominant feminist account of men's relatedness as "bonding without intimacy."

An ethnographic study by Peter Lyman (1987) has offered a focused analysis of the homosocial joking relationship in a college male fraternity. Lyman explores how the fraternal bond serves as a homosocial enclave, suspending the impending commitments and responsibilities of adult life represented by marriage and work. The possibility of a dyadic friendship with a woman implies loss of control and dependence, whereas the male group activity enables the maintenance of individuality and control. According to Lyman's analysis, the homosocial group forms a rule-governed aggression that enables the men to negotiate the tensions between their need for intimacy with other men and their fear of losing autonomy. The group engaged in sport activities, paramilitary games, or wild parties with the intention of forming suspense and thrill. Their solidarity was built around an "erotic of rule breaking" based on shared risk rather than on a social structure of shared intimacy. Eventually, this analysis reinforces the common notion of the homosocial bond as devoid of intimacy, a bond confined to "shared spontaneous action, 'having fun,' rather than to the self-disclosure that marks women's friendships" (Lyman 1987: 156).

In what follows I suggest a somewhat different perspective for the homosocial joking relationship, not as a rule-governed form of camaraderie struggling to retain a sense of *autonomy*, but rather as a semi-arbitrary, ambivalent language of relatedness striving to produce a sense of *intimacy*. Focusing on interactions between friends in public spaces of sociability I describe how they use verbal cues and physical gestures in order to communicate their feelings.

Exclusivity, a basic factor in defining and shaping the boundaries of close friendships (Simmel 1915/1950: 369), is dependent on private spaces and private meanings. Chapter 3 presented some unique examples of how two men can attempt to create private, exclusive spaces of friendship, described in "romantic" terms. But this is neither the common nor the practical alternative for homosocial relatedness. Because they often have a public focus, the dominant playground for male bonds is out in the open, in front of peers, colleagues, or strangers. Given these constraints, we need to look at how homosocial relations incorporate intimate emotions in public—in other words, how they negotiate *public intimacy*.

Public Private Talk

Male friends may develop a communication system that they can employ in public, in the context of their daily life, while still maintaining a sense of exclusivity. Yoram, a single college student, offered many examples of an exclusive form of communication he has developed with some friends. His interactions with his closest classmate involved special humor and word games that were unintelligible to those around them: "When the professor would talk in class we would laugh about the same things, things that no one else could understand. Our humor was unclear, using many word games that only we could grasp. We had a shared language, we would laugh, do fun things, talk."

The men repeatedly referred to the notion of "shared language," a homosocial lingo developing in the context of a dyad or, as is more often the case, a group of friends. It involves the use of special expressions and idioms, the result of shared cultural experience. In Israel, the widespread and most dominant manifestation of such lingo is unquestionably the one originating in military slang, including both professional military terms and macho discourse rich with rough, "dirty" talk about sex. It serves to create a common denominator, a factor that unites a group of men, blurring the differences between them while underscoring the boundaries that separate them from others. This lingo is so pervasive that it may color the way men interact many years after their military service, as Haim noted:

> I can call him up and he will talk to me exactly like in the old times. . . . For example, a year ago, I called him up on his mobile phone, and he's in the car. The language in the military was very dirty, sex and stuff, and he immediately talked to me in that way. I told him "Are you crazy, sitting next to your kids, is that a way to speak?!" . . . When we hear each other we instantly return to that place . . . the minute I call him up he would tell me "I'll suck your dick, suck my dick, who did you screw today."

It seems that the men deliberately use these shared expressions to incite their feelings and to intensify their present interactions on the basis of the common experiences they shared. The common basis, the shared knowledge on which this humor is based, varies from one case to another. It can be as broad as the general military jargon shared by almost all men, and it can be as narrow as the specific knowledge shared uniquely by two men. Yoram gave an example of a joking practice with Rani, his friend since high school. During their everyday life they continually employ a corpus of humorous citations that go back to their early school experiences: "Many things that were between the two of us, having been in the same places . . . making fun of our principal, just like some people recite parts from Ha-Gashash Ha-Hiver, we imitate the principal, recite incidents we had at high school. There are some we actually know by heart and that we turned into sketches about the principal or the teacher."

Yoram compared their practice to the prevalent custom among Israeli men of citing full passages from the popular sketches of Ha-Gashash Ha-Hiver. This legendary comedy trio, noted in chapter 2, introduced slang terms and expressions that have rapidly assimilated into general Hebrew slang, predominantly through male homosocial groups. Their best-known film, *Giv'at Halfon Eynah Onah* (Halfon Hill is not responding), is a light satire based on the social interactions among a handful of military reserve soldiers stuck in a desolate post on the Egyptian border. There is hardly an Israeli man who has served in the military and not been exposed to some of the ridiculous conversations, phrases, and nicknames heard in the film, not necessarily by actually viewing the film but by hearing these phrases repeatedly quoted by men around him, often devoid of any meaningful context or intention. On the large scale of the greater part of certain generations of Jewish-Israeli men, this shared knowledge of Ha-Gashash Ha-Hiver, a bible of sorts, serves to create an imagined shared-experience. Without saying anything of any significance, this type of talk simply reinforces a sense of mutual belonging. Yoram and Rani's joking ritual is, then, a particular case of the same phenomena, but is also a ritual that reinforces their sense of exclusivity: it marks and declares their common shared experience against the background of a general public sociability. Whether the public space of sociability is the classroom, the military unit, a wider circle of friends, or the workplace, this joking ritual carves an intimate enclave.

Tamir's case provides another telling example. Reflecting on the combat military background common to most of his present-day friends, he noted how they sometimes employed military radio communication speech protocols (the Hebrew military acronym is NDBR) when talking to one another in everyday life. Tamir recalled how he received a phone call from a male friend while working in his office with "his girls," i.e., female secretaries:

> We use a form of speech, you know, with a lot of self-confidence . . . sometimes you switch into NDBR mode . . . you might switch into total combat language, like "red 30, green 70, I'm in 40 attacking 50, 30, 20" . . . It's things that we are familiar with and use when we have an idle conversation, say, in the middle of a meeting when I'm sitting with my girls in the office, and suddenly the phone rings and I have this conversation, and they [the girls] tell me, like, "you're crazy, you're insane!"

The use of NDBR in military communication is employed in order to achieve accuracy in the usage of professional terms, sometimes using secret codes known only within a given unit, codes that neither the enemy nor other units could decipher. The reenactment of such communication in everyday, civil life creates a similar effect of special codes that surrounding people can not understand. It also makes a concrete reference to their imagined shared experiences in combat. And it is an *imagined* shared experience, because Tamir and his friends never were in the same combat units, hence never needed to use such language between them for any functional ends. Rather, this language serves expressive needs. It is a ritualized, coded mode of communication reinforcing the affiliation between the speakers. Creating an air of self-confidence, it proclaims their bond and demarcates those who belong and those who don't.

How do specific expressions *become* semipublic speech? Their distinguishing character is the ability to shift from one context to another. They may originate in specific shared experiences by two friends or by a group of friends. But in order to become homosocial codes, to gain their significance as markers of the bond, the expressions need to be used outside their original context and set against the backdrop of the surrounding public spaces. Consider the following example of a special whistle developed in Judd's military group: "We had this special whistle that belonged only to the group, and behind it were two words [demonstrates the whistle]. It was two words: wanna fuck. It started as a song and later we turned it into a whistle, so that we could pronounce it in public too."

The unison exclamation chanted by a group of men, "[We] wanna fuck, [we] wanna fuck!" is very common among soldiers. It is perhaps the ultimate macho cry, or rather, outcry, clamoring against the forced conditions of military service. It also functions as an informal anthem, sung during marches and social activities within the confines of the military encampment, creating a sense of alliance and unity among the men. Transforming this dirty talk into a whistle enabled Judd's group to use it in completely different contexts. Its original meaning no longer manifest, it became a unique code that they could now convey in public to signify their bond, reinforcing not only their alliance but also their sense of affiliation and closeness.

The diverse codes of exclusively shared language shift back and forth from private spaces to public spaces. They may develop privately between two friends and then become used in public. They may also develop in the public context of the homosocial group and then permeate the intimate discourse between friends, such as Haim's dirty talk with his ex-military friend when talking to him privately over the cellular phone in his car. The alternating usage of expressions, originally developed either in private or in public space and then employed in the complementary space, affords these expressions their unique significance. They become the "stamps" that give these semipublic interactions the value of intimacy.

Having discussed the origins of idiosyncratic language, I turn to explore some of its encoding. In various ways, the men apply an ambivalent, twisted coding system of contradictory messages to convey their emotions, sometimes communicating the opposite of what they feel. The distortion of emotions may go both ways; it often involves a displacement of distress by communicating high spirits that convey poise and strength.

Recall Haim Guri's poem noted earlier, as to how his Palmach friends lied about their physical well-being. Along these lines, Peter Lyman analyzed the stance of "being cool" as being in control and not responding with anger to an act of aggression (Lyman 1987: 160). But the distortion of emotions can also involve a displacement of positive feelings with a stance of offensiveness.

Consider the issue of nicknames. In the context of a private, heterosexual dyad, a nickname is a basic signifier of affection and intimacy. The Spanish novelist Javier Marias writes: "All couples have nicknames, often many, but at least one for each other, so that they could believe they were different and not always similar, and in order to avoid using their real names, which are reserved for moments of anger and insult." (Marias 1999: 140). The meanings of nicknames in the homosocial group may serve similar purposes, but in a complex and subtle way. From the outset, a nickname reflects one's status in the group. It is a basic marker of a person's acceptance into the homosocial group. Prominent figures in the Israeli public arena proudly preserve and nourish the nicknames assigned to them in the youth movement or their military service as testimony to their sociability and popularity. If you don't have a nickname, you don't belong. As described in the quote from Javier Marias above, nicknaming is used to differentiate the men from each other, ascribing to each person his special traits and unique place in the group. But unlike the clearly affectionate content of nicknames in the context of the typical romantic dyad, the homosocial nicknaming is a subtle and unclear marker of affection. In many cases the nicknames are essentially derogatory and offensive. The men often focus on the weaker qualities of their friends, especially on abnormal physical characteristics. Haim stressed how his closest friends from the military would use derogatory nicknames bordering on outright curses when referring to each other: "Our friendship was so close, a military kind of teasing-friendship. Everyone had a nickname. I was called, they both called me the small, negative, black electron . . . when he wanted to shorten it he'd call me the black . . . [I called him] the baldy, the fatso. He was small and had started to lose hair. Fatso and baldy, along these names—because that's how you expressed closeness, through nicknames and curses."

These nicknames could easily be misinterpreted by an outsider as an expression of rejection, when in fact they convey mutual acceptance among the group members. In a study of humor in a group of shop-floor men, David Collinson (1988: 185) notes that the use of exaggerated, ridiculing nicknames contributed to the group's cohesion by developing a shared sense of masculinity. Accepting highly insulting names demonstrated that one could take a joke and was man enough to laugh at himself. Similar to Peter Lyman's (1987) concept of coolness, playing along with the rules of the joking relationship marked conformity and acceptance. A similar account emerges in military settings. Liora Sion (1997: 45) argues that the aggressive humor is a mechanism of socialization in combat units that serves to promote a sense of belonging. The soldiers' full identification with and acceptance into the group are conditional on their willingness to accept pranks at their expense as a rewarding experience. But the aggressive joking behavior and the antagonistic nicknaming in particular are not only an act of conformity or part of a power struggle. They are perceived also as an expression of closeness and affection *disguised* in curse-form. As Haim reflected on his military friendships: "It's a boys' thing. They can't say something like 'I'm awfully glad to see you, how nice of you to come.' There's no such thing, it's all curses." He proceeded to tell an amusing anecdote of how such words, meant to express affection between friends, could be completely misinterpreted by outsiders, such as his parents:

> I was on leave for a few days. I took my parents on a trip . . . on the way we passed through [a base where a friend was stationed]. Knowing he'd be there I entered the encampment with my parents, so they could meet him. So I called out to him, "Mussa, how's it going?" and he called me back "You son-of-a-bitch, on your mother's cunt, coming here on your leave, huh?". . . So my mother said to me, "Why does he call you that?!" and as we entered the tent and he saw my mother and my father he was totally floored.

The curse-form is a standard way to communicate familiarity. It is simply a way to say hello with an edge. Why, then, use such twisted language to express affection? The easy explanation of this paradox of love-through-animosity talk is to interpret it as a reaction formation. Feelings of affection toward a close friend create a homoerotic anxiety, which in turn is transformed by a defense mechanism into an expression of aggression. But a more attentive way to make sense of this kind of communication is to see it as a deliberate intention to create *ambivalence*. The curse, a generic form of semipublic speech within male groups, can be viewed as a joke form in which the ordinary consequences of forbidden words are suspended by metalinguistic gestures (tones of voice, facial expressions, catch phrases) that send the message "this is a joke." Shifting between levels of meaning in the microworld created by the joke facilitates the safe communication of emotions that might otherwise endanger the social interaction (Bateson 1972). As argued by Gary Fine (1984: 97), the humorous interaction does not by itself create meanings, but rather plays them off, using the meanings previously implicit to present a novel, if metaphorical, situational one. To the extent that the meaning of a humorous remark may be separated from the teller's "true" beliefs, humor means *less* than what it says. But at the same time, precisely by being potentially disengaged from the teller, humor is capable of conveying powerful messages, and in this sense it means *more* than what it says.

Accordingly, the curse-form is an open-ended form of expression that in itself says very little about the emotional intentions of the speaker. It can be interpreted both as an act of hostility and domination disguised in a joke form and as an act of affection disguised in curse form. It is left to the respondent, not to an outside audience nor even to the speaker himself, to make sense of the expression and to resolve the ambivalent emotion in a direction that may eventually further the attraction or extend any animosity between the parties. The point is that the *ambivalence* created by the joking curse-form suspends a clear-cut emotional reaction by the respondent and at the same time draws him to respond in some way. The suspense it creates practically forces the participants to engage with each other. It draws them closer, encouraging them to further deepen their mutual involvement.

The diverse examples of semipublic communication presented so far suggest an emotional interplay that is often open-ended and eludes precise interpretation not only by an outside audience but also by the participants. Only in rare cases did the informants offer concrete illustrations of how specific homosocial codes conveyed specific intentions. Eli provided one such example, where he immediately interpreted his friend's hidden gesture in a way that proved useful in a business meeting: "He has this gesture, he doesn't wear glasses and he goes like that [puts a finger on his nose]. . . and I gather that the guy simply indicates that he isn't satisfied with how things are turning. Look, it helps because we were in certain meetings at work when something was said and he just did that, as if straightening his glasses if he had had any glasses . . . and I knew immediately where to put in a few words and then I could see how his hand disappears signifying his approval."

However, most illustrations of the communication recounted by the informants seemed to evade a clear-cut interpretation of the codes used by the participants. Eventually, it occurred to me that this vagueness was the name of the game. This has become particularly manifest in the story of Tamir and his friends. Tamir recounted how their homosocial talk could be placed under the general framework of *nonsense:*

> Nonsense is a shared language. . . . If I call up a friend right now, and you'd hear the way he talks you would send him to the shrink immediately. . . . You're in a restaurant with a few guys, men and women, and the waiter comes to take your order. So you tell him '*li-monada* [lemonade], *lo-bster* [lobster], *la-kerda* [smoked fish], and *la-chmania* [bread roll].' [The first syllable in each of these nouns—'*li*,' '*lo*,' '*la*'—also happens to be a homonym for a prepositional pronoun, meaning 'for me,' 'for her,' 'for him,' respectively]. It's like, the waiters don't get it, nobody gets it. It's our own humor, playing word games.

Nonsense talk is a mode of speech that is never meant to convey a clear message, an awkward encoding that evades any specific deciphering. Not only do these seemingly foolish word games create an effect of unintelligibility by an outside audience, they also create an *affect* of unintelligibility within the homosocial group itself. The nonsense talk is a projective mode of communication, resembling the arbitrary inkblots in a psychological Rorschach test: A stimulus is introduced, its meaning unclear. It invites the participants to respond by tossing loose, free-flowing associations across the table and enhances the interaction. Similar to the curse-form, nonsense talk is another form of ambivalent language characteristic of male joking interactions.

Nicknaming, cursing, and nonsense talk are all instances of game-playing. They might be totally neutral in their emotional content, like the nonsense talk, or more structured and provocative, like the curse. Yet as joking interactions, none of them convey the specific intentions of the speaker. The speaker can place taboo themes on the table without taking a stand. His speech defies a clear-cut judgment by the participants, but it teases, creates suspense, and draws the participants to engage deeper in the interaction. The men may engage in passionate arguments, attempting to get at each other. When challenged with a curse, they might feel provoked to fight back. When triggered by word games, they might be impelled to go along and join in the game. The homosocial joking interactions create an *affect* of senseless playfulness. It is a playfulness that eventually enables the men to carve out an exclusive enclave of intimacy. This intimacy is achieved not by an act of *disclosure*, not by conveying to the other party any particular message, but by an act of *seduction*, by pulling him into a game of pure pleasure.

Public Private Bodies

Men may express their affiliation, bonding, and love not only in verbal communication but also in bodily contact. Embracing customs among Israeli men seem to have expanded markedly compared to earlier generations. This may be the result of the growing influence of mizrachi Jews, originating from Arab cultures, who manifest a more easy-going, warm attitude toward physical contact than Jews of European descent. This trend may have permeated to the general culture through military socialization that is particularly prone to impose physical proximity. It also is interesting that this growing expression of bodily contact is not labeled as homosexual despite the increasing awareness of homosexuality in Israeli society, probably precisely because of the marked public focus of these interactions.[1]

The general frame for expressing physical contact is a context of instrumental action, when the men's involvement with each other has an outward focus apparently extending beyond their relationship in itself. Such circumstances, especially at distinct times of stress or victory, offer a legitimate context for physical contact that explicitly communicates a message of support. Yehuda, a college student and a fan of various sports, described such a circumstance: "Sometimes I take a friend with me to work, and when he realizes that I am under pressure, he can put a hand on me, that's one of the most relaxing things you can imagine. So in that sense it is intimate . . . and when we play [volleyball] and win the match together, then we hug each other."

But bodily contact between men is not limited to an embrace after scoring a goal in a football match. It also appears in situations that do not have a clear-cut outward focus but are related to the bond itself. The homosocial gestures may include a wide variety of physical contact, from handshakes, hugging, kissing, and caressing to backslapping, punches, and blows. Some of these gestures appear tender, even cuddly, while some seem harsh and brutal. I begin with the softer gestures, which seem a more likely candidate for expressing affection and pleasure. Whom do men feel comfortable embracing, and when might they embrace?

From the outset, the informants presented a diverse and contrasting picture of what kind of friends they might embrace. Ehud provided somewhat of an ideal when describing the hug as "coming from the heart." This ideal sets a clear line between close friends he would feel comfortable hugging and more distant friends he would feel less comfortable with: "I would feel comfortable hugging a close friend, but not a distant friend. It seems to me less genuine to hug an acquaintance. . . . A hug should come from the heart, either there should be a hug or there shouldn't be one." Eli, too, sensed that embracing friends is a natural expression of closeness, although not necessarily a significant one in terms of singling out one friend over another.

Indeed, some informants argued that the custom of embracing was of little importance, because it did not convey the extent of closeness they felt for a friend. Yoram noted that he refrained from hugging his best friend Rani, yet would hug other, less intimate friends: "I don't know why, but [with Rani] there is a taboo on the matter. . . I don't see the hug as an important act, it's not a principle. . . Through Rani I am now in contact with people from high school, and with them there is no such thing as guys who kiss or embrace . . . and yet with my friends from the military, who are not that close, I do embrace." Yoram's account suggests that the circumstances for embracing friends depend not so much on the nature of a specific friendship as on the social and cultural milieu, on the setting of the homosocial group that might reinforce or restrict male physical contact. Although the military setting seems to have facilitated such contact, among some groups of men it was a type of taboo. Judd explained the exact nature of this taboo—the fear of being perceived as homosexual. It is a taboo that constantly produced a *boundary* for male embraces, even among his relatively open military group: "We didn't hold hands because it wasn't trendy. But we would walk arm in arm, in a clowning manner, but it carried with it the need for touching. It was always within the boundaries so as not to be labeled as homosexual."

A subtle line is drawn: men relate to each other physically but also need to keep this contact guarded, for fear of exposing a desire for other men. It is the public private frame of the joking relationship that offers a safety valve for such bodily contact, allowing men to "walk arm in arm in a clowning manner." Practiced out in the open and in the manner of a joke, homosocial bodily contact defies immediate labeling as too intimate and therefore as homoerotic.

What does the homosocial embrace convey? In my earlier study of military culture based on interviews with gay veterans, one of the participants described two distinct physical interactions among his peers:

> We had this ritual called "goal." Some one who simply feels like it comes along and shouts "goal, goal, goal!" And he goes and leaps on top of another guy who was sleeping in the tent, and then everybody gets on top of him. . . . It was hilarious, it became so fashionable, you'd pass by any tent in one of the artillery battalions, no matter what your home unit was, alas, you go in the tent with everyone else and jump on the guy. (Kaplan 2003a: 172)

> A bunch of us were sitting between the beds and started to talk. All of a sudden one of them, Ofer, came on to me and started hugging me. There was nothing homosexual about it, but he loved me so much that he just lay on top of me for half an hour. It was the ultimate closeness you could expect in the army, with no fooling around and no games. (Kaplan 2003a: 209)

The first account describes a collective ritual of lying on top of another man, set in the form of a game with seemingly few expressive attributes. The second account describes a specific incident of lying on top of another man, interpreted by the informant as a sign of authentic love and closeness precisely because it exceeded the usual ritual of "fooling around" and "games." Note that in both cases the gesture appeared in public, within a group of men, but each received a different interpretation—the first a silly ritual, the second a unique act of love. Between these two widely disparate interpretations of the homosocial embrace lies a range of more subtle positions, which deserve further attention.

Having discussed the question of whom men might embrace and the general framework of semipublic spaces that affords the homosocial embrace, I would ask *when* men feel they can embrace. There are several specific boundaries that the men seem to set to differentiate between a "legitimate" embrace and an "illegitimate" one, between an embrace signifying a *ritualized* function and one expressing a *spontaneous* act of pleasure as described by Hillel above. The informants' accounts suggest a continuum of social situations that equip men with a boundary between the legitimate and illegitimate interpretations. The first and most prevalent boundary for restricting the homosocial embrace is to practice it only as an act of greeting during the initial moment of an encounter between friends, a sort of expansion of the official male handshake. Nachshon held his periodical rendezvous with his best friend Michael in remote places. This private, exclusive space seems to have necessitated clear boundaries for physical contact. Nachshon describes the sort of embrace they would use during these encounters, stressing how the contact was strongly ritualized and therefore lacking "real" meaning: "When we meet, first we'd give a small hug . . . an initial warm physical contact, only when we met, never when we departed. . . . So we'd meet, touch each other lightly. But this was definitely part of the ritual between us that we needed to touch each other . . . it is limited, almost symbolic . . . it confirmed a kind of warmth that we've decided to express that way. But it's a symbol, it's not real."

It follows, then, that the primary boundary for the male embrace narrows the need to touch and express warmth to an isolated instance when greeting each other. A renewed encounter after a long period of absence may create an even better opportunity to embrace in a less ritualized and more expressive manner. Eli described how such circumstances aroused a more vibrant practice of embracing among his friends than the backslapping they would regularly employ: "When we hadn't seen one another for a long time . . . we would jump one on top of the other, for example Nissim would stand behind me, and I wouldn't see him and he would suddenly leap on my shoulders." Distinctive social events offer another occasion for ritualized embraces. In public events such as a party, even men who regularly avoid any physical contact might feel practically compelled to embrace. Haim recalled that his own birthday party was the one occasion on which his best friend, Yitzhak, was ready to give him a kiss on his forehead: "He wouldn't give me a kiss on my cheek on my birthday . . . because guys don't kiss . . . on my birthday he was awfully excited, so the most he could do was a kiss on the forehead."

A more surprising aspect of male physical contact that has appeared in a few narratives is the issue of sleeping together, sharing the same bed. On the face of it, this would seem a definite homoerotic boundary that most men would never cross. The following account by Haim, trying to no avail to persuade Yitzhak to share a bed during their private vacations, demonstrated the anxieties at stake:

> We'd go abroad a lot. We would arrive at the hotel, we were often mistaken for a couple—'two beds please'. . . and sometimes I was the cheapskate and two beds was more expensive . . . what would happen if you slept with me in the same bed? . . . I don't know this person, let him think whatever he wants, what do I care if a fucking hotel manager somewhere in the US thinks we sleep in the same bed and have sex?

For most men, sharing a bed in private would be too suspect of homosexuality. However, the semipublic context of homosocial relationships affords a more protected possibility for such a practice. For instance, joking behavior such as pushing each other out of bed may alleviate homoerotic tensions. Hezi recounted sharing beds with his roommates in the dorms at preparatory school: "I had this big double bed so at night we'd sleep together and kick each other out of the bed, as part of the fun." Hezi then continued to provide an example of the atmosphere surrounding this custom of sharing beds, involving game-playing around the actual possibility of two lovers preparing to go to bed together:

> I think anyone in his right mind would see it from the outside and say "what a bunch of fools," but it was the atmosphere that created it. For instance, Ami always had this expression, "Wear your red shirt, I'm coming to you!" This was at night before I'd go to sleep . . . I had this red shirt, part of my work outfit. . . so he'd always say, "Wear your red shirt, I'm coming straight to bed," or things like that, he was totally nuts. Until at one point I asked him, "Tell me Ami, are you gay or what, what's the matter with you?"

Another way through which homoeroticism is negotiated and solved is through the mediation of women. Male bodily contact is often dependent on female mediation and involvement. Hezi provided a vivid example, describing a peculiar habit that he had developed with his best friend, Yoni, in order to tease Yoni's wife:

> And sometimes I see him, and give a hug or a kiss, and when his wife is watching we do it on purpose, because . . . I've gotta tell you this, I would always [eat] bananas so his wife would say, "Why do you keep eating bananas the whole day long?" So once I told her, 'I'll give one to Yoni as well' . . . I took it in my mouth and passed it to Yoni, mouth to mouth, and he ate. . . . Till this day his wife tells me, 'Go and eat your bananas together!'; it's like another example of the traditions [*havay*] I share with Yoni.

This extraordinary anecdote would have probably been analyzed by followers of traditional psychoanalysis as an illustration of a woman's penis envy—Yoni's wife envying the men's bond and decrying them for "eating bananas together." But the point is that Hezi and Yoni seemed to need the presence of the woman in order to express such blatant physical intimacy with its specific symbolic allusion to oral sex. The presence of Yoni's wife provided the backdrop for their act of physical closeness, spurring them to perform it as an act of teasing. It also prevented their gesture from expressing direct homosexuality, precisely due to the way it is staged in front of an audience, and a very important audience at that. It is through the presence of a closely affiliated woman that they could communicate their own intimacy.

Having discussed various aspects of the homosocial embrace, its boundaries, and some of the ways to play around the boundary, I turn to examine the harsher variety of gestures, such as backslapping, punches, and outright blows that men tend to engage in. Despite their seeming brutality, many of these gestures involve a stance of aggression and affection simultaneously, similar to the ambivalent encoding of homosocial talk. A case in point is the forceful backslapping known as the *chapkha*. Liora Sion (1997: 40) analyzes how this gesture, when performed by a commander on trainees at the military training graduation ceremony, can be interpreted as signifying "intimacy and acceptance": "After the forced march [to earn the beret] you placed the red beret on our heads. You gave us a *chapkha* on the chest and smiled at us for the first time." This contradiction between a violent act such as the *chapkha* and its plausible interpretation by the soldiers as an expression of intimacy illustrates the complexity of the interpretational process at play.

Once more, the possibility that men may hit each other to express affection or intimacy should be viewed in the context of public private meaning and the homosocial group. In this context, the employment of aggressive gestures is a response that *erases* homoerotic desire. The more obvious the aggression, the more blatant the violent act, the less risk there is of a symbolic collision resulting from the expression of desire. Instead, it is merely body parts that may indeed collide, as in the following account by Hezi: "I developed this hugging technique in prep college where we didn't hug but we actually bumped our bellies together, a kind of caressing . . . [demonstrates] you inflate your belly, and bump it against each other and that's how you say hello, simply butt your bellies. . . . One day, when they tried to do it one guy broke the other guy's teeth."

A stance of aggressive affection recurs in many kinds of bodily interactions, the more blatant examples being pranks and hazing activities, particularly in, but not limited to, the military. For instance, David Collinson (1988) studied aggressive initiation rites for new blue-collar employees on an English shop floor. Michael Housman (2001) studied hazing rituals in preparatory schools in France. In the military, hazing rituals are often performed on "green" rookies, soldiers beginning a new posting, or to regular group members as part of the power struggle between cliques. These rituals consist of a wide array of acts from pouring water, machine oil, or raw eggs on the designated man, all the way to virtual gang rape. Shuki, a veteran of an infantry brigade, described a particularly obscene example of such hazing:

> There were a couple of guys who invented a game. They called it Sado. The game was to have a couple of people hold somebody down on the ground. And one of these two guys—there were two good friends who always invented things to do to others . . . they would hold somebody down and one of them would come and play with his dick around . . . the mouth of the guy that was pinned down. Usually, they didn't get that close, but he would threaten with it. He would

bring his dick close depending on how strongly the other guy was
fighting. He got as close as maybe 20 cm. He even did it to me once.

Evidently, these gestures involve degrading and humiliating situations
of dominance and submission and may be experienced as such by some
soldiers. Shuki noted that "At one time one of the guys went to the officer
to tell him about it. After it happened. He said he was going to commit
suicide and stuff. It made him feel bad. Eventually he left the unit."

Yet that is not the common reaction to hazing ceremonies. In most instances, the participants—both the perpetrators and their victims—fail to
perceive these rituals as humiliating. What are they, then? The common
explanation for aggressive pranks situates them as a test case for taking
a joke, hence for being worthy of acceptance into the homosocial group,
another instance of proving one's masculinity (Collinson 1988: 189; Sion
1997: 62–64). Gary Fine (1988: 51–52) describes the importance of pranks
and dirty play in general as a status contest among boys, whereby the risk
involved in daring to perform a prank increases one's social status. Acting out jokes of domination and submission between men places them in
positions of unequal power, yet it also works to create a sense of potential
equality among them in comparison to other groups. The principle of rotat-
ing roles in these symbolic acts of domination and submission assures that
everyone gets to play attacker and attacked, to be audience and performer.
The men open up to a degree that enables them to be members of the group.
Along these lines, Liora Sion and Eyal Ben-Ari (2005: 661) suggest that most
jokes involving aggression "rotate" between the group's members, and in a
sense reinforce the wider backdrop of the cohesive unit. Under this reading,
acts of domination-submission serve in the long run to demonstrate the essential equality—and therefore unity—within the homosocial group.

As sound as such an explanation may be, however, it is still a functional
account. It does not address the question of the emotional, expressive attributes of such practices. As in the ritualized position of the greeting act,
it transforms the emotional context of the illegitimate physical pleasure
and pain involved in these sadomasochistic acts into an instrumental,
legitimate context, a test case for achieving masculine status. But such an
account does not examine how the men themselves may read this aggressive and obscene behavior. I asked Shuki for his own interpretation of
the "Sado" game preformed by his two fellow soldiers. He responded: "I
don't know. I didn't think about it at that time. They were very intimate.
I think they became friends in the army. And they were very intimate. "
Shuki could not explain their behavior; their language was ambivalent
and he could not read their signs. But he did sense that between the two
of them they were very intimate, and that something of that intimacy was
reflected in their misdemeanors.

Benny had a more decisive interpretation of the emotional intent of the
various violent homosocial practices he experienced in his own military

unit: "It was all out of love, I tell you, really out of love, I tell you, these are things that would look crazy to people from the outside." Throughout Benny's account as well as in those of many other informants, the men stressed that an outsider could not possibly make any sense of it. This recurrent stress on senselessness and unintelligibility from an external point of view is all the more intriguing, leading one to ponder once more what these interactions could mean from the men's own point of view. I conclude the analysis with a condensed account of the extraordinary interactions taking place in the military barracks of Benny's team in an elite reconnaissance unit:

> We would all go into the showers together, and then there were pissing con-
> tests, and if you could knock someone down everyone would pee on him.
> [laughs] And spitting, oh my God . . . it would start with some teasing,
> eggs would fly across the room, there were even accidental bullet discharges
> in the rooms. You can't imagine what it was like, insane, insane. . . . If
> some guy would go mad he would turn on everybody, then we'd go to the
> showers and piss and throw people then go sleep together in the same bed
> . . . it's not like fags or anything, but you give little love hugs. And we
> used to bite each other, too . . . There was one night where they grabbed
> me from behind and took a bite out of my neck. . . There was also this guy
> who had to get his punch otherwise he wouldn't go to sleep . . . he would
> talk endless bullshit all day long, so there was always someone on duty to
> go punch him. . . . You really would see a lot of things that could look, to
> an observer, really bad. Like, just for the hell of it, we would sleep with no
> clothes, always naked. . . . You would open the door and see three guys
> spread out naked in bed together [laughs].

This extreme account captures many of the bodily gestures of the homo-social joking relationship discussed earlier, from tender hugs to violent punches. It involves practices incorporating both physical pleasure and physical pain, some of which could almost fall under definitions of sado-masochistic behavior. Taken together, these practices create an extremely ambivalent emotional space of desire between the participants, placed in the context of game-playing, and taking place in the semipublic-semipri-vate setting of the military barracks.

These physical gestures illustrate perhaps more clearly the process of ongoing seduction involved in this kind of homosocial interaction, similar to the process suggested earlier in the case of public private talk. Benny described a whirl of frenzy taking place among the men, extending from knocking each other down while taking showers together, through piss-ing contests and all the way to love hugs in bed. The game begins with one man pushing another to a position of submission in a joking manner and so defying a clear interpretation of violence. But it spurs the attacked to come up with another aggressive joking act that retains not only his dignity but also the ambivalence of his intentions, provoking the original attacker and others to join in on the game and so forth. Eventually the game draws the men closer and closer until the whole incident may be experienced as an act of love, as Benny put it.

The dynamics of these instances of seduction in semipublic space relieves the men from succumbing to the so-called homosexual taboo, liberating them from anxieties of being vulnerable, and from fear that too much exposure will invite sexual domination, because it leads them to those very same spaces of intimacy *through* acts of aggression. The homosocial game sends an ambivalent message, something along the lines of "you can either beat me or join me." But the participants do not have to decide either way. The dynamics of the relationship transform the dichotomy of "if you can't beat them, join them" to an interaction where, in effect, to beat him *is* to join him *is* to beat him.

Interim Summary: The Public Management of Desire

The men's ambiguous joking relationship not only negotiates intimacy. It can be interpreted as a mode of interaction that unfolds feelings of love into displaced acts of desire. Whereas many heterosexual men might refrain from expressing closeness in the context of an exclusive, private relationship, it is the varying opportunities for semipublic interactions that paradoxically afford them more room to maneuver their feelings. The men's joking relationship creates a bizarre choreography played out in the open, in front of various types of spectators ranging from other friends to acquaintances to passers-by. The lingo of eccentric speech and bodily gestures renders their performance unintelligible to the outside spectator. It is left to the participants themselves to decipher these public private codes, not always quite sure what the exact cipher might be. It is this very stress on *ambivalence* in homosocial interactions that produces seduction. The men can exhibit ambivalent cues that suspend any clear-cut interpretation of their intentions by the participants but that entice them to engage deeper in the interaction, drawing them into a game of fun and pleasure.

This persistent miscommunication of feelings requires a mode of analysis different from that that of a phenomenological inquiry. In a way, my analysis has followed the framework of deconstruction, as it is employed to the homoerotic (Rumsey 1995). Deconstruction focuses on the implicit, on what is avoided and disavowed. It explores instances where human discourse and practices are structured by silences, by discontinuities and institutionalized defenses (Norris 1991). Michael Hatt (1993) explored such discontinuities in various artistic and literary examples of the homosocial gaze, the male gaze on another man's body. The aesthetics of the male body is immediately separated from the erotic through an implicit adherence to a stand of indifference. The silenced moment of homoeroticism in homosocial context does not affirm the male body as a sexual object of desire in the way heterosexual desire affirms the female body as sexual. Rather, for a male spectator to find aesthetic pleasure in another man's body he must find a response that *erases* any desire. Expanding Eve Sedgwick's (1985) formulation of homosocial desire, Hatt interprets the homoerotic as an attempt to differentiate between the homosocial and the homosexual, to create a sense of a boundary between the licit and illicit emotions. This usage of the term homoerotic needs to be carefully distinguished from a positivistic claim as to a hidden homosexual desire within homosocial relations, a naked truth that simply needs to be revealed. Eroticism is the process of veiling or containment, producing the very possibility of the naked or the "truth." Deconstructing the homoerotic implies "finding a place for certain desires between men, not as an already formed desire looking for an object, but as a desire that emerges from, or is actually shaped by, a disciplinary frame or method of containment" (Hatt 1993: 14).[2]

Many of the everyday homosocial interactions described in this chapter present a similar dynamic. The men's homosexual innuendos in semi-public settings are accompanied by aggressive language and rough acts of game playing, presenting a variety of responses that *erase* desire. But this containment is done in a way that simultaneously denies and signifies the homoerotic. Their ambivalent interaction does not reflect a prior sexual attraction. Rather, it presents complex ways of articulating a desire that *cannot* be validated. Desire in this context is not a precondition of male friendship, but one of its *emergent* outcomes.

The male homosocial performance provides a double layer of meaning set in both instrumental actions and expressive interactions. The previous chapters illustrated instances where the men engage in outwardly focused activities ranging from playing games and seeking adventures, to inventing patents, to discussing theories and ideologies. Consider the following account by Hezi, describing how he and his best friend Yoni like to build complicated theories in the air, resulting in a constructive outcome:

> Between me and Yoni there's this coordination that we are both wild in our thinking and we like to develop theories offhand . . . we always go to opposite directions, each one of us invents theories and builds them one on top of the other and of course there's always a clash and that's the fun thing, and the argument is over as if it never happened, we made it up, we created it. It could be on politics, on I don't know what, on how a certain building has been constructed, things like that, or why the hang-glider flies one way and not the other. Each one of us . . . will say exactly what he knows, and the other one will say why he thinks it's different, and at the end . . . the knowledge is formed or the final decision is formed from the argument more than anything, from the discussion and the radicalization.

Emerging from Hezi's account are two different meanings of the interaction. At one level, such interactions could be defined purely by their function, reaching a certain target or coming up with a new theory. But at another level, irrespective of the outcome, their motivation comes from the "fun" that they gain from the "clash" between the two of them in the process of debating. This dynamic becomes the very embodiment of the friendship, as Hezi points out:

> And then we reach a certain point or we don't reach any point and the argument is over, it doesn't matter really where it stopped. And that's the friendship. You never have to even things up . . . We're good friends and it doesn't matter what we say and what we do, or where we are, it's a friendship.

The juxtaposition of expressive ties with instrumental activity has implications that go beyond the joint pursuit of hobbies, or the idiosyncratic invention of theories, into the politics of male homosociality. The homoerotic displacement emerges precisely at that moment when a "nonfunctional" act of pleasure is placed in the more "legitimate" context of an activity that aims to achieve a "functional" end. For instance, when the spectacle of a commander gazing at the bodies of his youthful soldiers is established as an act of discipline, or when comradeship becomes an organizational means to cement the ranks, an inspiration for the men to fight—it is then that the frame becomes homoerotic (Hatt 1993: 14). Similarly, when beating someone up also means joining him in the homosocial game, as in some of the examples in this chapter, the institutional legitimacy of the violent activity conceals what it has also produced—an instance of an "illegitimate," nonfunctional context of pleasure, pain, or desire.

Taken together, these displacements of desire perpetuate male social networks and reinforce a politics of male homosociality. The public staging of a seemingly unintelligible language of relatedness is a collective display of power. It places the nonparticipating audience, both women and other men, in a position of inferiority and exclusion. The potential of experiencing these interactions in the utilitarian guise of "work" or "military action," and in the alluring guise of "pleasure," underscores the significance of these rituals of seduction in reinforcing hegemonic male social and organizational networks.

The communication, or rather miscommunication of desire between men suggests a continuum of possibilities for the emotional management of desire. It may start with outright denial of desire, the response of most men when asked about it explicitly; it might move through various forms of erasure and concealment of passionate emotions enabled by the joking relationship, reflecting the unfolding of love as a negation of desire; and it may end with the potential of actually acknowledging desire. So far we have seen little, if any, instances of the latter possibility—that of a straightforward acknowledgement of homosocial desire. In the following section I explore this direction further, in the context of heroic friendship and national commemoration. In these circumstances, the celebration of male homosociality is no longer an implicit aspect of friendship in everyday life, but rather is an explicit rhetoric for nation building.

Notes

1. For additional analysis of public homoerotic bodily contact in the military see Kaplan (2003a: 201–209).
2. There is a vague, tricky line to be drawn here between apparently contradictory approaches to the study of emotions, and the homoerotic in particular. On the one hand, a poststructuralist, queer-theory approach would argue against universal theories that presuppose essential human drives and rely on covert underlying psychic processes. On the other hand, queer theory in its turn often assumes a set of cultural constraints that apriori guide and structure human experience, such as homophobia. This inevitably results in what may often seem, yet again, an essentialist notion, as in the case of "homosocial desire." Along these lines, Michael Hatt's (1993) account of desire as the product of a disciplinary containment presents a universal paradigm for desire, which seems quite farther afield from an *in situ* anthropological interpretive approach. When placed in a localized context, it is difficult to evaluate how well it is attentive to the "constant swirl of reality-constituting activity" (Holstein and Gubrium 1998: 153). Without attempting to resolve the theoretical complexities at stake, I have nevertheless found Hatt's formulation useful in interpreting the underlying homosocial emotions in the current narratives. A similar analysis of homoeroticism in cinematic representations of masculinity in the Israeli military has been offered by Raz Yosef (2001).

Part III
Sacred Friendship

How is nation building implicated in fraternal friendship? In his renowned address in 1946, Itzhak Sadeh, the first commander of the Palmach troops, wrote:

> Combat comradeship (*re'ut halochamim*) is probably the peak of friendship (*re'ut*). . . . *Re'ut* is doubly needed in combat. Fighting for an independent Hebrew force—that is our fulfillment, it is also the building of a better future, the building of the whole country. In this building the bodies of friends are the building bricks. The cement for the building is the blood of brothers to the cause; the man standing next to you and willing to give you cover with his mere body, willing to carry you in his arms at times of deadly danger, willing to fall at your side for the sake of erecting that building that only fighting can maintain—he is the true friend. (Cited in Almog 1997: 379)

This quote is perhaps the most explicit account in Zionist thought linking *re'ut* to nationalism. Nation building is envisioned as the construction of a concrete building made from the bodies and blood of brother-friends to the cause. This extreme image underscores two aspects of fraternity in national context: heroism and death. I devote the next two chapters to each of these concepts, respectively.

The various negotiations of intimacy and passionate interactions between men are limited by the obligations of everyday life. Some of the men's stories feature notions such as "shared destiny" and spaces for exclusive pairing between men that were reminiscent of a full-fledged romance (see chapter 3). Yet just as apparent was how the daily routines of heterosexual lifestyle and norms pose constraints on such homosocial unions. Dorothy Hammond and Alta Jablow (1987: 255) discuss the incongruity between the tradition of heroic male friendship and the institutionalized settings of contemporary industrialized societies. The social networking that most men encounter seldom provide an arena for dramatic and heroic exploits of devotion between friends.

Haim shared a deep and long-lasting relationship with his best friend Yitzhak that came to an abrupt end with Yitzhak's tragic death in a car accident, just a few months prior to our interview. As soon as he began to talk about his dear friend, he burst out with the following declaration:

> Dear Yitzhak, I am talking to you now [sobbing]. I can't believe this. When I will speak of Yitzhak I will often cry. Because I loved him very, very much. Hell, I shouldn't say this. Boys aren't allowed to love.

When is it actually allowed? When does the possibility of male lovers cease to be prohibited and become feasible, at times even a cultural manifesto?

The distinction I make throughout this book between *haverut* and *re'ut* reflects a move from social experience of everyday life to that of heroic life. The former involves diverse patterns of relationships set in various life periods and social institutions, with little cultural recognition. The latter involves well-defined, culturally acknowledged, and politically dominant bonds related to male sacrifice. It is a "love sanctified by blood" (*ahava mekudeshet be-dam*), to quote a well-known phrase by the poet Haim Guri in his popular song *Ha-re'ut* (Guri 1950/2000: 147–148). Indeed, the move from *haverut* to *re'ut* can be likened to a move from a "secular" relationship to a "sanctified" or "sacred" relationship. This distinction resonates with a key notion in Jewish tradition distinguishing between the sanctified (*kodesh*) and the secular (*hol*). I suggest that this differentiation is not only, as in Durkheimian terminology, an "elementary form of religious life" (Durkheim 1915), but also a common understanding of "national life," read as a civil religion.

As noted in chapter 1, the rise of nationalism is associated with romanticism, most noteworthily in Central Europe (Greenfeld 1992). In terms of social relationships, the romantic perspective embraced the idea of a deep interior within each individual, a soul, which could ideally unite with another deep interior, another soul. A man's soul may erupt and spill both in heroic action and in heroic expression such as poetry, song, and mourning. The expression of grief gave voice to one's very depths. The loss of a loved one legitimizes profound grief, for it signifies the capability of profound love (Gergen 1991). Haim echoed this view in a touching manner, describing how he had expressed grief over the death of his special friend Yitzhak in the presence of his (female) work colleagues. He explained to them how the pain he felt reinforced the significance of the love that he was lucky to have had:

> I sat there for an hour and simply wept, telling them that "with all the agony that they see me in . . . . we walk on this earth and we don't form such bonds for fear of being hurt, the way I appear hurt right now," and from

the depths of my pain I told them, "I can tell you, each and every one of you, don't give up on it, because the gift is so much greater, the experience is tremendous for someone who can feel it . . . but we apparently don't feel it because we fear that it will happen to us, that someone will suddenly pass away."

Haim considers people's fear of experiencing loss as an inhibition that prevents them from experiencing the precious gift of profound love. Framed in romanticist terms, the ability to overcome this fear, to love and to grieve, is viewed as ennobling and heroic. Taken together, the romantic approach to social relationships considers the expression of deep emotions in relationships as sacred (Gergen 1991: 249).

Chapter Six

DAVID, JONATHAN, AND OTHER SOLDIERS:
THE HEGEMONIC SCRIPT FOR MALE BONDING

Introduction: The Romantics of Heroic Friendship

Whereas friendships originating in childhood and high school were often the most lasting in individual men's narratives, bonds associated with the military and particularly with combat experiences carried with them a stronger symbolic significance. Haim chose to begin his long interview with his military experiences, having served as an infantry officer in the 1982 Lebanon War. His story began in the following way:

> Military friendships, especially after the war, it's a relationship I term "love sanctified by blood." Really, that's my understanding. It's these kinds of relationships, where we might not see each other for years, but if I were to call one of the boys now I would feel this kind of excitement that can only happen when coming from there. Seven years ago they did an event for the company, and I was to call up all my men and all the staff. It was amazing, we haven't spoken for ten years, and yet in most of the cases they just needed to hear my voice, and their reaction was, again, we haven't spoken for ten years, "I don't believe it, I don't believe it, is it you calling me?" It was something you just couldn't explain. Of course there was a big party for everyone, an amazing evening. It's a kind of thing that could never happen anywhere else. It's something that formed there within the large group that is beyond any rationale. Apparently, in my analysis, it arises from a situation where men face the danger of death and as a result their thrills are very high. And then the emotional attachments become extremely strong, extremely strong.

Haim offers here almost a full canonical description of a military heroic friendship: A bond forged under stress, in the shadow of death, and including extremely high thrills. Such bonds are deep and long-lasting, even if the men meet only at unit reunions.[1] Throughout his story Haim repeatedly alluded to this kind of friendship as a bond that defies any explanation and that couldn't happen anywhere else.

Unlike the limitations, silencing, and contradictions surrounding the expression of love between men in other contexts, love between fellow warriors has enjoyed enduring cultural representation. The general scheme of heroic male friendships can be traced to ancient times. David Halperin (1990), following Dorothy Hammond and Alta Jablow (1987), analyzed three ancient epics of male friendship emerging in the Near East, all of them at similar periods—the Assyrian scheme epic of Gilgamash and Enikdu, the Greek Homeric epic in the Iliad of Achilles and Patroclus, and the Hebrew biblical story of David and Jonathan. All three stories depict a close bond between two comrades-in-arms who operate as an exclusive pair. The men's relationships involve the following structural aspects. First, they are forged under harsh conditions, embedded in action, as the men battle against enemies. Second, the two men act as an isolated pair excluded from their surrounding. Relations with women are relegated to the background and prove no distraction. Finally, it is not a private relation; it is a public act with an outward focus, a purpose beyond itself, and it aims to accomplish glorious political ends.

Gabriel Herman (1987: 58) notes that the bond between David and Jonathan could be placed within the framework of ritualized friendship, or the Greek term *xenia* (guest friendship) between high-standing families that was practiced throughout the Eastern Mediterranean during the archaic period. Ritualized friendship was characterized by long-ranging and long-term alliances maintained by the reciprocal exchanges of favors, hospitality, and gifts. It was the forerunner of political and military alliances in classical Greece (Hornblower and Spawforth 1999: 612).

The Near Eastern epics of heroic male friendship provide a potent, long-lasting model for homosocial relationships in the Western tradition. Dorothy Hammond and Alta Jablow (1987) note that representations of heroic friendship, usually in the form of a dyad, have been continually dramatized in canonic literature such as the *Song of Roland* in eighth-century France, in the near-mythic heroes of frontier America, in the bush 'mateship' of Australian folklore, or in the 'comrades-in-arms' films of the First and Second World Wars. The epics provide a predominantly vague concept, such as friendship with a symbolic dimension for collective self-understanding and social labeling (Halperin 1990: 76). As meta-narratives, these stories represent culturally shared knowledge. They may reaffirm moral values and provide frames for clarifying and resolving conflicts, similar to myths: "the purpose of a myth is to provide a logical model capable of overcoming a contradiction" (Lévi-Strauss 1963: 229). Likewise, Victor Turner (Turner 1980: 168) has stated that "the narrative component in rituals attempts to rearticulate opposing values and goals into a meaningful structure, the plot of which might make cultural sense." In this vein, heroic bonding affords cultural legitimacy to the limitations and tensions of love between men.

But in what way could we consider the frame of heroic friendship as a *romantic* script? The term "romantic" is associated with the literary-historical roots of the medieval romance and the ensuing eighteenth and nineteenth-century ideas of romanticism, offering a Western cultural schema for masculine values of emotional self-expression. The category of the romantic does not focus on a bond between two men. It is typically placed either as an ideal of solitary escapade—an individual and personal rite of passage to manhood—or as a group ideal. In both cases it often emphasizes passionate heterosexual love. However, as noted by Mary and Kenneth Gergen (1995: 224), the romantic vocabulary has gradually been interwoven into myriad patterns of relationships, ranging from heterosexual unions, family relations, and teachers-student dynamics, to friendships.

Erich Auerbach (1953), a literary critic of the medieval romance, analyzed the structural aspects of the romantic quest. Some of these aspects resemble closely the features of the above-mentioned epics of heroic male friendship. First, the protagonist moves through successive stages involving perilous encounters toward a crucial test. When not confronting the enemy (other men, giants, dragons, ogres), the hero devotes himself to constant practice and proving. Second, the setting is a fixed and isolated landscape distinct from the setting of the normal world. Lastly, the romantic quest employs a style that separates the heroic and sublime from everyday reality, and serves a sociological-political purpose. Those engaged in the stylized pursuits of the heroic acquire inner values of nobility and become a circle of solidarity, "a class of the elect, which at times indeed seemed to constitute a secret society" (Auerbach 1953: 139). In Auerbach's reading, love gradually becomes the sole motivation behind the hero's actions, the driving force behind the plot. Just as the hero "can not for one moment be without adventure in arms," so too he must be constantly involved in (heterosexual) "amorous entanglement" (Auerbach 1953: 140–141). In courtly love, the feudal code of service and devotion to the noble lord was transformed to the ideal of devotion to a lady. The knightly virtue of courage and sacrifice in battle was transmuted into display of heroism and moral worth in the quest of love. Romantic love signified both moral striving and social rebellion (Swidler 1980). Denis de Rougemont (1940/1974: 276) viewed it as a code of adulterous love that put the hero in conflict between his love of a lady and his loyalty to the lord to whom she is married.[2]

Despite variations in themes, and beyond religious and cultural differences, the medieval romantic quest projects earlier ideals of heroic friendship. It propels a tradition of friendship made by and for aristocrats. In contrast, modern versions of the heroic myth spread the aristocratic code of friendship to the lower classes. Modern protagonists, at times heroes in spite of themselves, are often common soldiers, seamen, cowboys, prospectors, and even criminals. However, the ideals of friendship remain similar, depicting situations of danger, isolation, and attachment to a fellow friend (Hammond and Jablow 1987: 252–253). The romantic quest, combined with the myth of heroic friendship, provides a prototype of male friendship, a precursor to the modern concept of brothers-in-arms. Paul Fussell (1975: 135) analyzed images of combat fraternity in the British literature of the First World War, delineating many structural aspects of the romantic quest that parallel and echo Auerbach's (1953) analysis of the medieval romance.

In a similar vein, selected segments in contemporary narratives of Israeli men's friendships, predominantly during their military experiences, subscribe to a dominant script of male bonding with structural features similar to those shared by the heroic epic and the romantic quest. First, the bond originates or is reinforced by a harsh setting, a stressful, dramatic shared experience, most pronouncedly in war or combat-related activity. The men engage in perilous action, helping one another up to the point of risking themselves. This setting is interpreted as a trial for the friendship. Second, there may be a certain formative moment when the men act as an isolated pair cut apart from their surrounding and go through a liminal emotional state that brings them closer to one another. In this instance the men enact a symbolic pact. Thirdly, the pact is maintained over time and tested in various kinds of reunions. At the wider, collective level, the bond has a public focus. It creates an exclusive circle of solidarity between the men, with political implications. In what follows I elaborate on each of these components based on some narrated examples.

Harsh Circumstances

Jonathan falls in love with David in one crucial moment, when David has just achieved one of the most heroic deeds in the biblical ethos—the slaying of Goliath the Philistine. The new hero is presented to King Saul, carrying Goliath's head in his hands. Infatuated by David's marital prowess, Jonathan, Saul's son, lays eyes on him for the first time, and in that moment "[t]he soul of Jonathan was knit with the soul of David and Jonathan loved him as his own soul" (1 Samuel 18:1). Other than this single sentence the biblical narrator offers us little in the way of an actual account of the first encounter between the two men. In contrast, some of the stories I collected from the interviewees recount in great detail the dramatic, intense encounter with a new friend, and the feeling of an immediate "click" between the two of them, as analyzed in the narrative structure of "shared destiny" in chapter 3. This narrative structure is confined to situations where one or both of the men has arrived in a new setting, most notably in the military. They confront harsh circumstances that force the men to act together under stressful conditions. Amnon recounted a canonic story of a pure combat scenario, which formed the basis for his bond with one of his fellow officers, Sharon. The two men fought together in the 1973 Yom Kippur War. While they had known each other casually from a previous yearlong service in the same artillery unit, their bond developed in the ten days they spent together after crossing the Suez Canal to Egypt:

> During our advancement beyond the canal we discovered an entire artil-
> lery battalion abandoned by the Egyptians who fled and left the whole
> battalion with all the equipment . . . We improvised temporary teams
> and started to operate the cannons against the Egyptians. Now, while we
> were at it one of the ammunition trucks, loaded with fifty-sixty shells,
> suddenly caught fire and started burning. It stood in the middle of the site
> where the battalion was deployed and it was clear that any minute now it
> would explode, and the question was what should we do. Do we cease our
> fire and get the hell out of there . . . and the other option was to try and
> attach an APC [Armored Personnel Carrier] to the burning truck and tow
> it away. . . . Clearly we couldn't order one of the soldiers to do it, you
> couldn't give such an order; and so being the only two officers there one of
> us had to do it. . . . He attached the APC to the truck and towed it away,
> got back, and two-three minutes later the truck exploded. No more than
> two-three minutes. It was a huge risk. And that moment is the moment of
> our friendship. . . .

I will return to discuss the significance of this moment in forging the bond between Amnon and his friend. But let us first consider additional examples. Under less heroic, yet still dramatic circumstances, Gadi re-called the tragicomic incident that marked the beginning of his bond with Gideon in basic training:

> In the end of November or December, as the first rain began, it turned out
> that our glorious camping ground . . . was situated in the middle of the
> Yarkon riverbed. And at the first rain we were simply flooded, washed
> out. We almost drowned. And I was in a scouting tent, feeling like I was
> drowning or something. And I cried for help. And Gideon was on guard
> duty outside the camp, and then he helped me, we moved the tent, and
> saved some of my stuff, and relocated in a different place, and laid down
> some padding. I think this must have been the beginning of our relation-
> ship. And since then we, like, never parted.

The common thread in such accounts is that the formation of the new friendship, or in some instances the transformation of an existing ac-quaintanceship, is explained by dramatic circumstances that either bring the two people together for the first time, or draw them closer under unexpected, harsh conditions. The men help one another while engaged in perilous action, and this situation is understood to forge their bond. But what exactly is forged here? What is the new emotional interaction emerging between the men?

At one level, the dangerous situation highlights the meaning of friendship as a trial. Resonating here is a prevalent understanding of masculine ideals as an ongoing performance that constantly needs to be achieved and affirmed through a set of trials (Ben-Ari 2001; Gilmore 1990). The ultimate test of manhood is the test of battle (Badinter 1995; Kellet 1982). Therefore, the "true" essence of male bonding is revealed in times of trouble and hardship, particularly in combat. The men are expected to help one another up to the point of risking themselves. Once again, Itzhak Sadeh's address on *re'ut ha-lochamim* in the Palmach phrased this explicitly:

> . . . The man standing next to you and willing to give you cover with his mere body, willing to carry you in his arms at times of deadly danger . . . he is the true friend. This friendship needs to be fostered and indoctrinated. The day of trial is to be felt all year long. You must memorize and cherish the understanding that your friend is your brother in the deepest sense, a brother in deeds, devotion and readiness. (cited in Almog 1997: 379)

Male friendship is constructed as a trial "to be felt all year long." Its true essence is revealed in times of danger, but it can be tested in other settings that simulate the combat experience. Indeed, the IDF expanded and perfected this code of *re'ut*. It established a training routine that provides a continuum of situations that simulate the combat scenario, instilling an "emotional work" of soldiery through a series of physical and mental testing. Eyal Ben-Ari (1998: 47) studied the underlying organizational logic of action, which he termed "the combat schema." The combat schema depicts a threatening situation of extreme stress and uncertainty in which soldiers perform their assigned tasks of physical and technological performance, while mastering emotions of fear and aggression. *Re'ut*, as a military logic of action, emphasizes an additional component of the combat scenario—that of mutual responsibility between fellow soldiers, the readiness to sacrifice oneself for the sake of fellow soldiers. It fosters this organizational logic all year long in simulations of the combat situation, reaching a climax with the imperative of *hilutz ptsuiim*—rescuing wounded soldiers under fire and never leaving them behind under any circumstances, as defined in the IDF's official ethical code of conduct (Kasher 1996: 230).

Indeed, Amnon's earlier story about the heroic action of his friend Sharon provides the perfect example of combat performance as a trial for manhood. After towing away the burning truck, Sharon returned and jokingly said to him: "Listen, I don't care what, I want a 'badge of honor' . . . he didn't do it because he wanted the badge . . . he did it because at that moment it was very important for him to reinforce his self-image, and he was willing to pay a heavy price for that." Sharon's courageous act complies with the ultimate trial of manhood: mastering fear and aggression in the face of danger and volunteering for missions up to the point of self-sacrifice. As readiness for combat is a sought-after asset, men feel obliged to compete in volunteering in order to reinforce their masculine social status. Sharon felt that his trial deserves a badge of honor by the military system that would serve as an external proof of his manhood.

Yet in addition to asserting manhood as a social status, the combat experience involves the transmission of an additional set of emotions that deserve further attention. Elsewhere I have analyzed the combat situation in the face of danger as an individual experience of thrill bordering on the erotic. This thrill creates a sense of elation within the group of men, who, affected by intensive anticipation of the thrills of combat, combined with the obvious anxieties of war, may succumb to a quasi-religious atmosphere of ecstasy (Kaplan 2003a: 188). In the interpersonal sphere this thrill forms a newly emerging sense of *intimacy*. In chapter 4 I described a core aspect of intimacy as the possibility for total exposure, letting down defensive walls and feeling naked, expressing truly what one is (Josselson 1992: 165). The men referred to this as a state of "net" exposure. It is strongly reinforced under the harsh circumstances of combat. General N. defined *re'ut* in the battlefield as: "bringing down all the barriers, that is, in those split seconds . . . when what is at stake is human life or an emergency situation, then naturally other barriers . . . or inhibitions will be removed." Judd Ne'eman, one of my more critical informants, described the six agonizing months that he and his peers endured during their commanders' course. The strong friendships forged between some of the men turned into lifelong companionship. Judd went so far as to define the military training as a framework of sheer torture and terror, but he emphasized how this system of hazing forged a close-knit, total experience of bonding that covered many aspects of their lives. This bonding, in turn, enabled them to further accommodate the continual traumatic experiences: "The friendship was shaped in long and gray months that had no climax, nothing in particular, but for the suffering and torture and psychological terror . . . and at the same time you process and cope with the suffering . . . so the group was a kind of enclave that really helped in going through all this traumatizing experience."

Finally, a third possible emotional outcome of the harsh setting involved in the hegemonic script is a new kind of attraction toward the fellow men. The notion of "net" exposure, the letting down of barriers and the feeling of openness, may stir a sense of homosocial attraction. In another series of interviews focusing on military culture, one of the soldiers I interviewed, at the time a self-defined bisexual, noted how at their lowest state of exhaustion and shock his friends had suddenly "become beautiful": "At certain points you do feel extreme love and closeness towards the people serving with you. They are sometimes the most beautiful in the world. They may be ugly, but suddenly they become so beautiful to you, just because, you know, they are their true selves. There is a point that they may be so exhausted, they may be so shocked, so depressed, that they don't try to hide anything. You know, you see a person, netto, with no walls around him (Kaplan 2003a: 72)." Judd Ne'eman took this attraction one step further and reflected on the homoerotic potential of his own combat training setting: "It was a true love that if it weren't for all the social prohibitions would have been realized in homosexual relationships, I'm almost positive . . . the attraction was very strong and yet the prohibition was even stronger. But we were aware of this; we didn't talk about it, but we sensed that we were close to it." The erotic potential embedded in the homosocial situation is reinforced by the harsh setting, but in most cases it is left on hold, not to be performed nor discussed.

Crying and Hugging: Enacting a Conjugal Pact

Immediately after describing the sudden click between Jonathan and David, the biblical narrator moves to recount the ritualized pact that the two of them make. Like a newly wed bride moving to her husband's household, David is transferred from his own house to the house of King Saul. Jonathan and David sign a pact to enact this union, and instead of a ring or an ornament Jonathan bestows on his beloved the gift of his most personal belongings, his own clothing and arms: "And Saul took him that day, and would not let him return to his father's house. Then Jonathan made a covenant with David, because he loved him as his own soul. And Jonathan stripped himself of the robe that was upon him, and gave it to David, and his armor, and even his sword and his bow and his girdle" (1 Samuel 18:2–4). This ceremonial act has been interpreted as an initiation ritual between two friends forming a pact of ritualized friendship (Herman 1987: 58). Similarly, John Boswell explored the historical circumstances of ritualized pacts between men in the early Middle Ages in Europe as "same-sex unions," ceremonial acts of commitment between "soul mates" in order "to become brothers" (Boswell 1994: 24, 27). In some European societies the two men would pledge undying friendship and even exchange blood in the sacred precincts of a church. The exchange of personal belongings might symbolize the gift of the friend's personality (Brain 1976: 9).

The present stories of Israeli men do not offer any ritual of this sort, but a specific symbolic instance in the narrated accounts of some bonds may emotionally convey such a pact. When I asked the interviewees how the notion of combat fraternity (*achvat lochamim*) related to their experiences, Shuki came up with an interesting analogy for the emotional experience that results from a harsh, extreme situation:

> You know, in adventure movies, the hero always falls in love, because it's an extreme situation. The man and the woman . . . while they are running away or being hunted. It bonds. So maybe you get true love that isn't romantic, like *achvat lochamim*. Going together through some kind of an

extreme situation just bonds people. Because you went through something very exciting together. People fall in love on trips; you go through something very special. Something you never saw before with someone.

Is there a special situation where these feelings can happen?

Sex.

You mean sex as an adventure?

[laughs] Yeah. Sometimes.

Shuki positioned the sexual act as an extreme, exciting adventure and therefore a basis for strong bonding. Reversing the analogy, one could compare the heroic adventure shared by the two men in combat bonding to a passionate situation, passionate in the sense that it unites them together, if only for a brief moment. Situating this notion in the present context, what would be the specific, formative, binding moment within the hegemonic script? What is this special moment, which, like sex for the first time, unites the men together and may symbolically "conceive" their union?

Haim gave the following account of a key moment in the development of his relationship with Barak, a paramedic in his company during the Lebanon War:

> At a certain moment, after the air raid, Barak was called up to tend the wounded men. When he got back he passed next to me, with his armored vehicle next to my armored vehicle. We stared at one another for a split second, a moment that we certainly won't forget for the rest of our lives. And we did not speak. Somehow we reached a resting area for the night and went to sleep. In the morning we gave each other a similar stare. And then he signaled me with his head, to get down from the vehicle. We were in waiting. I got down. We went and hid behind a small stone shed, in the middle of the field, we went behind it and hugged one another and cried and cried and cried. . . . We hid from the other soldiers. We were ashamed for them to see us hugging and crying. . . . We shall never forget that moment for the rest of our lives, I mean we share this bond that, wherever we meet, there is this something which is intimate.

This account describes a formative moment, an emerging pact between Haim and Barak, set against the background of the traumatic death scenes surrounding them. The act of embracing and crying next to the scene of carnage is construed as an enactment of their bond, an act that shares some of the structural characteristics of the marriage act. The two participants are the protagonists of a public event—the ongoing battle, in which the canopy is the battle scene. They single each other out, then go aside to confer in private, hidden from the public in a shed, suggestive of the exclusion room that the newlyweds go to as part of the ceremony in a traditional Jewish wedding to consummate their marriage. And there are also the vows—in this case an unspoken understanding in which they acknowledge their commitment to one another, a commitment that in sorrow or happiness they shall not part.

Along similar lines, Amnon defined his war bond with Sharon as centering on the specific moment surrounding the incident with the burning truck: "And it came down to a moment. . . that today if I were to define the core of our relationship . . . was a very, very significant moment." Then, after describing the details of the event, he noted that: "When he [Sharon] returned we laughed, we hugged each other."

There are some striking recurring characteristics of this specific moment of crisis and the ensuing symbolic pact. Ehud recounted a crisis situation in his military unit, where he was the officer in charge, together with a subordinate commander who became his friend, Danny. Their subordinates were mostly women soldiers serving in a field unit at a border post. Ehud and Danny's superior was a woman officer, Tamar. One day, one of the female soldiers was raped by a male soldier. Ehud had just returned from a home leave, when Danny told him how he initially handled the event: "He saw that she was looking kind of funny and acting funny and was very silent. . . . He just stayed there and talked with her for hours . . . until he got it out of her. Think about it, the woman had been raped and couldn't say anything not even to her close girlfriends. And at the end she tells it to the guy that is her commander in charge . . . so it was mostly thanks to his sensitivity that it even came out at all." The commanding officer, Tamar, decided to retain the female soldier in the unit and refrained from giving her special treatment. The situation became more and more complicated as the soldier who was raped made repeated attempts to commit suicide. It became essential to confiscate her personal gun and take her away from her post in the field, without traumatizing her even further. Ehud felt he had to act as a "part-time psychologist" and be firm and authoritative about it at the same time.

On the face of it, this situation is very different from the combat scenario, involving something of a reversal of male roles. Both Ehud and Danny acted as attentive psychologists or social workers, not as soldiers under fire. Yet in terms of the stressful experience and its impact on their own bond it suggests emotional attributes similar to those of the conjugal pact. Ehud described a key moment in the course of events. He and Danny confronted Tamar, insisting that the solider should be transferred for her own sake, and Tamar harshly refuted them. The argument heated up until Ehud said that he just couldn't take it anymore: "At a certain point I couldn't talk anymore and simply stood up, turned around and then the tears started running . . . and I couldn't show her I was crying; I simply went out and went into my car and started crying there. And then Danny came by, and first of all he felt relieved to see that I was a human being too, that I was crying too after he had gone through many nights of distress and crying." This moment presented a turning point in their bond and drew them much closer together: "We went through this moment of crisis that was the only time in the army that I wept. . . and yet with him [Danny] you could talk with no masks. . . [after the event] I felt it was much easier to talk about so many other unrelated things, once you talk about such issues. The fact that we see each other in all sorts of situations, including situations of weakness."

Another informant, Noam, formulated on a more general level the emotional significance of such moments of weakness in the context of the difficult experiences he and his friends went through in Paratroops training: "You got closer to people in such a way that there are no more games, if you cry then you cry, and if you hug then there's nothing to it, you see people get killed. . . . So that's when it cracks, it cracks when you go through something really tough. . . . It's much easier to show compassion for someone when he shows you his weaknesses. . . . It's when you see something human in a person that you are ready to open up, and it's mutual." Noam's account draws implicitly on the recurrent metaphor of the hegemonic male body as an "impenetrable" body, a body that is typically impassive and serves as an iron shield defying physical and emotional penetration (Bordo 1994). The special circumstances of a stressful experience shared by the men *legitimize* sudden cracks in this iron shield. The situation forms structured moments where the walls of invulnerability crack, where people allow themselves to hug each other and cry in the presence of others, and therefore legitimize the mutual demonstration of compassion and openness between them.

To reiterate the point, the act of crying together, which recurred in several narratives, serves as a binding moment within male relationships in such crisis situations. Peter Lyman notes that crying in front of other men is a moving symbol of male intimacy that rarely occurs in practice, for it is an admission of vulnerability, a violation of the ideals of "strength" and "being cool" (Lyman 1987: 155). To a certain extent, the possibility of crying in front of other men is a taboo. In his poem on Palmach-style friendship, *A few words in praise of my friends* (Guri 1981: 230), Haim Guri lucidly describes this taboo:

I had peculiar friends.
When they laughed everyone saw them and heard them,
When they wanted to cry they hid their faces
And went aside.
I had dangerous friends

Guri then commented to me that this was the ethos of a whole culture that restrained itself from crying in public—unlike the present-day generation, in his view. But perhaps precisely because of the taboo, the occurrence of the crying act in the midst of the hegemonic scenario becomes

the emotional signifier of the conjugal pact. It is an act that attains sacredness. Its function is twofold. It records the depth of the trauma that the
men go through and at the same time offers them the best "opportunity"
to experience intimacy, an opportunity that may never return. Exposing
them in their highest state of weakness, it cracks the walls of male invulnerability, and offers the most extreme instance of male intimacy.

The intimacy of friends who share this experience for the first time can
be likened to the intimacy ideally involved in passionate, erotic experience.
It does not capture the full psychological meaning of a sexual experience,
that is, the wish for union or oneness (Josselson 1992: 73–74); but it may narrow the space between the two men in a dramatic way. Furthermore, this
binding moment of turmoil and intimacy can be understood in the context
of a liminal adventure, a hazy, ambiguous state cut apart from the normative structures of everyday life. The secluded space of this fleeting moment
of intimacy, set against the backdrop of their public actions, forms a unique
emotional state of both vulnerability and availability. This liminal state may
stir nonconforming emotions, bordering on the homoerotic.[3]

Irrespective of any erotic interpretation, the formative moment conveys
the quality of a fetish, a ritualized deed marking its significance as a conjugal *pact* and not only a conjugal act. The biblical formulation depicts and
summarizes the emotional and performative features of the conjugal pact,
describing another key moment in the epic of David and Jonathan, when
David is on the run from King Saul and meets Jonathan in a hide-out:
"And as soon as the lad was gone, David rose from beside the stone heap
and fell on his face to the ground and bowed three times; and they kissed
one another. And wept with one another, until David recovered himself;
then Jonathan said to David, "'go in peace, forasmuch as we have sworn
both of us in the name of the Lord, saying, the Lord shall be between me
and you, and between my descendants and your descendants forever'"
(1 Samuel 20:41–42). The act of mutual kissing and weeping conveys a
double function. It is construed as an enactment of the heroic male bond,
confided in private and loaded with emotions. At the same time, by mentioning the three bows and the act of kissing, a recurrent mark of tribute in
biblical narration, the narrator underscores its ritualized nature, its significance as a social pact, an oath for a long-lasting commitment between the
two men and between their kin. In the modern Israeli context, the conjugal
enactment between men may serve a similar function as a pact of social
and political significance, forming a circle of male solidarity.

The Tent Metaphor: A Circle of Solidarity

The significance of the conjugal pact can only be realized over time, when
special occasions put it to the test of male solidarity. The pact between David and Jonathan lasted throughout their lives and beyond. Following the

death of Jonathan and King Saul in battle on the Gilboa, David is anointed king of Judea and embarks on a political conflict with the House of Saul in order to extend his kingdom to the northern tribes of Israel. When Jonathan's son, Mephibosheth, is captured the biblical narrator emphasizes how David spares his life, honoring his pact with Jonathan: "But the king spared Mephibosheth, the son of Saul's son Jonathan, because of the oath of the Lord which was between them, between David and Jonathan the son of Saul" (2 Samuel 21:7). Once again, this practice echoes the archaic customs of ritualized friendship. The promise of friendship between families provided enduring support and protection through the generations. A son or a grandson could tap the symbolic credit accumulated by his ancestors (Griffith 1995), overriding other considerations of rivalry and hostility.[4] Subsequent European traditions of heroic male friendship have also resulted in bonds that transcended local obligations. For instance, in late medieval Europe the men who engaged in the romantic quest formed an elect class of solidarity (Auerbach 1953: 139).

In the Israeli case, the social status attained by serving in elite combat units carries with it a similar "romantic" aura. The bonds between men who have gone through significant military experiences often result in extensive social networking and may further facilitate economic and political negotiations. The "good ol' boys" network reinforced through shared generational experiences in combat units is based on a sense of exclusivity separating those who were "one of us" from those who weren't (Horowitz 1993: 143–144). As noted by Edna Lomsky-Feder (1998) and Orna Sasson-Levy (2000: 143), the rarity of the combat experience reinforces this sense of exclusivity and belonging to an elite circle of solidarity.

The establishment of these norms goes back to the Palmach circles. Moshe Shamir, the prominent author of the Palmach generation, reflected: "Perhaps one of the secret charms of the Palmach is the full social equality between the men and women of the time. And indeed, in a few years the Palmach sprouted from its ranks not only the military but also the political and economic leadership of the state. Statements like 'we slept together in the same tent' are typical of the Palmach generation" (Shamir et al. 1994: 8). The tent metaphor still holds a prominent place in the perceptions of later generations and offers a rich symbol for the cultural norms involved. Judd Ne'eman began the story of his long-lasting bond with his military *havurah* by describing how: "The closest and strongest friendship is the friendship I had in commanders' course . . . it's a group of men that I shared the same tent with." He then drew a clear line from the shared tent to their ongoing relationships: "It's amazing how these bonds lasted for years, and till this day we have certain connections and the vitality of the bond has not declined."

Judd also emphasized that from the beginning this group of men held a high standing in his unit, both socially and professionally, and that this combination of high social status and mutual experiences of hardships solidified their bond "in cement." Over the years the group developed, transformed, and incorporated many other men from various social networks: "Each guy brought some friends from different sides of his life . . . and at the same time there was the core group, with all the memories and internal language . . . the special smiles and glances, and the formation of myths . . . There were definitely many men there, from the military, including a few who later on became the chiefs of staff. It was very intensive, very heterogeneous, at the level of the elite of course . . . again, it's the way that the elite crystallizes itself." The male *havurah* owed its status not only to the men's social background and achievements but also to the way it crystallized through the myth of its inception, the "shared tent," a myth of origin perpetuated by shared memories and internal codes, forming a cohesive group as strong as cement.

In this sense the hegemonic bond can be analyzed along the lines of the Israeli concept of *gibush* (cohesion, crystallization), as suggested by Tamar Katriel (1991: 18–21). Katriel explored the key concept of *gibush* through the root metaphor of the crystal. First, similar to particular initial conditions that encourage the formation of a solidified crystal, *gibush* depends on shared experiences and concerns that mobilize the people's sense of involvement. Second, it captures a sense of internal strength based on the stable integration of the constituent elements that make up the crystal. Third, the members of the social group are ideally undifferentiated in terms of social values or standing. Finally, the social group has well-demarcated boundaries and entails the exclusion of outside people.

The metaphor of sleeping together in the same tent carries within it similar attributes that turn the hegemonic male bond into a cohesive, crystallizing force. First, the bond originates in particular initial conditions of hardship in which the men are strongly involved, sharing experiences, concerns, and goals. Second, the men acquire internal strength from being together in the tent, which reinforces a sentiment of cozy togetherness and belonging (*beyachad*), a sense of stable integration. Third, sharing the harsh conditions of a tent emphasizes the undifferentiated, egalitarian status held by the men. Men of unequal social status would not share the same tent. Finally, and perhaps most importantly, the tent metaphor reinforces the exclusivity of the bond. It is they who slept in that tent, not others. The tent draws a clear boundary between those who shared this intimacy and those who didn't, and are therefore excluded from its rewards.

The following account by N., a senior air force commander, corroborates these structural aspects of *gibush* as the underlying mechanisms of *re'ut*: "There's a process of selection . . . a guy who passed through this incubation within the unit . . . he was there; other's weren't . . . theoretically the screening is according to objective parameters, but in practice it's a group who selects itself; they accept the people who are most similar to themselves . . . and there's strength in this similarity . . . and then it paves the way for better communication . . . so you can say it's *re'ut*, it's not *re'ut*, I don't know." Under this formulation, military *re'ut* is related to the selection process of *gibush*, a selection of friends, continually demarcating those "who were there," in the combat setting, from those who weren't. It creates a "crystallized" similarity and paves the way for future cooperation based on facilitated communication.[5]

Altogether, the tent metaphor encapsulates the myth of the origin of the male bond as well as an elaboration of its implications for future life. Following Tamar Katriel (1991), it is a "summarizing symbol," expressing and representing the underlying cultural meaning for the participants in an emotionally powerful way without them giving it much thought. But it also is an "elaborating symbol" offering not only the image of origin but also socially valued modes of action that promote the continuation of the bond over time. It facilitates a certain type of male networking and legitimizes the elite social status of the men who shared the hegemonic military bonds, producing the cultural construct of *re'ut* as the Israeli version of a "private men's club." By alluding to the bonds of *re'ut*, their social status attains its legitimacy not from their individual background and qualifications but from their success in being part of this male bonding.

However, there is a manifest gap between the descriptions of a deep bond created under dramatic circumstances reinforced by a symbolic conjugal pact, and the subsequent evolvement of the relationship. Unlike other examples of close friendships originating in various life circumstances, many of the strong bonds that developed in the military were soon to dissolve after the men finished their service. Ehud summarized his relationship with Danny:

> It's not nice to say it but it's really a bond that has more to do with [the army]. In the army we were really, really close friends, especially because of the tight interaction, the joint work. And now there's the physical distance and more than that, it's not the same anymore. For instance, take my relationship with Tzur and Yair—it's funny that friends in fourth grade are in touch as if nothing has changed, whereas a friend from the army, it's like you look at it from a different perspective . . . today he's not close enough for me to come and confide in him, as he was back then.

Lillian Rubin notes a similar phenomenon in her study of friendship among US veterans of the Vietnam and Korean Wars. She argues that wartime friendships are rarely maintained as intimate relationships when lives return to normal (Rubin 1986: 168). Even General N., who had a long career in the air force, noted that his military bonds did not necessarily constituted close friendships in his civil life: "Your choice regarding your circle of friends, as your life rolls on down the years it creates different sorts of attachments; you won't necessarily keep on with these people . . . to say that it is a factor that is enough to form a bond that will shape your close friendship over the years—I don't think so."

In this sense, heroic friendships present a complex picture when compared to other, nonheroic close friendships across the life-course. For most men, meetings with military friends are restricted to official or unofficial reunions. Gadi is a case in point. He sustained a long-lasting relationship with his childhood group of friends, whom he meets with regularly despite their dispersal across the country. In contrast, no such efforts were invested in keeping in touch with his military pals. Nevertheless, in his rhetoric he employed strong terms to underscore his deep bond with his best friend from the military, Gideon. He used the loaded concept of twinship (discussed in chapter 3) to describe their common paths and common fate throughout their military career, both in regular service and in the reserves, including the Yom Kippur War: "[Gideon] was a twin in terms of the paths we went through throughout our service, and in meeting after leaving the army. Everywhere, I mean in boot camp, in the platoons . . . we found a connection between us, a connection of closeness, of understanding . . . and it's the same path all over again. We both flunked out of officers' school, went to be instructors in the same battalion."

In practice however, Gadi noted that they rarely met outside the military: "As soon as I stopped doing reserve duty there hasn't been hardly any contact, neither by phone, and not in any other way . . . it's a bond that doesn't exist, in my case, beyond the reserve period." Their sole attempt to meet again was in the pretext of a large official reunion of their whole army division: "There was a big reunion of the artillery corps in Latrun . . . I called up Gideon in advance, because it was important for me to make sure that he came, so we could meet up. He wanted to come, but couldn't make it. . . . We said we must meet. I still have his phone number here. I have this small basket of urgent things, and I don't know, if and when it will happen." As the planned meeting couldn't take place Gadi has been left with an ambivalent desire to see Gideon. On the one hand it has become an "urgent" need on his things-to-do list; on the other, he did not go into any effort to actively make contact.

What emerges is an interesting paradox. If military bonds are often confined to rare reunions, considering them to be friendships seems rather odd. A telling example of this paradox can be found in Amnon's story of his bond with Sharon in the Yom Kippur War following the incident of the burning truck described earlier in this chapter. When initially introducing the story of Sharon, Amnon termed him a "good friend." As such, his account of their relationship gave me the impression that they were continuously in touch after the formative war incident. But it soon became clear to me that they were hardly in touch at all. Indeed, Amnon had not even mentioned Sharon in his "relational map" of friends at the beginning of our interview. In fact, they only met by chance during a visit abroad many years later: "The next time I met him after 1973 was in 1993 . . . he was serving in an official position in the US and I was giving a talk in a nearby town, and one day I am notified by the consulate that I am invited for breakfast at the consulate . . . and I arrived and I had a surprise. It was he."

Why does such a bond deserve a significant place in Amnon's narrative; why should he at all define him as a good friend? Amnon gave a simple answer, when describing the intensity of their renewed encounter: "and that meeting was so exciting, it was like, we almost wept there. And for me it's an indication of a certain depth, a certain intimacy that evolves, and that in specific circumstances doesn't blur; it doesn't fade." What lay behind their renewed meeting was the same binding experience around the burning truck that originally forged their bond. It triggered similar emotions, almost forcing them to weep, recreating a commitment to their unspoken pact: "And that moment is our friendship . . . and even when we were sitting there, 5,000 miles away from where it all happened, talking about other things entirely, still somewhere in my mind I was picturing him. And I was in that same place and same moment when the decision had to be made who is to tie up to the burning truck and tow it away." The war incident has remained the core of their relationship, casting a shadow on anything else they might do together. As Amnon put it, that moment is their friendship. Indeed, it is nothing else.

A very similar pattern emerged in Haim's case. He drew a detailed emotional picture of his continuing bond with Barak, the paramedic, although it turned out that they are hardly in touch anymore. Again, in their scarce reunions they reconstructed their binding experience around the death scenes in the Lebanon War:

> There was a period when I hadn't seen him for some five-six years. We were on a trip up north . . . he came in to give us a lecture; he took a seat in front of me, because the previous lecturer hadn't finished yet. He turned his head and saw me, and at that second we singled each other, went outside, hugged and started crying. It was very emotional, being at the Northern border. That entire experience had suddenly surfaced within us.

The unspoken oath taken by these men on the battlefield in the Lebanon War is reflected yet again in this outburst of emotions. They replayed their original act of crying and hugging, reconstructed through the same ritual of singling each other out to go aside and confer in private. Later on, when Barak had become a high commanding officer, Haim was to be interviewed by him as part of the official procedures when terminating a job. Again, he described the dynamics of their relationship as a resurgence of the preliminary experience. Barak could barely complete the interview, finding it hard to treat him as simply an officer in the corps. These instances demonstrate the emotional intensity involved in some of the social networking between men who shared war experiences, and how this kind of trauma-based bonding overshadowed, and at the same time reinforced their professional conduct.

To recapitulate, the circle of solidarity grounded in the heroic script is strengthened by an intensely emotional sense of familiarity and intimacy. The social, economic, and political benefits attached to the "private men's club" of military veterans are accompanied and culturally reinforced by an expressive construct called *re'ut*. And even when the friends refrain from actively maintaining their bond later in life, they often perceive it as enduring and everlasting.

Replicating the Hegemonic Script

The obvious accounts of hegemonic bonding were connected with battle experiences, or with military settings set to simulate the combat trial. But such a simulation is not restricted to military organizations alone: men themselves often initiate various aspects of the hegemonic script when left to their own devices. Amnon reflected on the curious and remarkable way that he, his best friend Binyamin, and another friend chose to spend their short leaves during officers' school: "At one time, in a weekend break in the middle of the course, instead of taking a rest we met at three in the morning, on the Haifa-Tel Aviv highway and climbed up the hills, to a tree grove between Zichron-Yaakov and Bat-Shlomo, to see the sunrise. . . . The physical exertion of doing such a strenuous trek, three people, in the middle of officers' course . . . that is something I can't understand anymore." The men reenacted the harsh setting of their military training by carrying out a solitary trek, in a way that served to forge their bond. Their choice of staging is also revealing: it replicates the *sabra* ethos of touring the land that has developed into a ritualized declaration of love to the homeland (Almog 1997: 277).

This ritual incorporates values of masculine performance, such as stamina, adhering to the mission, and mischievousness. More significantly, since it was performed outside of the organizational setting and lacked any instrumental goal, it celebrated the homosocial enactment in its own right. Judd Ne'eman recounted how four of his *havurah* of friends embarked on a risky adventure over the Egyptian border, echoing a trend that led many of his generation to cross the Jordanian border to see the ancient city of Petra (Almog 1997: 286). Their own trip, taken after they terminated their military service, reenacted their war experiences anew, this time without the "excuse" of the military setting:

> In '57 we went together on a camel trip . . . we crossed the border and encountered an ambush, and it wasn't pleasant. We were shot at and we ran away. It was a sort of adventure, a provocation such as the walks to Petra. . . . The idea was to repeat the adventures we had in the Sinai Desert [in their military service during the 1956 Sinai War] . . . on the way

> we told ourselves, we should go, we shouldn't go, but when we actually
> arrived, and stood there, saw the sunset, it was a remarkable view. . . . So
> as you can see it remained with us as a certain memory.

Capturing the characteristics of the hegemonic script, the event was
assigned the official "seal" of their friendship. It became an exemplary
story, a legitimate and worthy event to remember and cherish as part
of their evolving internal tradition. In chapter 3 I delineated building
blocks that explain the maintenance of male friendships across life,
among them the notion of "shared past." Incorporating these pseudo-
combat activities into the "canon" of the group's shared past reinforces
their solidarity along the hegemonic values of *re'ut*.

But perhaps even more intriguing were those accounts of hegemonic
bonding that had nothing to do with the military, whether directly or indirectly, yet still shared the same characteristics. Yehuda, aged twenty seven,
is a striking case in point. Yehuda's friendship with Rami evolved in high
school from a casual acquaintance in class, accompanied by a covert rivalry
in sports and in dating women. At a certain point Rami got seriously ill
and was hospitalized for a period of time. Yehuda felt a need to visit him
in hospital and from that point on their friendship gradually grew stronger.
Eventually, although school was over, they started to see each other of their
own accord. It seems that their acquaintance based on high school activity
was transferred into a stronger bond forged under the anxiety over Rami's
sudden injury. Later in their adult relationship they sought to experience
adventures together, such as going on a mini-tractor voyage in the desert,
bungee-jumping, or diving, with an underlying motivation to overcome
challenges and "proving themselves." Having had little opportunity to
practice this scenario during their military service in non-combatant positions, they seem to put themselves deliberately in states of danger where
they could create a trial for their bond. In a specific example of a diving
incident Yehuda recounted how Rami made a reckless, forbidden dive
and Yehuda followed him reluctantly, feeling he "couldn't leave his friend
behind" and had to "guard his safety" in action and "take a risk in order
to save both of them."

The hegemonic script is particularly evident in the folk scenario of the
"jack test" discussed in chapter 4 as an illustration of mutual support
in everyday life. The readiness to drive out in the middle of the night
from the other end of the country to come to the rescue of the friend
stranded in his car without a jack draws on a military logic of total readiness, availability, and sacrifice for a fellow soldier in physical distress,
a logic associated originally with life and death situations. As ways
are found to replicate the military codes of *re'ut* and *hilutz ptsuiim* (the
rescue of wounded soldiers under fire) in everyday life circumstances,
the hegemonic script is established as a trial of friendship to be felt all
year long.

Interim Summary: A Case of Post-Traumatic Love?

*Two friends went out together on a journey, bim bam bom/ one
got hit on his knee, bim bam bom/ . . . then his friend told him
"it's not too bad, my friend, there's greater trouble than this."*
—Yoram Taharlev (1993), From "Bim bam bom"

Throughout this chapter I have drawn parallels between contemporary
hegemonic scripts of male friendship and the biblical epic of David and
Jonathan, which is essentially a case of a ritualized pact of brotherhood
and loyalty between families of different estates or tribes (David coming
from the tribe of Judah, Jonathan from Benjamin). I have also compared
it in passing to the romantic quest of the medieval romance. I do not pur-
port to make historical comparisons. Obviously, practices and perceptions
of heroic friendship underwent significant changes from biblical Israel,
through the European knights of the Middle Ages, through the merce-
nary-soldier, hired to fight in any army, and up to the development of the
modern nation-state instituting mandatory military service for all male
citizens. Rather, I intended to demonstrate how contemporary notions of
collective solidarity are heavily dependent on culturally available traditions of friendship, whereby ancient myths are reinterpreted by national
consciousness. The story of David and Jonathan stresses not only heroism,
but also personal affection and commitment strong enough to overcome a
harsh rivalry between families or tribes. In this sense it serves as an ethos
for national solidarity.

In a nutshell, the crux of the hegemonic script is captured in the
children's song above: two men partake on a joint venture; one of them
gets hit on the way, and is told by his friend that there are greater troubles
out there. Under this reading, men's companionship is dependent on the
shared ability to endure hardship, and on the promise of an ongoing "adventure," with the potential for continuing trouble. This homosocial voyage is based on trauma, which has a lifelong effect, as summarized by Air
Force General N.: "Now what could be more turbulent than a life-bound
experience, where there are people who just die around you, or were injured, or taken captive. It's a life experience that never leaves you."

Haim vivid illustrated the strong resurgence of his war experiences,
describing them as "flashbacks": "These flashbacks bring you back there,
as if it happened yesterday . . . the issue of combat fatigue, I think in my
view in trauma the thrills become so high, that you connect very deeply
to people next to you." Simply put, Haim described his war bonding
along the lines of post-traumatic syndrome. In his personal case, this is
probably a viable formulation of his concrete experiences in one of the
worst battles of the Lebanon War. Most men I interviewed did not go
through such manifest traumatic experiences. Moreover, even those who
endured varying degrees of grueling conditions in their military service

rarely stressed their traumatic effects. Judd Ne'eman reflected on the harsh combat training that forged his military group bonding: "At the time I wouldn't even think of seeing it as traumatic; it was *gibush*, meant to strengthen us, instill us with soldiery." Indeed, based on systematic interviewing of Israeli war veterans, Lomsky-Feder (1992) argues that the majority of combatants fail to internalize their war experiences as a traumatic event in their life-course.

Nevertheless, the harsh, stressful setting that forms the context for these hegemonic bonds, and the dynamics of how these relationships are maintained over time, suggest, at the symbolic level, a "post-traumatic"-like relationship. Irrespective of how dramatic the events that forged their bonds may have been, and of how traumatic they are retrospectively perceived as being in the men's life stories, the homosocial bonds could be best described as bonds inscribed by the drama and trauma of military, heroic life. The binding pact is transformed into a relationship that is frozen in time, preserved in memory like a flashback so that every renewed meeting vividly reconstructs past experiences.

Many interviewees reflected that even after long breaks from their military friends, feelings of intense closeness emerged immediately once they met. As Gadi put it: "Perhaps there's something about the nature . . . of military service, and sometimes it's under fire, and life threatening situations, that these breaks don't spoil the bond. You meet someone after half a year or a year . . . and you feel exactly the same feeling of closeness." Gadi has not gone through real combat experiences of life and death situations with the specific military comrades alluded to in the quote above. But as a certified veteran of an artillery combat unit, he can formulate the bond as a relationship forged "under fire" and involving a "life threat." This framing enables him to perceive his past military ties as enduring, despite the lack of close, continuous contact over time.

To recapitulate, the unfolding of the hegemonic script of *re'ut* conveys an interesting kind of relationship. On the one hand, it involves an intense set of emotions during the original enactment of the pact and the sparse consecutive reunions. On the other hand, unlike many other accounts of male friendships developing in everyday life, the bonds of *re'ut* are rarely maintained and actualized in ongoing contact and interactions. Nor is there an expressed need to maintain such a relationship. One is reminded here of the notion of an "unfulfilled bond," implicated in the tensions between shared past and shared destiny discussed in chapter 3. The relationship carries a promising potential, based on the conjugal pact, tested only at rare reunions, yet the pact colors these reunions with an immediate click and a sense that the broken bond may resume immediately. Furthermore, the hegemonic script partly lends itself as a prototype, a framework for making sense of male friendships more generally. Even when occurring in nonheroic settings, sometimes not even in the military at all, important moments in the relationship are made sense of along the lines of this dominant script of male bonding. At stake is a recursive process involving both top-to-bottom and bottom-up effects, whereby hegemonic scripts reinforce national subjection precisely by exercising their power on what are seemingly personal emotions of friendship. Yet *the* crucial feature linking individual friendship with hegemonic sentiments and collective practice is still missing from the puzzle of the national: it is the ideal of death, with its rituals of commemoration. It is there, I suggest, that the promises of these unfulfilled bonds are finally realized.

Notes

1. Similar accounts can be found in Edna Lomsky-Feder's (Lomsky-Feder 1998: 100–102) narrative study of the 1973 (Yom Kippur) war veterans.
2. The newly emerging European middle class of the eighteenth-century developed a different, bourgeois conception of romantic love. While retaining the theme of love as rebellion against social life, the bourgeois novel no longer contradicted love with marriage. Rather, it tied love to the quest of inner experience, the search for the "true self" and one's proper place in the social world. It also became a liberating form of expression for bourgeois women (Swidler 1980: 121–124).
3. Auerbach (1953: 135) notes, following Simmel (1911/1971), that in the modern understanding an adventure refers to an "unstable, peripheral, disordered situation," one that is "outside the real meaning of existence." Victor Turner (1992: 48, 142–144) analyzes the liminal state as a collective or individual transitory position between two steady states within society. It may involve unruly behavior, nonconforming experiences of antistructure that explore alternatives to social norms. Elsewhere I have analyzed homosexual emotional experiences in the military as situated in such a liminal period (Kaplan 2003a: 157).
4. For instance, in book 6 of Homer's Iliad, the heroes Diomedes and Glaukos are about to engage in combat. When Glaukos presents himself by mentioning the name of his ancestors Diomedes halts immediately, and "[w]ith one thrust in the field he fixed his long spear like a pole, and smiled at the young captain, saying gently: 'Why, you are my friend! My grandfather, Oieneus, made friends of us long years ago.'" Diomedes then proclaims, "I am your friend, sworn friend, in central Argos. You are mine in Lykia, whenever I may come. . . . Let those around us know we have this bond of friendship from our fathers" (quoted in Wilken 1994).
5. Unsurprisingly, the IDF recruitment organization employs the term *gibush* for the official selection procedures to elite units. The choice of this term for what should have been individual aptitude testing reveals the significance that the military organization attributes to a "crystallized" match between the candidates and the unit.

Chapter Seven

"SHALOM, HAVER":
COMMEMORATION AS DESIRE

Let us sing to the dead before they die, for what use is in your singing to them when they are deaf of hearing and dense of understanding . . .

For if great they were in death—in life sevenfold so, and if holy after death—holy were they afore . . .

Know this: Among you walk all tomorrow's dead.

If know you that your friend dies tomorrow, what would you not do to make his last day pleasant? . . .

Gathering round the body of the dead and digging in it crumb by crumb—so be the manner of all maggots and worms. But they who love the dead truly—they should quench his thirst and nourish him of their goodness while he yet lives. Anointing the body of the dead with perfumes and fragrances—that be the trade of embalmers, but the good friends of the dead would anoint his shield with oil before he heads off to battle!

—Yitzhak Shalev (1951: 172–174), From
"Let us sing to the dead before they die"

Introduction:
"It is thanks to death that friendship can be declared"

The hegemonic perception of re'ut suggests a bond that is both *static* and *eternal*. It presents a relationship that does not develop and transform across the life course. Rather, its maintenance is based on a resurrection of past events. In this sense, the feelings invoked by *re'ut* are reminiscent of those invoked in *commemoration*. In this chapter I expand on the interrelations between these two emotional settings and on their joint institutionalization in Israeli culture, moving the focus of my analysis further into the collective, national level. I do so in light of a specific framing of masculinity as a moral code associated with male expendability and self-sacrifice. David Gilmore has suggested that in many societies the idea that men's lives are expendable seems to hold a central value in the cultural construction of masculine identity (Gilmore 1990). The question I explore is how such ideas appear in concrete male friendships on the one hand, and how they are endorsed by national practices on the other. Beyond the men's narrated experiences, I draw more closely on canonic literary sources, cultural artifacts, participant observations, and media coverage of national commemoration rituals.

In chapter 1 I briefly introduced Jacques Derrida's study of the politics of friendship, based on explicit and implicit "correspondences" with a range of Continental philosophers, both dead and alive. In one of his essays Derrida quotes and addresses a sort of epigraph written by the French philosopher Morris Blanchot, following the death of yet another philosopher, Michel Foucault. Derrida writes (1997: 302):

> This friendship could not have been declared during the lifetime of the friend. It is death that 'today allows me' to 'declare' this 'intellectual friendship'. . . . May thanks be given to death. It is *thanks* to death that friendship can be declared. Never before, never otherwise . . . and when friendship is declared during the lifetime of friends, it avows, fundamentally, the same thing: it avows the death thanks to which the chance to declare itself comes at last, never failing to come.

The friendship can be declared thanks to death. More than that, if that death has not yet arrived it is still imagined, in order that the friendship could be declared. Typical of Derrida's style of writing, this phrasing invites a series of additional questions. In particular, I have become preoccupied with the term "declaration." What is the nature of this "declaration"? To whom does the speaker make it? Is it an issue of public legitimacy? Do we need to wait for the friend's death in order to publicly legitimize our relationship with him? Or is it perhaps not only a public acknowledgment, but also an internal one? Does the mourner rely on his friend's death to acknowledge the depth of his feelings toward him? In what follows I attempt to frame these universal questions of friendship and mourning in the Israeli context of heroic male bonding. I explore what it takes for male love to be "declared" within the hegemonic national discourse of friendship.

Derrida's deconstruction of the philosophical canons of fraternal friendship underscores a fundamental opposition between what is public, manifest, and testimonial and at the same time private, secret, and illegible. The opposition between illegibility and testimony is highlighted in what is perhaps the first modern Israeli poem to explicitly address *re'ut* and commemoration, "The stranger remembering his friends" by Natan Alterman (1941). Alterman was a leading Israeli poet whose ascent in the 1940s strongly influenced the younger 1948 generation (Almog 1997:

104). The poem provides an elaborated artistic framework for describing the relationship between the dead and the living, based on a literary construct known as "the living dead." The living speaker longs for his three friends, who lie underneath a stone memorial (*gal'ed*), and is conversing with them. In a specific verse explicitly contemplating *re'ut*, the speaker exclaims (Alterman 1941: 46): ". . . Re'ut is a wolf / I could not calm it down, my brother / It has widened to no limits/ The most modest in the passions of the living. / The most silent in the world's passions/ How did it suddenly become so full of words? / To my friends, oh lead me / Oh remove the mountains from me . . . ". Alterman poses the question that is at the heart of the present discussion, namely, how does the modest and silent passion of friendship become an untamed, wolfish hunger? Moreover, how does this passion that is so silent and illegible transform into a testimony, a declaration of desire?

The Jewish-Israeli culture of commemoration developed elaborate mourning rituals. A range of studies discuss the tension between national practices endorsing hegemonic, collectivistic values in Israeli commemoration rituals, especially during the formative years of the pre-state and early state period, and the growing attempt in subsequent generations to express individual values.[1] However, it seems that the emphasis on images of friendship has remained steady in the culture of commemoration throughout the years. Ever since 1948, memorials depict fallen soldiers in situations of closeness and intimacy, stressing personal, individual pain over collective mourning. The verse "in life and death they did not part" (2 Samuel 1:23) from King David's lament has become a common inscription on memorials for fallen soldiers (Almog 1997, 38).[2]

In his analysis of collective memory during the 1948 War of Independence, Emmanuel Sivan (1991: 166) noted that the rituals emphasized personal traits of the fallen men, and not only the glory of the war itself, as a collective euphoria of masculinity or nationalism (Sivan 1991: 229). Despite the rhetoric of "us"—the stress on collectivity that dominated the discourse of the 1948 generation in general—the basis of commemoration by both parents and friends was nevertheless situated in personal, primordial feelings of a grievous loss following the death of their loved one (Sivan 1991: 166). Such notions were expressed in the numerous commemorative booklets produced by the agricultural training settlements (*hachsharot*), youth movements, and military units. In one such booklet published by the prominent yeshiva *Merkaz Ha-rav*, a religious student laments the loss of his friend in poetic phrasing drawn from a mixture of biblical verses (especially Jeremiah 31:20 and Ezekiel 27:35) and the lament of David for Jonathan (2 Samuel 1: 26):

> Whenever I talk of him I do remember him still, my heart yearns for him, and my lonesome soul, orphaned from such a dear, old and beloved friend (re'a), will not be consoled. Therefore I allow myself to sincerely use the

verse from David's lament for Jonathan "very pleasant have you been to me; your love to me was wonderful [also mysterious]," and not only to me, for all your friends and acquaintances became desolate, and their hearts stormed, their faces were convulsed and they were horribly afraid (cited in Sivan 1991: 166).

Why is it that only now, after the friend's death, does the mourner "allow himself" to "sincerely use the verse from David's lament"? What is so special about this verse that it is so frequently quoted in these circumstances? I propose that the lament, with its combination of hegemonic battle scenario on the one hand and revelation of a mysterious love on the other, is repeatedly used because it *legitimizes* homosocial love. By subscribing to the hegemonic script of friendship bordering on death, men are "allowed" to experience a passionate love hitherto silent and unacknowledged. National discourse provides a framework for transforming this illegible emotion into a testimony.

A Friend to Die For

We formed an intimacy of two people whose throat was bound up by the same rope; there is no greater intimacy than that

—Amnon

In the ancient epics of heroic male friendship, as well as in the romantic quest of courtly love male performance is associated with the specter of death. In all three epics of heroic friendships analyzed by David Halperin, the weaker or less favored friend dies. The subordinate friend is the expendable friend, and his death paves the way for his friend's further adventures (Halperin 1990). In the great love stories, from Tristan and Iseult of the middle ages to Romeo and Juliet of the romantic period, the forbidden love ends in tragic death (Swidler 1980: 122). According to Denis de Rougemont, the death wish is the ultimate, hidden desire behind the lovers' bond in the romantic myth (Rougemont 1940/1974: 46). The love that the living for the dead by is shifted to a new and possibly more devoted plane. It is unending love, linking them together in an eternal bond (Gergen and Gergen 1995: 225). These ideals have been incorporated by modern national ideology, and specifically in terms of homosociality. The hegemonic script of male friendship implies that *ideally* male bonding can only be attained through death. The confrontation with death offers the ultimate staging for homosocial bonding. It is based on the logic that the more traumatic the agonizing experience may be, the stronger the emotional impact on the men, and the stronger the possibility for an intense sense of bonding among them.

In a journalistic interview, Efi Eytam, a retired IDF brigadier-general and a leading figure in ultra-right-wing national religious circles, described the experience of combat as an expression of the sublime, connecting it with the biblical image of Abraham's sacrifice of Isaac (Shavit 2002):

> Till this day the one thing that makes my eyes moist is when I see young men loaded down with military gear on the way to a mission and becoming silhouettes on the horizon. I find it so dramatic, for me it the most exciting thing in the world. Because it is the trial of the *akeda* (binding for sacrifice). And there is some kind of *aliyah* (elevation) in it, an *ola* (burnt sacrifice to God). Take the word *la-krav* (into battle). On the one hand, it contains the most terrible connotations of loss of life. On the other hand, it contains a sense of *hitkarvut* (coming closer), it has something that brings you closer to your inner truth.

Eytam's account describes combat motivation in romanticist terms, presenting the desire for battle as an act of romantic bonding with one's true, inner self. His wording plays on various associations. First, there is the plausible linguistic association between *krav* (battle) and *hakrava* or *korban* (sacrifice). Although Eytam chooses to use more specific biblical terms for sacrifice associated with sacrifice to god (*akeda* and *ola*), the underlying thread is the general association between *krav* and *hakarava*, based on the same root *k-r-v*. The result is a linkage between the combat thrill and a death wish. Elsewhere I discussed the recurrent association between the combat thrill and sexual desire as a building block in the organizational construction of combat emotions (Kaplan 2003b). Death is the third element in this association. As one Israeli soldier was reported to claim: "I am willing to die to get a thrill" (Sasson-Levy 2000: 141).

Eytam draws yet another, perhaps less evident associative link between *krav* (battle) and *hitkarvut* (coming closer), again based on the same root *k-r-v*. His phrasing links battle and sacrifice with an act of closeness. Although he speaks of closeness to one's inner self, a romantic ideal of solitary male performance, the combat scenario he alludes to is clearly one embedded in homosocial experience. The image is of a group of young men on their way to their military mission fading into mere silhouettes on the horizon. The forceful death wish contained in this image is a *collective* one, and it is mediated by the *closeness* formed between the men.

Efi Eytam's powerful image echoes earlier representations of the Zionist fighting spirit. In his poem on Palmach-style friendship, discussed throughout his interview with me, Haim Guri (1981: 230) mentions the acclaimed Palmach spirit of volunteering for a mission: "And so did I have deaf friends. / When one volunteer was called for, there came ten / For they didn't hear well."

What is intriguing in Guri's semi-ironic yet sympathetic depiction of this spirit of volunteering is the association that led him to this metaphor of his deaf friends. Guri clarified to me in our conversation on his poetry and life experiences that the verse was based on a prevailing joke in the Palmach: "You'd say of certain women, this woman is deaf, when you tell her to sit down she lies down" (in Hebrew *la-shevet* and *shochevet*). The term *shachav* means both to lie down and to have sex. The men's persistence in demonstrating their fighting-spirit is likened to a deliberate deafness of a woman who may not be permitted to express a direct desire but in fact is eager to have sex. Guri associates the guys' eagerness to join battle with the desire to have sex. Whereas lying down, *shachav* refers to sexuality it is also closely associated with dying. A common expression in biblical Hebrew is *"shachav* (lay down) with his fathers"—passed away and joined one's ancestors. As argued by Judd Ne'eman (1999), the 1948 generation involved in the War of Independence were suppressing a collective death wish. What is at stake, then, is a complex relationship between the enthusiasm to set out on the combat mission and a silenced sexual desire related to a death wish. Similar to the women in the Palmach joke, the young fighters could not express a direct desire to die or to have sex. Hence, they played deaf and behaved as if they were called on for the mission, all the while acting on a silenced desire to die in battle, summoned by a national call to literally join their ancestral line of men by dying on the battlefield.

By this reading, death in battle is implicitly associated with a sexual union. Indeed, a few of the 1948 poets linked death in battle with the imagery of a wedding night. Dan Miron (1992: 225) referred to another poem by Guri, *Till Dawn* (Guri 1949: 73), illustrating a fantastic-realistic picture of battle and death told by the dead speaker to a female lover. The speaker portrays the battle scene with colorful metaphors of a wedding, "a wedding of blood," but explains that the sexual union does not occur between the soldiers and their women lovers, but rather between them and the primordial mother earth that takes in their bodies as a loving woman would take her man in her arms. This interpretation places the enthusiasm to set out on the combat mission and the erotic death wish it involves around heterosexual desire. But the framework of heroic male bonding suggests an alternative interpretation of the death wish based on homosocial desire. Death is where the male friendship is truly attained. Halperin (1990: 79) formulated the pact between the two men in the epics of heroic friendship in terms of the wedding metaphor, whereby the ultimate wedding is achieved only when one of them dies: "Death is the climax of the friendship, the occasion of the most extreme expressions of tenderness on the part of the two friends, and it weds them forever (in the memory of the survivor, at least)." Under this interpretation the men's eagerness for battle may act on a silenced, inexpressible desire to symbolically lie down together, body next to body, united in their deathbed.

It is interesting to follow some of these notions in the narratives of concrete, real life friendships. Although only a few of my interviewees had had close contact with death, some of them offered some explicit and implicit insights as to its place in their male relationships. Death shapes the notion of what true friendship is about. Reflecting on one of his bonds during the first stages of his conscript military service, Modi relayed a canonic definition of the "true friend" as a friend "to die for": "He [the friend] was a true friend . . . the kind of friend you'd be willing to die for, definitely . . . what I felt with him was that kind of feeling that if we happened to arrive at a situation . . . where one of us had to defend the other one, then we'd do that . . . that I could really lose my life for his sake."

How is death associated with intimate friendship? An interesting window into male subjectivity in this regard is offered in the following, detailed reflection by one of my most outspoken interviewees, Amnon. At a certain stage during his interview, I asked Amnon what the points of similarity and difference were between him and his friend Binyamin, his buddy from officers' school, with whom he resumed contact only many years later. After some reflection he pointed out that the essence of their similarity is in mutual feelings of existential fear and anxiety: "In the situation where you're by yourself, totally, utterly alone, it is precisely there that you experience fears and anxieties that I think formed the similarity between us. I think that in those situations where we're alone we are afraid of the same thing . . . maybe that's the explanation for the deep bond between us." Then, trying to clarify the source of this deep, deep dread that bonded them together, Amnon referred to the notion of death: "We would talk a lot about death in our conversations . . . about the fact that life is transient and the end is predetermined. And old age is predetermined and what will happen to us in old age is predetermined, and perhaps the way we both sense how the end is in the air. . . . When I say that when we're alone we are afraid of the same thing, I think that's what I mean.

Beyond the philosophical-psychological contemplations that Amnon shares here with his friend, he considers a concrete example related to death that served as a catalyst for their growing closeness: "One thing that really brought me closer to Binyamin is the dying of his mother, she had been dying for three years ... the fact that he shared with me his mother's death, and perhaps the worst moment of all when there was a decision to help her die. And the way he shared with me his struggle and his feelings and the terrible pain of a son who loved his mother so much after four years of taking care of her this way, and now he reached the conclusion that there's nothing to be done and she should be freed from her suffering. This experience was simply very, very strong." Following this story of Binyamin's treatment of his mother, Amnon offered the following analogy to explain the essence of their bonding: "We formed an intimacy of two people whose neck was bound by the same rope; there is no greater intimacy than that . . . because that situation of total helplessness when you confront death is truly very intimate. And in that situation when you fear death, the fear of death is so revealing . . . in that moment there are no more defenses, no faking it, no games." Amnon's words draw on a recurrent notion that the confrontation with death creates a newly emerging sense of intimacy. It offers the possibility for total exposure, for letting down defensive walls and inhibitions, feeling bare, and expressing truly what one is.

At this stage Amnon turned to illustrate this very idea by way of another friendship story, unrelated to his intimate friendship with Binyamin, that of his contact with Sharon in the Yom-Kippur War. As discussed in the previous chapter, beyond their shared encounter with the burning truck his bond with Sharon was very limited. It is striking that Amnon associated both bonds with the notion of "two men bound by the same rope." His intimacy with Binyamin following his friend's treatment of his dying mother does not involve a hegemonic account of male combat performance. On the contrary, it depicts a counterhegemonic performance of nurturing and tending, traditionally associated with the female role. Yet to make sense of his bond with Binyamin, Amnon associated it with, indeed subordinated it, to the war experience, defining these two very different relationships as an illustration of deep intimacy in the face of death. In other words, instances of deep closeness between men, whether in actual instances of "sacred" combat scenarios, or in instances of less hegemonic cases, are made sense of in light of the ideal of death. In this regard, although only a few of the interviewees in the present study discussed explicit life events related to death, the symbolic function of death as an ideal of friendship recurred in between the lines. Similar to Jacques Derrida's (1997: 302) suggestion, the men need to envision death in order to fully acknowledge the deep meaning of their friendship. Anticipating death, actually preparing for it, is understood to be the path to ultimate intimacy: The true friend is a friend to die for.

Gazing on the Friend

A eulogy pays homage to the dead. The mourner tends to present and view the deceased in a more positive light than during his lifetime. This is a phenomenon most people are aware of. Sometimes it even hinders them from determining what their true opinion of the deceased really was, had it not been for his death. One of my interviewees, Eli, reflected: "I had friends from elementary school, who in retrospect were more high quality guys . . . one fell in the Lebanon War, so he was really, I don't know whether I think of him as the most high quality guy because he was killed or that he was high quality simply because that's what he was . . . but he was really an awesome guy!" In this case, having died in heroic circumstances such as war, the deceased acquires added virtues and is assigned greater value. His "real" qualities are even more difficult to evaluate.

Most personal eulogies pay homage not only to the friend's personal virtues but also to the friendship itself. Again, the mourner may tend to exaggerate the magnitude of their relationship, or may experience it in a new light. John Berger (1967: 93) notes that when people recall their dead friend, they might recall such banalities as "he always maintained that a front-wheel drive was safer; and in their memory this now acquires the value of an intimacy." Yet I suggest that Derrida's notion of *declaring* the friendship only after the death of the friend, or while anticipating his death, implies more than that. It implies that a certain aspect of this friendship appears for the first time only at the deathbed. What is this new emerging aspect of the relationship?

In everyday life, the experience of emotions between men is bound by incongruity, discontinuity, or "aporia" in the narration. In the framework of deconstruction, aporia are blind spots in the text, betraying a tension between what the men *manifestly* mean to say and what they are *constrained* to mean (Norris 1991: 100). From a narrative perspective, death, whether real or imagined, transforms this complex, ambivalent language of relatedness. Emotions that have been ambiguous, silent, or even absent, during the lifetime of the friend may enter new grounds following his death. The narrated grief may produce a one-dimensional picture, one that can invoke explicit emotions of yearning and passion. This is one way to make sense of the "romantic" narratives of male friendships offered by some of the interviewees. In chapter 3 I followed a few singular narratives that referred to an immediate click between the men, developing into a deep dyadic relationship set in exclusive spaces, reflecting a sense of shared destiny. Although many accounts of male friendship describe intimacy, in these particular cases the men painted their bond in much more intense, passionate colors. Interestingly, in most of these stories the friends were no longer in touch by the time of the interviews.

I suggest that these men described their bonds in such a passionate manner precisely because they experienced them as dead. Haim's love story with Yitzhak is unquestionably reinforced and colored by Yitzhak's sudden death two months earlier. While no other interviewee referred to a close friend who actually died, some spoke of a close friendship that had died out, and this symbolic death played a role in coloring the bond in romantic terms. Two such cases in particular brought about simultaneous feelings of both yearning and rage over the breaking up. Such is Nachshon's account of his intimate and exclusive relationship with Michael beginning at the age of eighteen during military service and developing into an intensive relationship until its deliberate termination. At a certain stage, after each of them had settled down with a family and career, their meetings gradually transformed into a mundane relationship between the two families. Unwilling to accept the new circumstances of their relationship, Nachshon actively broke the bond:

> And suddenly I felt the need wasn't symmetrical and that he could manage without it or that there were more important things . . . and suddenly the

whole affair lost its meaning . . . because at a certain moment I said I didn't want to meet under these conditions. As far as I was concerned it was all or nothing. I wasn't ready for the four of us to meet once every two months on a Saturday to go on a picnic, taking the kids to pick anemones. I didn't want that . . . I wasn't prepared to be a foursome and not have the real thing.

Nachshon gave a detailed account of his feelings regarding his breakup with Michael: "I appeared extreme in my reaction, as overreacting. . . . And you can definitely see it perhaps in terms of a love between a man and woman, where he can't continue seeing his lover, remain friends, as they say. No, I wasn't ready to remain friends. It was too hard for me . . . I definitely took it as a lover breaking up from his beloved." Whereas most men would probably talk of separation from friends in terms of the fading of their relationship, Nachshon experienced the change in his bond with Michael as an extinct love relationship, describing it as the pain of a lover abandoned by his beloved. Throughout his story of their bond, his words were suffused with feelings of grief and rage over what he experienced as Michael's abandonment. Consider the imagery he used to convey their punctual meetings every three weeks:

We'd meet, I would unload my charge and he would unload his. A conversation would develop, but the whole thing would exhaust itself in two or three hours, and then it's gone, it's heavy, it's the kind of oil that could last for three hours and it's clear that after that there's nothing more to say. It's like I brought mine, and you brought yours; you crucified me and I crucified you, and now we have nothing more to put together. You know what . . . you could actually call it a kind of alienation; it's like we ended the sexual act (or fucking), pardon me, and we both discharged and there's nothing else to do together, just like that.

The homoerotic potential, left as an aporia in most homosocial narratives, suddenly surfaces explicitly in Nachshon's account. He retrospectively describes their meetings as a performance charged by sexual energy, brief encounters coming to a halt once the "sexual act" is over. His anger over the loss of their bond, combined with mourning, seems to have induced an expression of desire toward the friend, which might have not appeared had the friendship been retained.

Meir's story is another unique example of a eulogy of a friendship that has symbolically died. His best friend since early childhood, Baruch, had converted to ultra-orthodox Judaism (*hazara bitshuva*), a process that gradually cut off their bond. From Meir's Zionist-secular point of view the ultra-orthodox way of life represents a threat that could be best captured under the orthodox self-assigned phrase of "dying under the tent of the Torah" (*lamut be-ohala shel Torah*), alluding to a lifestyle devoted to the study of the Torah with no room left for anything else, including friendship. For Meir, Baruch's disavowal of their friendship brought about feelings of

rage, which in turn imbued their previous friendship with dramatic, passionate emotions:

> The first crack I can think of, I call it the first nail in the coffin of conver-
> sion, I put it in such extreme words because for me it was a very difficult
> event . . . [the friendship today] is so miserable and difficult compared to
> the magnificent past, it's like impoverished Italy compared to magnificent
> Rome . . . I feel I had something phenomenal, we would think alike, want
> the same things, love the same things, in nuances, in nuances . . . we had
> this amazing closeness, and I ask where has it all gone. For me only death
> matches this situation. Perhaps it would have been better had it happened
> that way, really. I have a lot of anger, as you can tell.

The breaking up or drifting apart of male bonds, of any kind, are a natural course of adult relationships. But Meir and Nachshon perceived their
friendships as symbolically dead, and in so doing colored the bond in
romantic, passionate emotions. Their retrospective, postmortem accounts
marked the bond as the perfect, ideal relationship, as Meir put it: "Me and
Baruch, he was the real and definite thing."

These postmortem narratives draw on the issue of the male gaze.
Twentieth-century (predominantly continental European) philosophy
has been preoccupied with two alternative formulations of (male) desire:
desire as sex and desire as power. These two opposing views would often
complement each other (Silverman 1999). Sexual love, at least as it has
been viewed within the cultural horizons of the male world, is all about
penetration and therefore all about position, superiority and inferiority,
rank and status, gender and difference (Halperin 2002). As analyzed
extensively in feminist thought, representation of erotic desire in the
Western artistic traditions reflects a hierarchical structure between subject
and object. Desire is understood to be a gendered gaze: The one who sees
and the one who is seen are gendered positions. The dominant thesis of
the male gaze has been that the ideal viewer is male, occupying the domi-
nating and objectifying position toward women (Berger 1972; Kern 1996;
Rumsey 1995).[3] This thesis excludes the possibility of desire as a mutual
gaze between the two partners. As such, it echoes the traditional cultural
assumptions underlying male bonding. Unlike the familial and heterosexual bonds that are grounded in fundamental difference, male bonds
are constructed as egalitarian, nonhierarchical, and reciprocal precisely by
the careful removal of any hint of subordination on the part of one friend
to the other (Halperin 2002).

How is it possible, then, for a man to objectify another man, to strip
him from a culturally regulated position as a subject, whether a compan-
ion or a rival, and treat him as an object of desire? Following David Halperin (1990), I argue that experiencing a friend's death institutes desire
by repositioning the homosocial bond as an asymmetrical relation. As
much as the hegemonic plot of friendship celebrates a bond between two

equals, the outcome of the plot is dependent on the breaking of this symmetry. In the case of the heroic epic of David and Jonathan, it is the latter's death that affords David's celebrated declaration of desire: "your love to me was wonderful, passing the love of women" (2 Samuel 1:26). The tension between the two partners is relieved through death—the dead friend is now officially and permanently assigned the subordinate position.[4]

By this reading, we can understand that Nachshon's relationship has been transformed precisely because of his feelings that their balance of symmetry has been violated: "As far as I was concerned the equality, symmetry and mutuality was a dramatic aspect of the relationship, and so when it was violated I cancelled the whole thing." And because of this transformation his retrospective account of their relationship could suddenly be colored with erotic shades. Within the hegemonic framework for male friendship, the death of the friend, or his imagined death, dissolves the potential of sexual symmetry between the men. It is thanks to death, that the affirmation of the social order of desire is achieved. It is thanks to death that the friendship can then be declared.

The Mask of *Re'ut*

Having examined some personal narratives of friendship and loss I return to the collective sphere of *re'ut* and commemoration. Artistic representations of the Zionist military struggle and rituals of commemoration reflect a tension between alternative meanings of war and sacrifice—war as an integral part of the national struggle and war as a source of horror. Following Dan Miron (1992), I suggest that the tension between the two poles of the war experience is mediated by the idea of *re'ut*. Miron notes that the war poetry between World War I and the 1948 War of Independence shifted from an emphasis on the war situation as a source of trauma and terror to an emphasis on its national, collective ideals. The early depictions of war by early Israeli poets were influenced by the modernistic antiwar approach of their European counterparts following the World War I, but as the Zionist enterprise grew more and more dependent on military power, especially after the first Arab Uprising of 1929, the depiction of war gradually switched to an epic, heroic, and sacred style.[5] This is best captured in a poem by Shaul Tchernikovsky "On the Hills of *Gilboa*," echoing the biblical lament of King David over King Saul's death by his own sword, rather than falling in the hands of the enemy (Miron 1992: 16–41).

A psychological interpretation of the epic would suggest that David suffers pangs of conscience for seizing the crown from the house of Saul and atones with a public lament that lauds the earlier king and his son Jonathan, emphasizing their virtues both as war heroes and as dear friends. His manifested expression of personal grief can reinforce his own political legitimacy. Modern-day rituals of commemoration in Israeli society may follow similar psychology. Dan Miron suggests that the community of men who have participated, either directly or indirectly, in the national experience of war, and for whom the death of their peers paved the way for their own survival, have developed a unique, ambivalent space of commemoration, represented by the centrality of *re'ut* in the war poetry. The survivors' guilt feelings could be somewhat redeemed by consistently placing the bond of friendship in combat in close association with the sacrifice of war. *Re'ut* created a kind of emotional balance for the agony of the dead. It helped the survivors to endure, and partly conceal, the severe sacrifice of casualties by emphasizing the eternal promise of friendship (Miron 1992: 95).

Since the death of the fallen soldiers can not be viewed as a complete and total death, it is masked by diverse ritualized symbolism. One recurring metaphor in war poetry is the replacement of the dead with red flowers.[6] Another central theme for masking the reality of the heroes' death, especially after the War of Independence, is to connect the dead to the living by the artistic image of the "living dead" noted earlier in Alterman's poetry. Miron (1992) distinguished between Alterman's stylistic use of the living dead as a predominantly romantic-metaphysical schema, an abstract philosophical exploration, and its usage in Guri's writing, which deals directly with concrete war experiences and the realities of the human condition. For Guri, who actually participated in the war, the metaphor of the living dead serves to repress and blur his realistic gaze on their dead bodies: "But while looking he is partly covering his face. His living dead is like the fingers on his eyes—partly concealing and partly opening and enabling a real glimpse" (Miron 1992: 224).

The image of the living dead is a literary-cultural solution, attempting to bridge the acute paradox of a society that sacrifices the lives of its sons in the name of collective values, even as the preservation of life and survival are lauded as one of its central values (Hever 1986). This notion can be expanded to the general association of *re'ut* with commemoration. George Mosse (1993: 128) argues that despite the almost unprecedented prevalence of memorial sites across Israel (about one for every sixteen fallen soldiers), this national effort does not signify, as it did in Europe, "an effort to make war acceptable through masking or disguising its terror." However, the public consumption of, say, poetry, songs, and memorials for fallen men through the emphasis on *re'ut* does suggest the ritualized function of a *mask*. Tomas Scheff (1977) discusses how rituals, much like theater masks, offer distanced reenactment of situations that evoke collectively held emotional distress. They form the aesthetic distance necessary for the restimulation of repressed emotions. By experiencing distress within the *dramatic* frame, the grief becomes more bearable. As both participants and observers of their own distress, the dramatic frame enables people to acknowledge a large spectrum of repressed emotion from a distance. Along these lines, the rituals of *re'ut* become a collective theater mask that serves to stimulate emotions and at the same time refine them. The image of the living dead is an ever-present mask that continuously serves both to hide and to signify what it means to hide.

The Friend Yitzhak Rabin

Most of the aforementioned studies centered on the formative years of commemoration rituals following the War of Independence. Yet to this day, Israeli collective rituals use a similar rhetoric and dramatic style, commemorating dead warriors in terms of personal attributes of friendship. The electronic media repeatedly deal with the continuing death of soldiers (and, in the case of the *intifada*, of Israeli civilians) by broadcasting interviews with "best friends" of the deceased to tell of the great friendship they enjoyed. Rituals of commemoration based on the rhetoric of longing for "the friend" reached their climax with the memorial rites for Prime Minister Yitzhak Rabin, who was assassinated in 1995 by a national-religious extremist who opposed the Oslo Peace Accords initiated by the government. Rabin, the first prime minister of *sabra* background, had served as a Palmach commander during the War of Independence. In a 1994 television interview for Independence Day, Rabin said that Guri's song *Ha-re'ut* (Guri 1950/2000: 147–148) was his favorite song because it came out right after the war and signified the friendship and solidarity crucial for the founding of Israel. He also noted that the song reminded him of the period following the war, signifying his fellow soldiers' wish for peace.

The political rally where Rabin was shot involved pop singers, and included the song *Ha-re'ut*. The rally ended with a collective singing (*shira be-tzibur*) of "Song for Peace," written in the early 1970s by Yaakov Rotblit (1973). The song became an unofficial hymn of the Israeli peace movement. Rabin joined the singing. The sheet with the song's lyrics was found in his pocket following the assassination, stained in blood. Another song preformed at the rally was "Crying for you"(Geffen 1995), a rock ballad whose chorus runs: "For ever, my brother / I'll remember you / And we will meet in the end, you know that / And I have many friends / but they all fade away / in front of your stunning light." The ballad, written by rock singer Aviv Geffen in memory of a friend who died in a car accident, nevertheless employs some military slang terminology, which together with the term "brother" draws on the classic themes of fraternal friendship and commemoration. Upon Rabin's assassination, the song was immediately transformed into a kind of updated version of the earlier *Ha-re'ut* song, a vehicle for public mourning. It became the most popular commemoration song among youth and, eventually, in institutionalized school commemoration ceremonies (Vinitzky-Seroussi 2001: 262).[7]

In addition, at Rabin's funeral, attended by an unprecedented number of world leaders, US President Bill Clinton eulogized Rabin as a fighter for the freedom of his people and for peace. Then, in what seemed like a simple, straightforward act of tribute to a political ally, Clinton ended his speech with the words "*shalom, haver*" (Goodbye/peace, friend). The combination of friendship with commemoration could not have been made more explicit. These two words struck a chord among the Israeli public. The term *haver* symbolically placed Prime Minister Rabin on a par with all other members of the community, his death representing yet another sacrifice on the national altar, similar to that of all other fallen soldiers. It also placed the sacrifice of each solider as tantamount to that of the nation's leader, reinforcing the image of the nation as a deep horizontal comradeship, as argued by Benedict Anderson (1991: 7).

The phrase "*shalom, haver*" immediately became a slogan and a popular bumper sticker, with many variations that developed over the years, from "Friend, I remember" to "Friend, you're missed" to "Friend, you're missed more and more," adding additional levels of interpretation to the original commemorative act.[8] The framework of friendship has meanwhile served to mediate the tension between two alternative representations of Rabin: the consensual image of Rabin as a warrior of the Palmach generation and the IDF chief of staff who led Israel to its 1967 victory, and the less consensual image of Rabin as a politician who launched a controversial peace initiative. Rabin was to be remembered first and foremost as a friend, not as a warrior or a politician. Taken together, the public rituals around Rabin's figure and the related national repercussions of the assassination reinforced the unifying theme of friendship already established in earlier generations. Even among a left-wing peace watch group who continue to gather at the posthumously renamed Rabin Square on a weekly or monthly basis (among them a group titled *Shalom Haver*), the cornerstone of their commemoration was the chanting of Guri's *re'ut* song, as well as many other *Eretz Yisrael* (Land of Israel) songs centering on themes of war and comradeship (Dekel 2001).

An anecdote hinting at the continuing role of friendship in the collective ethos can also be found in the choice of winners of the 1998 song competition for the 50th anniversary of Independence (*shir ha-yovel*) conducted by *Reshet Gimmel*, the national radio station specializing in Hebrew music. *Jerusalem of Gold* by Naomi Shemer (Shemer 1967: 40) was chosen as the all-time favorite Israeli song. It was written shortly before the 1967 Six-Day War and gained immense popularity immediately after the war, symbolizing the reunification of Jerusalem under Israeli sovereignty and reflecting the public elation following Israel's victory. This was followed by Guri's (1950/2000: 147–148) *Ha-Re'ut* song. *Song for Peace* by Rotblit (1973) came in third. It is as if, on the collective subconscious level of the Israeli public, the value of male friendship mediated between the two opposing poles inherent to the Zionist collective enterprise: the military struggle for a national home as portrayed in *Jerusalem of Gold* on one hand, and the craving for the end of war depicted in *Song for Peace* on the other. In other words, the emphasis on values of friendship can be viewed as an enduring attempt to compensate for the horrors of war by establishing its personal and humanistic aspects. The sacrifice of life for the national cause is staged against the backdrop of eternal friendship and the sanctity of life.

Absence Turned into Presence

National commemoration practices strive to transform the absence of the dead into various representations of their presence (Handelman and Shamgar-Handelman 1997). The enduring contact of Israeli society with death, the special religious character of Jewish burial customs, and the primary role of the military organizational logic in the national death scene—all of these factors join together to form a highly dramatic setting for the transformation of absence into presence.

The arrangements for Jewish burials in Israel are conducted almost exclusively by Hevra Kadisha (Holy Society), a religious-orthodox civil organization authorized by the government. Jewish orthodox law (*halacha*) assigns extreme importance to the presence of all body parts of the corpse, as the body represents the site of potential resurrection at the End of Days (Handelman and Shamgar-Handelman 1997: 91). Following military actions every effort is made to retrieve the remains of soldiers for proper burial. A special unit of field rabbis under the Military Rabbinate follows the troops in combat. When a soldier is killed they assist in locating the body parts and transporting the body for identification procedures at the national Institute of Forensic Medicine (Weiner 1990: 105). According to *halacha*, the blood is the soul. If possible, even drops of blood from the body are collected to be buried with the corpse. Since 1994 the gruesome circumstances of terrorist attacks on civilian crowds carried out by Palestinian suicide bombers have often resulted not only in mass fatality but also in devastating mutilation and scattering of the victims' bodies. This presented a new challenge to the identification and recovery of the bodies for the purpose of proper Jewish burial. A special private volunteer organization run by ultra-orthodox Jews and associated with leading figures in both Hevra Kadisha and the Military Rabbinate was founded in 1995 under the name ZAKA (acronym for *zihui korbanot ason*—Identification of Disaster Victims). They arrive at the site of each terror attack, assist in searching for severed limbs of survivors that can be rushed to the hospitals for reattachment, and patiently scrape all the remaining bits of flesh and blood off the sidewalks and buildings so that the dead can be buried in full accordance with Jewish tradition. ZAKA volunteers working side by side with the emergency medics at scenes of carnage have become a standard sight in television coverage of suicide bombings. At times the ZAKA volunteers seem to be the first rescue workers to appear at the scene, even before the medical staff. Such images, even if unintentional, symbolically communicate a preference for sanctifying of the dead over the treating of those still alive.

Indeed, this symbolism turned into a reality in May 2004, when in a series of incidents in the Gaza Strip roadside bombs set off next to Israeli armed personnel carriers killed all the soldiers within the vehicles. In the first explosion body parts of the dead soldiers were torn up, and some were viciously removed and tampered with by a group of local Palestinians in front of television cameras. The second incident resulted again in extensive scattering of the remains, and this time the military rushed heavy reinforcements to rescue the bodies. Infantry soldiers were instructed to crawl bare-handed on the sand dunes in order to scan for any possible remains. Other soldiers provided cover for their activity, demolishing houses from which Palestinian fire was aimed. The crossfire resulted in ten Palestinian casualties and two more Israeli soldiers dead.[9] The use of such extreme measures to recover the dead, at the expense of additional Israeli and Palestinian lives, is revealing. Israeli state institutions have always followed Jewish tradition, attempting to honor the dead by recovering body remains for proper burial. Yet the gradual amalgamation of ultra-orthodox zeal and military organizational logic has turned these actions into a national obsession with the sacrificial dead. It would seem that the military code of ethics demanding the rescue of *injured* soldiers under fire (*hilutz petsuiim*) and associated with *re'ut* (Kasher 1996: 230) has inconspicuously mutated into a nonwritten code of ethics, driven by both national and religious sentiments, demanding the recovery of all bits and pieces of *dead* bodies under fire. In the words of one of the soldiers participating in the operation above, in response to the public criticism it roused: "One of the most important values in the IDF is to return the boys home . . . returning them healthy or injured, dead or alive, but returning them at any cost. This way, every soldier knows that if something happens to him, he shall return. Every soldier and every soldier's family know that the military will not desert them."[10]

Necrophilia and Homosocial Desire

The infatuation with recovering bodies can be viewed through the lens of the wider ideological value attached to male bonding. The interrelations between *re'ut* and commemoration act as a mask not only for the ideological tension between nation building and the sacrifice of life discussed earlier, and not only for the national-religious sentiments about the sacrificial dead, but also for the built-in tensions of homosocial desire.

In everyday life, male-to-male physical attraction is neutralized or repudiated in various ways. Indeed, in some instances, it is outright eradicated. I recall an interesting slang idiom used by my peer group during adolescence: when a boy wanted to note that another guy had an attractive body he would say, "what a corpse (*gufa*) he has"; in contrast, an attractive girl could always be referred to directly with, "what a body (*guf*) she has." In other words, referring to another male in physical terms that connote attraction creates a desire that needs to be immediately concealed through transforming his attractive body into a corpse. It is as if male-to-male desire is so uncanny it evokes, in Freudian terms, an unthinkable anxiety, an anxiety that must be annihilated by imagining the object of desire as already dead. The move from everyday life to the sacred spaces of mourning, from living friends to dead friends, relieves these homosocial tensions through the ritualized act of commemoration.

Steve Neale (1983) analyzed cultural representations of the male-to-male gaze in film imagery, noting that the male body can be objectified and eroticized by another male protagonist only at extreme moments in the plot.[11] The erotic, objectifying gaze on the male body is masked by the ritualized nature of the scene, "by stopping the narrative in order to recognize the pleasure of display, but displacing it from the male body as such and locating it more generally in the overall components of a highly ritualized scene" (Neale 1983: 12). I argue that the collective emotional space of *re'ut* in practices of commemoration is a similar ritualized mask, a mask for the collective gaze on the dead heroes as an object of desire.

In what way is such a gaze necrophilic? The common psychoanalytic and psychiatric definition refers to necrophilia as an individual perverse desire to have sexual intercourse or other kinds of sexual contact with a (dead) body (Fromm 1973: 6) and an obsession with obtaining sexual gratification from cadavers, mostly from morgues (Kaplan, Sadock, and Grebb 1994: 678). Yet in their original usage in ancient Greek, *nekro* (corpse) and *philia* (love) referred to love of the dead spirits in the underworld (Fromm 1973: 6). Hence, it is not necessarily a sexual attraction to actual corpses, but also a more generalized transformation of commemoration to desire. Along these lines, one of the expressions of necrophilia refers to attraction not only to corpses but also to objects connected with the grave, such as flowers and pictures, keeping in mind that in many cultures it is customary to exhibit a portrait of the deceased on the grave (Hentig 1964; cited in Fromm 1973: 326).

Erich Fromm emphasized yet another feature of necrophilia related to everyday life: the shifting of focal interest from living creatures to nonliving artifacts, to the worship of purely mechanical objects. He suggested the example of taking *snapshot* pictures, which has become for many tourists a substitute for seeing: it transforms "the act of seeing into an object—the picture to be shown later to friends as a proof that 'you have been there.'" (Fromm 1973: 343). It is noteworthy that in common English shooting is not only associated with hitting a target but also a synonym for taking pictures. Similarly, in Hebrew slang, on-the-spot passport photography stands are called "murder photo." I contend that the act of *declaring* friendship through death is analogous to the snapshot scenario. The declaration is a *necrophilic* act that kills the subjective experience it has meant to represent. The elimination of the temporal and physical contingency of the original emotional experience enables the mourners to experience the relationship with the deceased as passionate precisely through and by its termination. The telling and proclaiming of the past relationship represents a new kind of desire, erasing the earlier bond. By acknowledging the death of the friend, or by acknowledging his symbolic death, such an erasure can take place. At stake is not merely public acknowledgement and legitimacy for a love that the speaker dared not claim prior to the friend's death. It is also an internal declaration signifying this love for the first time for the speaker himself, in a sense creating a desire toward the friend for the first time, a desire that "never was."

The mask of *re'ut* serves both to conceal and expose male desire. The death of the friend signifies the cultural notion that sexual love between men equals death. But for the same reason it also enables this desire, allowing it to appear in the same instance when the person, the object of this desire, has disappeared.[12] Carrying male desire from the personal to the public sphere, the rituals of commemoration through *re'ut* cleanse homosocial friendship of any physical-sexual significance. Only when the other man is dead can he be touched physically, stripped of his armor and uniform, and be addressed collectively as *yefey ha-blorit ve-ha-toar* (handsome of forelock and countenance).[13]

In his discussion of homoeroticism Michael Hatt (1993) offered various strategies of containment that mitigate desire within the homosocial gaze. Among them is the strategy of a pretension to a purely aesthetic, disinterested response by reducing the male body to a representation such as a sculpture. Another strategy is the deployment of hierarchy, using the gaze as an instrument of power relations. Hence, the object might be of a different ethnic group, age, class, or, in the case of the military, a different rank, such as a colonel reviewing the troops. All these strategies redefine the object as a legitimate spectacle, and the pleasure of viewing becomes distinct from mere desire (Hatt 1993: 13). The ritualized commemoration of *re'ut* is likewise an erotic gaze involving two strategies of the male gaze. The dead male body is represented in the various forms of commemorative art, from poetry and literature to pictures and monuments, thus placing all erotic aspects of the collective gaze in the framework of the *aesthetic*. It becomes, literally, a sculpture, placed in the national pantheon on the pedestal for all the spectators to observe. And it is also a hierarchical gaze: the dead man is both subordinated to the viewers, having died whereas they remained alive, and also superior to them, as his heroic death secures his entry into the realm of the sublime.

"And when the friendship is declared during the lifetime of the friend . . . "

Just as collective spaces of commemoration draw on the emotions of friendship, the construction of individual friendship may in turn be colored by commemoration. As a cultural, symbolic schema, the desire for the dead may be transferred from the national rituals of *re'ut* to the hegemonic script of male bonding between men who are, in fact, still alive. In order to demonstrate the depth of military bonding and its persistence over time, Air Force General N. compared it to the bond between the pilot and his old combat jet:

> There is something here even deeper that people don't talk about. I'll tell you more than that, of all the types of aircrafts that I have flown in the Air Force, and I have flown almost all of them, I still approach the Phantom that I flew during the Yom Kippur War. There's this hidden winking between me and the aircraft, "you and I went together through this hellfire." You see, it's a mutual experience. . . . You go with your machine together. Sometimes you have to bail out it and she's gone and that's it, and you fall or get injured. And then there are guys who survived, both the pilots and their aircrafts. And so if you see the Phantom, it's like patting the horse you went to [battle] with. So I think that the extent of mutual experience is strong enough to form components of a bond that apparently lasts for life.

N. offered here two interesting analogies for *re'ut*: the relation between a rider and his horse and that between a pilot and his aircraft. While the first relation evokes an affectionate patting of the horse, relating to its emotional needs as a living creature, the second relation is a man-to-machine relationship. Erich Fromm discusses the latter as another illustration of the mechanistic, nonliving necrophilic-like relatedness of men toward love-objects such as their cars (Fromm 1973: 342). By offering this analogy in the context of *re'ut* and male bonding, N. reinforces the notion of a static, non-developing bond between the military pals. N.'s analogy equates *re'ut* with the rusty monument of a seasoned combat aircraft, a monument residing outside the realms of real life. It is a living-dead bond, resurrected anew as a fresh memory much as the memory of the fallen soldiers is retained forever in the minds of their friends.

Judd Ne'eman (1999) has suggested that representations of Israeli wars in the art of the "modernistic" filmmakers of the "state generation" can be interpreted as a "death mask" on the face of the living—a formula in which the living-dead fallen soldiers of the 1948 generation are the object to be fanatasized about by the living youth of the subsequent generation.[14] Yet the fantasized object is magically evoked by way of its very renunciation. The filmmakers' modernist approach "developed as a positive cast that congealed inside the soft wax negative, wrapping the face of the dead, in order to cast the death mask, place it on the face, and live" (Ne'eman 1999: 121).

The dominant artistic representations of *re'ut* may likewise act as the *spectral* shadow, the cast of the death mask, that the living men employ in order to apprehend their relationships. After reciting to me his poem *A few words in praise of my friends* (Guri 1981: 228–231), which I repeatedly refer to in this book, Guri concluded that there was a strong similarity between the poem and his famous song *Ha-re'ut* (Guri 1950/2000: 147–148), despite the fact that *Ha-re'ut* is an explicit lament for those who died, whereas this poem refers also to his living friends. It is as if the experience of the men who live retains the emotional aura of those who died. They cast their friends' death masks, place them on their faces, and live. The hegemonic script of male bonding is dependent on this experience of death among the living. Its framing as a semi-post-traumatic relationship, discussed in chapter 6, suggests that the men relive the bond again and again by placing a mask on their faces. The mask sends them back to the harsh moment of the bond's inception, a moment bordering on peril, danger and death. They observe, share, and rejoice in the stories of their companionship as if they were players in a theater performance. By replacing distress with a dramatic frame, their grief turns into a celebration of friendship.

I return to the second aspect of Jacques Derrida's (1997: 302) argument on declaring the friendship:

> . . . and when friendship is declared during the lifetime of friends, it avows, fundamentally, the same thing: it avows the death thanks to which the chance to declare itself comes at last, never failing to come.

Following Derrida, I suggest that even when death does not hold an explicit place in Israeli men's friendships it is *always already imagined*, so that the friendship can acquire the idealized form of *re'ut*. *Re'ut* seems to cast a long shadow that impinges on collective attitudes toward *haverut*, the practice of friendship in everyday life. The deep meanings of the tests of friendship, of intimacy and exposing oneself, of support and sacrifice, are made sense of along the lines of the heroic script.

Notes

1. See for instance Dan Bar-On (1997: 92); Billie Melman (2001: 433); Hannah Naveh (1998); Meira Weiss (1997). For a general overview of national commemoration see Eli Wiztum and Ruth Malkinson (1993).
2. Interestingly, George Mosse (1990: 215) noted a similar pattern in Germany after World War II. Memorials after the war tended to replace the nationalistic values attached to fallen soldiers as sacrifices on the altar of the Fatherland, with those of personal loyalty. The warriors were portrayed as decent and loyal to their friends rather than to some abstract entity like the nation.

3. In psychological terms, women were viewed as objects of male desire failing to experience desires of their own, the assumption being that one could hold only one role in the relationship—either as an observer and actor, or as the observed and acted upon (Gilligan and Stern 1988; Mitchell 1975). As discussed by Judith Butler, this view, based in psychoanalytic thought, assumes that desire and identification are two opposing and mutually exclusive phenomena. Butler rejected the notion that one can only be in one place or another within the relations and that desire toward one gender—whether the opposite gender or one's own—automatically assumes identification with the other (Butler 1993: 99, 239). Along these lines, Sue-Ellen Case (1989: 283) delineated how the feminine gaze in the lesbian couple could enable both partners to inhabit the subject position.

4. In David Halperin's (1990) analysis of the epics of heroic friendship, one partner is always subordinated personally, socially, and narratologically to the other. In the biblical plot David is Jonathan's superior, being God's anointed, whereas Jonathan is the scion of a doomed royal house. When Jonathan dies in battle, he paves David's way to the kingship.

5. Dan Miron (1990) presents the case of Uri Zvi Grinberg, the poet associated most strongly with revisionary-nationalist circles. Grinberg initially wrote poems that stressed the experience of war as one of total disintegration, despair, and breakdown of societal order, but later shifted to glorify war for the Jewish cause.

6. Echoing the universal masking procedure for mourning by placing flowers over the graves, it partly replaces the dead with new life and partly signifies their very absence. In the British poetry of World War I the combat moment was contrasted yet often blended with the pastoral, with images of flowers, pasture or the sea. Roses and poppies signifying blood and battle scars were an indispensable part of the symbolism of the war (Fussell 1975: 243). In Haim Guri's poem "Here Our Bodies Lie" (*hineh mutalot gufatenu*) (Guri 1949: 77) the soldiers return and reunite as red flowers. In his popular song *Bab El Wad*, celebrating the conquest of the road to Jerusalem, the red flowers are a promise of times of peace (Miron 1992: 246–247).

7. Aviv Geffen, a popular artist among youth who at the time was propagating an image of an "enfant terrible," originally endorsed refusal to serve in the military as part of his public relations, but rapidly made his way toward more consensual views. An interesting psychoanalytic analysis of the meeting point between Geffen and Rabin, as the two embrace in the peace rally in front of the cameras, is offered by Shmuel Erlich (1998). He suggested that their embrace represents the meeting point of the first and third generation of Israeli collective memory, and that the widespread mourning rituals performed for Rabin by adolescents represented a wish to unite with the grandfather generation of 1948 and a need for historical continuity. Another analysis of Rabin's commemoration and youth culture has been suggested by Haim Hazan (2001).

8. As noted by Michael Feige (2000), at stake are complex dynamics of commemorating the very act of commemoration, employing a variety of rituals from alternative, often contesting viewpoints. For a detailed sociological analysis of the various frames of meaning through which the narrative of Rabin's assassination has been commemorated see Vered Vinitzky-Seroussi (2001; 2002). Eventually the variations on the *haver* bumper sticker transformed to apply in a range of other political contexts. For instance, a sticker following the trial on bribery charges of Ari'eh Der'i, a leading politician of the religious Sephardic party *Shas*, read: "Friend, he is innocent" (Dekel 2001: 7).

9. Sources: http://en.wikipedia.org/wiki/Al-Aqsa_Intifada and Hebrew version: http://he.wikipedia.org/wiki/%D7%90%D7%99%D7%A0%D7%AA%D7%99%D7%A4%D7%90%D7%93%D7%AA_%D7%90%D7%9C_%D7%90%D7%A7%D7%A6%D7%94 (accessed 5 December 2005).

10. From an Israeli youth website: http://www.bariqada.co.il/show_item.asp?levelId=457 31&itemId=393 (in Hebrew, accessed 5 December 2005)

11. Laura Mulvey (1975) noted two types of looking when watching a movie—a narrative identification with the story protagonist, and a more detached look of pleasure at visual

display, structured by the way characters within the narrative may look at each other. Applying this approach, Steve Neale suggested that the one moment when the film audience is allowed to look at a man's body as a spectacle is in moments such as the shoot-out scene in a Western film, where the protagonists exchange aggressive looks, often parodied through the use of extreme and repetitive close-ups. It is an erotic look between the male protagonists, its eroticism repressed by the narrative motivation behind it, the act of fighting. Along these lines, Raz Yosef (2001) analyzed the ways through which homosocial relations in Israeli cinema reflect homoerotic moments structured in conjunction with sadomasochistic fantasies.

12. Another interesting hint for such a process can be found in the terminology used to refer to men in the British literature of World War I. Paul Fussell noted how "as men grow more attractive, they are seen as boys, until finally, when conceived as potential lovers, they turn into *lads*." Lads were associated with erotic heat more than simply men, or boys. A lad was "a beautiful brave doomed boy," used in phrases such as "we have lost some very adorable lads" (Fussell 1975: 282–3). It would seem that while men may have been transformed into soldier boys in the war, it was only when facing death that these boys became lads, hence only on their deathbed did they become an object of an erotic male gaze.

13. As one of the most cited phrases from Haim Guri's song *Ha-re'ut* (1950/2000: 147–148), the forelock has become a symbol for the Palmach and *sabra* style of masculinity (Maoz 1988). The reference to the hairstyle of the fallen soldiers is a persistent motif in war poetry. For instance, in the British poetry of World War I, influenced by Victorian iconography, the blond hair of the young lads stood for beauty, bravery, purity, and vulnerability (Fussell 1975: 275).

14. Judd Ne'eman (1999) analyzed the cinematic representation of Israeli wars, suggesting a defense mechanism and compensatory structure in the artistic representation taken by the filmmakers of the state generation. Their modernist approach in the "new sensibility" cinema constructs a death mask, embodying a well-balanced formula for managing the death wish of their generation.

DISCUSSION:
NATIONALISM, FRIENDSHIP AND COMMEMORATIVE DESIRE

The Overshadowing of Friendship

I had friends who were alchemists / who turned water into wine / and road into song/and exhaustion into iron / and youth into an open wound . . .

—Haim Guri (1981: 231) from
"A few words in praise of my friends"

Many scholars have noted the unsettled status of friendship among the various forms of social relations. Throughout Western sensibility, friendship has existed outside the more thoroughly codified social networks formed by kinship and conjugal ties and is therefore more dependent on ideological definitions (Halperin 1990). However, whereas female friendship has been almost altogether absent from the dominant cultural discourse, male friendship continually provokes the ambiguity of being at once overdetermined and refused. It has attained cultural saliency through specific ideologies such as nationalism, and yet its emotional qualities in the national context have been elusive if not silent.

The emotional-ideological space of *re'ut* set in the Israeli national context offers an exemplary case for this ambivalence. National discourse aims to capitalize on the concept of friendship by magnifying its quality as a collective attachment and not only as an interpersonal bond. National solidarity merges two narrative building blocks of friendship, echoing the individual experience: shared past and shared destiny. As described in chapter 3, the notion of a shared past resonates with a *familial* rhetoric of friendship and a reconstruction of tradition. The friend is perceived as having been part of the family for years. The notion of shared destiny is set in the context of a dramatic encounter with a stranger who immediately and miraculously transforms into a friend. Echoing the rhetoric of the chemistry metaphor in interpersonal bonds, this encounter is perceived as an act of alchemy. It represents a *romantic* longing for a shared future. Both senses of friendship are merged in the national pot of solidarity, blending the vertical ties of the family rhetoric with the horizontal ties of the stranger-friend rhetoric.

In the Israeli-Jewish case this metanarrative could be roughly summarized as follows: A traumatic shared past, inscribed in Jewish familial-tribal history and tradition, is transformed into, and reinforced by, a magical encounter with strangers who are recognized as lost brothers of the same tribe. The old/new brother-friends go through binding events of hardship set in life-threatening circumstances and form a political alliance and solidarity, where they share not only civil rights and obligations, but also their destiny.[1] The ideology of *re'ut* builds on two other key symbols in Zionist ideology, *hagshama* (self- and collective actualization) and *gibush* (crystallization and social cohesion), discussed in chapters 2 and 6. These two concepts add psychological and social dimensions to the metanarrative and serve to reinforce this sense of a shared destiny.

Present-day Israeli men continually subscribe to the ideals and metanarrative of *re'ut*. Consider the following report by journalist Chen Kotes-Bar (2004) of an incident in 2003 where two company commanding officers were shot in the Gaza Strip.[2] The company soldiers erected a spontaneous memorial at the site where they were stationed, a simple sign quoting the lament by King David (2 Samuel 1:19): "Thy glory, O Israel, is slain upon the high places! How are the mighty fallen! In memory of Captain Hagai Bibi and Lieutenant Leonardo Weissman." One of the soldiers has also written a poem for his cherished commanders: "For you who knew no fear / And you who never experienced sadness / The two of you hold hands together / As always in the path of *re'ut* . . . " (Kotes bar 2004).

This example illustrates the complex interrelations between the narrative and the performative. Following Judith Butler (1993: 225), it demonstrates how hegemonic sentiments come into being through repetitive acts that are embedded in the discourse and practices initiated by the subjects themselves, not only through the power exercised by authorities.[3] The grassroots memorial suggests a series of repetitive acts: a poetic verse on fallen men written some two or three millennia ago, compiled in numerous versions of the Bible ever since, memorized and recited by modern Israeli school children, and then resurrected a few years later by these same youths in the form of an ad hoc memorial plaque at a military post . The plaque does not refer to the abstract, distant death of the biblical figures, but to the concrete death of two close friends and commanders whom these men knew very well and prized. The result is a *circular performativity*, whereby it is no longer clear which is a representation and which is reality; what is the original and what is a replication. Does the present-day fighting between Jews and Palestinians replicate the "original" biblical struggle between Judeans and Philistines referred to in the biblical epic? Or is the use of the biblical narrative simply a replication of current national understanding? Furthermore, which is *re'ut* and which is friendship, or *haverut*, in the example above? Does the modern, national interpretation of the biblical narrative view the relationship of David and Jonathan (and therefore of Hagai and Leonardo) as one of "real" friendship along the lines of the concrete interpersonal bonds of *haverut*? Or is the concrete relationship between the two commanders prior to their death a re-enactment of the heroic friendship of Jonathan and David, and therefore an instance of *re'ut*, as implied by the memorial? In that case, when did it cease to be *haverut* and transform into *re'ut*? These kinds of paradoxes and circularities *are* what national affect is made of: interpersonal friendship and personal loss subscribing to national narratives, and, vice versa, national narratives drawing on the experience of friendship and loss. The indeterminacy of time-space in this circular performativity serves to produce the monolithic, monumental hegemonic sentiment that is a requisite for national consciousness.

The national subtext of *re'ut* partially surfaces in everyday life. As much as commonsense understanding entails a differentiation between "sacred" and "secular" bonds, between the heroic and the mundane, national subjectivity incessantly blurs these two dimensions of friendship. Certain scenarios associated with concrete male relationships subscribe to the hegemonic script of *re'ut* even when evolving outside of any heroic activity. For instance, the folk scenario of the "jack test," presented in chapter 4, depicts the meaning of friendship as the readiness to drive out to the other side of the country to help a friend stranded in his car without a jack. Although hardly a life-and-death situation, this scenario symbolizes limitless availability for a friend in distress. It depicts sacrifice for the sake of the other simply because of their alliance, disregarding simpler solutions such as calling for professional roadside assistance. These instances of *haverut* create a repetition, a reenactment of key emotional moments related to combat and death, in order to foster a similar "deep," primordial sense of commitment and attachment, a love sanctified by blood.

The essentializing ideology of *re'ut* is fraught with contradictions. The all-abiding, persistent cultivation of *re'ut* as a national emotion creates an intense, collective *homosocial fantasy* overshadowing the subjective experience of Israeli men. It does so through a double bind. *Re'ut* acts as a hegemonic script for Israeli men, a frame for interpreting their friendships under the model of life-and-death situations. Veteran friends who rarely meet share a sense of closeness and intimacy and attribute this intimacy to their military history (although in many cases they never went through life-and-death situations together). Yet the flip side of this very same phantasmic shadow is that many men actually refrain from associating the term *re'ut ha-lochamim* or *achvat ha-lochamim* (combat comradeship or combat fraternity) with their own friendship stories in the military. Interestingly, even among men who served in elite combat units, especially those of the younger generation, some tended to play down the significance of combat fraternity in their personal experiences, suggesting I should speak with other men, from other kinds of units, to look for this kind of comradeship. For instance, Shuki, who served in an infantry brigade unit and fought against the Palestinians during the first *Intifada*, thought that his generation experienced such bonds only on the Lebanon front, which was more representative of a life-and-death situation. And yet Tamir, a seasoned naval commando officer who did serve in Lebanon and in combat operations, referred me back to the infantry brigades to look for the kinds of bonds related to combat comradeship: "We engaged in guerilla warfare, in Lebanon for instance we'd do 'mosquito operations,' that is, you hit at the enemies' home front, you come prepared, do what you do and go back, so you're not exactly on the battlefield . . . I also happened to serve in Lebanon in army posts where you'd see a Golani platoon [an infantry unit] take up a post . . . so I think that it's mostly there, in the brigades and battalions, that you'll find this friendship, what I call combat friendship."

This going back and forth from one unit to another "in search" of combat comradeship has been a constant aspect of my research. Benny of *Sayeret Matkal*, the most demanding infantry reconnaissance unit, presented yet another surprising rebuttal of combat fraternity: "You know what, in my team it wasn't combat fraternity, it was a fraternity of good friends. We simply happen to fight together as well . . . I think combat fraternity is when there's someone from another team in the unit that I would feel toward him . . . that he is one of us . . . that is, if such a thing even exists." Benny went so far as to *negate* the concept of combat fraternity as applicable to personal friendship bonds developed in his team, associating the former with a code of soldiery demanding commitment and solidarity among unit members. He could not relate to the idea that the friends he fought with, and with whom he had shared concrete, intensive, and intimate moments of friendship, comradeship, and combat thrills, were his very own "brothers in arms." It is as if the national image of comradeship has become so domineering that, regardless of actual life experiences, many men felt either that their own narrative did not match up with it, or else preferred to disassociate themselves from it. On both grounds—the modeling of everyday friendships after the hegemonic script of heroic bonding, and the reluctance to attribute the very same heroic model to friendships involving real life-and-death situations—the national ethos of *re'ut* creates an ambivalent emotional space for Israeli men.

The discourse of *re'ut* and its role in nation building is colored by *magic*. The quote from Guri's poem in the heading above underscores the mythic link between friendship and the miraculous willpower of youth, set in a rural landscape of settlement and military activity. Guri's friends were alchemists, turning their harsh conditions of living into a celebration of nation building by adding wine, song, and iron will. Yet at the same time, their endeavor transformed the youth into an open wound. To my mind, this is one of the most lyric representations of *re'ut*, a magical homosocial bonding, subscribing to the core fantasy of Zionist masculinity but carrying with it a grief-stricken open space of ambivalence in the memories of those who have survived.

The Black Treetops of Desire

> *The two of us come from the same village / we have the same height, the same forelocks, the same way of talking / what's there to say, we come from the same village / . . . And on Friday nights / when a quiet breeze passes through the black treetops / Then I remember you.*
>
> —*Naomi Shemer (1967: 34), from*
> *"We are from the same village"*

Fraternal rituals of commemoration provide a crucial link between individual friendship and national solidarity, not simply because they are gendered, but because they are *eroticized*. This is the central argument of this book. As I have tried to demonstrate in chapter 7, commemorative desire is a significant emotional construct in national identification.

The interrelations between commemoration and desire can be further interpreted by way of Freud's seminal differentiation between melancholic incorporation and object relations, associated with the distinction between absence and loss (Gay 1989: 586). In contrast to grief and mourning that follow the loss of an object, in which separation is recognized and the libido attached to the original object is successfully displaced onto a new, substitute object, melancholy reflects a failure to grieve. The loss is internalized and is therefore rejected. Judith Butler reformulates these dynamics as the key to gender identification, suggesting that the homoerotic within homosocial desire is a cultural marker, a displacement of ambivalent emotions; it is a love that "never was," a repudiated love that cannot be grieved (Butler 1997: 138). Underlying these dynamics are complex possibilities for overlap between identification and desire. Rather than assuming that subjects are in a position of either identifying with the other as a subject (typically of the same sex) or else desiring the other as an object (typically of the opposite sex), identification and desire can be directed toward the same object. Following the failure to grieve over the unacknowledged loss of a primary object of desire: "Identification is a phantasmatic trajectory and resolution of desire . . . a territorializing of an object which enables identity through the temporary resolution of desire, but which remains desire, if only in its repudiated form" (Butler 1993: 99).

This ambivalence in object relations between self and other can be extended to the collective sphere, bringing to full force the potent tensions embedded in male homosociality and its relation to the national. Homosociality is situated in fluid spaces around the public/private split. It extends beyond matters such as sexuality or interpersonal friendship that

are heavily freighted in the private sphere, into a question of membership in a community. In his notes on the "Mechanism of Paranoia" Freud
speculated on a mechanism of social regulation related to the repression
of "homosexual drives." These drives, he wrote, help to constitute "the
social instincts, thus contributing an erotic factor to friendship and comradeship, to esprit de corps and to love of mankind in general" (Freud
1953/1974: 31; cited in Butler 1997: 80). Carefully evading essentialist
claims along the lines of a latent homosexuality, Judith Butler identifies
here a "desire to desire," "a willingness to desire precisely what would
foreclose desire, if only for the possibility of continuing to desire" (Butler
1997: 79). I suggest that this "desire to desire" is publicly exposed at the
collective deathbed, transforming identification between fellow men into
that desire that never was.

Don Handelman and Lea Shamgar-Handelman (1997: 110) have analyzed how national commemorative practices strive to turn the absence
of the sacrificial dead into the presence of their absence in memorials.
They suggest that the lesser the degree of presence of the actual body in
the memorial site, the more elaborate its representation. A similar mechanism might underlie the declaration of friendship for the dead. Feelings
that were silent during the lifetime of the friend are marked as an absence
turned into presence. Through the very elimination of its object, the declaration of friendship for the dead may produce an eroticization of the homosocial bond. It forms a new site of desire; hence my allusion in chapter
7 to a semiotics of collective necrophilia.

The greater the public scope of the declarative act, the greater its significance as an act of revelation. By eliminating the object of desire, heroic
death becomes *the* cultural marker that prevents the continuity between
the homosocial and the homoerotic, yet at the same legitimizes and
celebrates desire between men. The idea that repudiated emotions may
produce an erotic component fits with the cultural notion of eroticism as
based on the fetishization of what is socially forbidden and silenced. Simone de Beauvoir argues: "Eroticism implies a claim of the instant against
time, of the individual against the group; it affirms separation against
communication; it is a rebellion against all regulation; it contains a principle hostile to society" (Beauvoir 1953: 187-188).[4] In a sense, the present
case turns this equation upside down. It presents a mode of eroticism
that claims the eternity of the dead against the transience of the living;
the triumph of the group against the ambivalence of the individual; a
regulatory regime against all rebellion. Far from being hostile to society,
it represents a central principal for the very continuation of society. No
longer refused, homosocial desire is transformed through collective acts
of commemoration into an ideologically recognized emotion, also known
as nationalism.

The collective, necrophilia-like commemoration of the sacrificial dead
and its fundamental significance for national awareness can be traced

back to early European nationalism. For example, during the French Revolution, conceived by many as the first, self-declared, contractual formulation of the nation (Singer 1996: 318), the revolution authorities sanctioned in 1792 a design for a new cemetery in Paris, according to which the ashes of the fallen men were to be mixed with those of France's great men and placed jointly in a central pyramid (Mosse 1993: 17).[5] In this sense, there is nothing unique in the Israeli case of commemoration. The enduring Jewish-Arab national conflict and its renewed stimulation of tragic circumstances of death and loss simply offers the national collective continuing institutionalized "opportunities" for mourning the dead. What is still an open question is the extent to which other national movements employ such an explicit framing of commemoration based on the rhetoric of friendship.

In closing I would like to restate the significance of this framing in the Israeli case of *re'ut*. Several of the men I interviewed noted a popular song written by the late national songwriter and composer Naomi Shemer, "We are from the same village," as reflecting their experiences of friendship. I came upon another forceful reference to the song in the following story by Pini, a combat pilot who had been held captive in Syria for several years. Pini was asked to talk about *re'ut* at a high school assembly on national Memorial Day.[6] He began by mentioning a reunion with two high school friends he hadn't seen for twenty-seven years, realizing how despite the years their "true" bond stayed intact, warm, and alive. The students, he said, should likewise appreciate the bonds of *re'ut* formed during their period of youth that once felt and recognized, could accompany them throughout their lives and build their character. These values had enabled him to withstand the pressures of captivity and to form deep bonds with fellow captive soldiers.

That is the bond embodied in "We are from the same village," as Pini proceeds to explain:

> Each time I hum this song to myself, I can't reach the end of the song. It moves me to tears. . . . The song talks about the same two people at any point in time, in any possible situation, who have a bond between them, a bond formed in a thousand ways . . . consider a moment early in the morning of March 1970, at the peak of the War of Attrition [with Egypt, following the 1967 war]. . . . Four guys still exhausted from the combat of the previous night are once more boarding on their Phantoms [jet planes] loaded with bombs and heading on a bombing mission deep into Egypt, in order to relieve the pressure on our soldiers on the ground at the Suez Canal . . . although we have no personal connection with these other soldiers, they come from "the same village" as we do. We know them because we know the children of our neighbors, our boys who gather in Friday nights in the village square during their leaves from the army, the boys of the neighboring village or the boys coming out of a movie in the neighboring town. We know—they're one of us. A deep bond of *re'ut* binds us; I

almost replaced this word with the word nation. But no, the word *re'ut* has its own significance and uniqueness. It wraps within it a lot of emotion—and an emotion is an undeniably a personal connection.

This explicit reflection on the interrelation between *re'ut* and nationalism underscores the intensity of the emotional experience at stake. It also expresses puzzlement at how such deep emotions, usually associated with a personal connection, could be substituted for the national. What Pini does not address is the crucial resolution of this puzzle, a resolution provided by the chorus line of the song and perhaps hinted at by Pini's bursting into tears in place of the words. The song underscores the mythic notion of twins, the emblem for total identification of self with his closest other, placing it in national context. Not only do the two men come from the same village, they also look alike and talk alike. Chapter 3 depicted the cultural significance of twinship as a bond stronger than brotherhood, two bodies connected in one soul, sharing the same preferences and engaged in total understanding. Most significantly, twins are expected to share the same destiny. Yet this is where the song presents a dramatic twist, as the chorus line changes from the previously overstated description of the quality of sameness in the men's friendship to an understated quality of absence represented by "a quiet breeze passing through the black treetops." The speaker then moves to address the friend in the second person, telling him simply that he remembers him. What he does not talk about is the unacknowledged emotion underlying the novel feelings of loss and loneliness felt on Friday nights, an absence hidden in the blackness of the treetops and marked only by the blowing wind. This twist in the narrative is an absence turned into presence and a move from identification to desire, a desire that could only take place following the death of the twin brother in the war.

In his writing on the politics of friendship, Jacques Derrida (1997) delineates a core model for fraternal friendship as a bond between two mortal men who have a contract according to which one will survive the other. One will, in a sense be the *heir* of the other and commemorate this inherited relationship. As analyzed by Michal Ben-Naftali (2000: 97), at stake is a polarity that Derrida's treatment of friendship draws between a political-economical bond and an *ultimate*, noneconomical, asymmetrical bond. For Derrida, ultimate friendship is one-sided, for it "is first accessible on the side of its subject, who thinks and lives it, not on the side of the object." Hence, the friend being loved can "belong to the reign of the non-living" (Derrida 1997: 10). At its extreme level of possibility friendship can survive its object and be colored by death and mourning.

National discourse exemplifies this core model of fraternal friendship through the act of declaration. Declaring the lost and eternal friendship symbolizes a passionate "blood pact" between men. The declaration of friendship echoes traditional rituals practiced in diverse cultural settings where two or more men exchange drops of blood to signify a pact between them (Brain 1976: 76). Blood symbolizes the perils of death as well as the promise of an eternal bond, an attempt to model the fraternal bond after the natural blood ties of kinship. Only when this pact is experienced as passionate desire can we begin to understand how the imagined ties of the national take precedence over the natural blood ties of kinship and the sexual ties of marriage unions. Fraternal friendship is a source of not only identification but also desire, whereby the citizen brother becomes, via national commemoration, the desired brother. If fraternal friendship is, following Derrida (1997: 14), "the grieved act of loving," national consciousness can be read as a homosocially-based emotion of commemorative desire. In Hebrew the terms commemoration (*hantsacha*) and victory (*nitsachon*) stem from the same root. The act of commemoration reflects the mourner's victory over the dead brother. It signifies the end of their rivalry and symbolizes the beginning of a new, beautiful friendship.

Notes

1. Destiny is a crucial factor in the rise of national consciousness. As argued by Robert Wohl (1979) the generational consciousness associated with the nationalism springing up in Europe at the turn of the twentieth century was closely dependent on a sense of common destiny shared by members of the generational unit.
2. Capt. Hagai Bibi and Lt. Leonardo Weissman of the Giv'ati Brigade were killed on 22 December 2003 when a Palestinian gunmen opened fire and threw a hand grenade at them as they emerged from their jeep near the former Israeli occupied area of Gush Katif junction (north of Khan Yunis) in the Gaza Strip (Israel Ministry of Foreign Affairs 2003).
3. Performative acts are forms of authoritative speech that hold binding and conferring power on its subjects. Performativity rests heavily on discursive acts, on the power of naming to define reality. It implies the production of ideological indoctrination in a way that is primarily indirect and unacknowledged by members of the social group. Judith Butler's analysis follows Althusser's (1971) well-known example of a policeman hailing a passerby walking down the street with the words "hey you there!" As the one who recognizes himself turns around, he acquires is so doing he a certain identity. The very act of recognition becomes an act of constitution. This recognition stems from the "interpellation" of the external ideology into consciousness.
4. Perhaps not very differently, Peter Lyman views the joking relationship of the male homosocial bond as an "erotic of rule breaking,"resulting from the collective violation of moral rules (Lyman 1987: 160). Such formulations are further consistent with the perceptions of sexuality in the Judeo-Christian tradition. Yishai Rosen-Zvi (1999) offers a similar interpretation of sexuality as the erotization of the forbidden in the Jewish Talmudic tradition.
5. Mosse notes, however, that the design was never actually executed. The widespread phenomenon of the military cemetery as a shrine of egalitarian, collective worship did not appear prior to the First World War.
6. I would like to thank psychologist Amia Lieblich for handing me the transcript of the talk.

STUDYING A NATIONAL EMOTION

The Topic, Field, and Research Group

This study is not a holistic exploration of a localized culture, organization, or group as a whole, but rather a holistic exploration of a *localized emotion* within that given culture: the emotion associated with fraternal friendship. As a result, the field of study is both narrow and broad. It is limited to a single emotional space and yet aims to study its expression within the overall hegemonic male constituent of Israeli society. I have aimed to resolve this tension by carefully choosing my core group of informants, and evaluating their place vis-à-vis the field, as elaborated below. Additional sources that I have used to corroborate and expand my interpretations include: participant observations in an IDF military cemetery, in Rabin Square, and in university campuses in the greater Tel Aviv area during Memorial Days for Fallen Soldiers and the commemoration day for Yitzhak Rabin; compilation and analysis of written and electronic media coverage and Internet forums alluding to selected national events and commemoration rituals associated with fallen soldiers; some forty interviews focusing on diverse kinds of friendship set in specific social or organizational contexts, made by my students during two research seminars that I held on friendship during my post-doctorate training at the Hebrew University; 22 in-depth interviews I conducted in an earlier study on gay and bisexual veterans of Israeli combat units (Kaplan 2003a); and finally, an analysis of popular Israeli poems and songs that refer to friendship and specifically to *re'ut*.

The study combines a phenomenological perspective with an ethnomethodological approach. It stresses the cultural context of psychological experience and explores interpretive procedures and practices that give structure and meaning to everyday life. These practices are both the topic of and the resources for qualitative inquiry (Holstein and Gubrium 1998). In the present case, it involves exploration of the subjective meanings assigned to friendship interactions and cultural analysis of underlying emotions. The interactions are not understood as the mere communication of a more important social phenomenon. Rather, the emotion formed during a given interaction becomes in itself the topic of analysis. Although most of the study does not involve direct observations of naturally occurring interactions of friendship in line with traditional ethnography, it partly employs one of the key tenets of the ethnomethodological approach, namely, the focus on the discursive aspects of the interactions. When subjects or informants talk, their utterances are not taken as mere reports about conduct or state of mind, but are considered "the very action through which local realities are accomplished" (Holstein and Gubrium 1998: 143). Along these lines, I have examined both emotional *practice*—emotional responses expressed either verbally or through bodily gestures and postures, as these were reported by the informants—and the explicit and implicit *discourse* of emotions, the ways informants made sense of their emotional life and of emotional constructs in Israeli society at large.

My core group of informants was selected through purposive sampling (Denzin and Lincoln 1994: 202). It consisted of thirty self-identified heterosexual men that I chose based on various procedures and a range of theoretical considerations. First, between 1998 and 2000 I set out to gather a pool of possible interviewees, asking people I met, both men and women, whether they knew of men with "interesting stories of male friendship." I exposed myself to a relatively diverse range of contact people based on the social and organizational networks that I could access. A non-exhaustive list of these social networks includes: acquaintances, people I met at varied social events, people related to my academic work, clients from my work as an occupational psychologist (involving screening for predominantly blue-collar jobs), men I met during my service in the military reserve, and hitchhikers. Second, I attempted to reach additional interviewees who could serve as generational representatives, either as "cultural copy writers" or "charismatic leaders" (Almog 1997: 386) The concept of the "generational unit," introduced by Karl Mannheim (1928), suggests that generations tend to crystallize around a nucleus group that shapes new perceptions, motivates other members of their generation, and forms a widely shared pattern of response to collective experience. Among my final group of informants were a poet, a playwright, a film director, a senior military general, an athlete, and a corporate business manager. The role of these men was tantamount to act as "professional complicators" (Geertz 1983: 89) able to contemplate and reflect on the subject of male friendship in its localized, Israeli context.

Appendix 2 summarizes the biographical details of the final research group. It consists of men from middle-class and a few from lower middle-class backgrounds; most had some higher education. All were employed; their occupations were diverse. They consisted of roughly equal numbers of *ashkenazi* Jews of European descent, *mizrachi* Jews of North African and Middle-Eastern descent, and men of mixed backgrounds, a phenomenon that is becoming more and more widespread in Israeli society. This variety of factors directed my selection process, which attempted to balance the sample in terms of characteristics that are relatively representative of this hegemonic group in contemporary Israeli society. Hence, the purpose of the selection was not to explore how each of these important factors separately shapes men's patterns of relatedness, but rather to draw on the men's common background and to explore recurrent dominant views regarding men's friendships.

In this respect, my study of hegemonic masculinity differs from common approaches in the field. It does not follow Robert Connell's approach (Connell 1995; Sasson-Levy 2002) in exploring the interrelations between a hegemonic identity of masculinity and alternative forms of masculinity that negotiate their identity in relation to the hegemony. Nor does it take a historical approach by following changes in the images of hegemony over time (see for instance Dan Bar-On 1999; Maor 2001). For the most part, I did not try to systematically distinguish between different "voices" of male relatedness in terms of class, ethnic, or ideological divides, nor did I assume that each individual represents either a hegemonic cultural voice or its 'othered' counterparts and can never hold both simultaneously. Rather, the study emphasizes the possibility of various voices within a single person, treating a single narrative or performance as a thick, multilayered subjective process.[1] It suggests that often—but not always—a "hegemonic" voice may dominate the exterior and occupy front stage in the narrated experience, relegating less dominant ones to the background. But its key conjecture is that individuals carry within them these 'othered' voices that can surface alternatively at different places in their emotional and cultural experience.

The sample is characterized by a uniform shared background pertinent to the current analysis. The interviewees were all brought up in line with the hegemonic, Zionist arrangements of Israel as a Jewish nation-state: They were either born in Israel or immigrated to the country in early childhood, studied in state-run Jewish schools (most of them in the secular system and a few in the modern-orthodox state school system), were drafted for three years of mandatory military service at the age of eighteen, and had engaged in annual military reserve duty throughout much of their adult lives. Half of the men had served in combat units and the rest in noncombat positions. Unlike most modern societies characterized by a sharp distinction between military and civilian structures (Moskos 1993), the Israeli case presents persistent blurring between the military and civilian sphere at both the political and cultural levels (Kimmerling 1993). Although its influence has slightly declined in recent years, prestigious military service is still socially esteemed and can encourage certain career opportunities and promote social networks. In particular, the military serves as a key agent of socialization into hegemonic arrangements of masculinity (Ben-Ari 2001; Kaplan 2000; Klein 1999). These cultural constraints are reflected in the men's friendships. Although their stories straddle a variety of homosocial interactions taking place alternately in the military and in civilian life, both spheres offer similar characteristics of male relatedness colored by a military male culture and a relatively undifferentiated military/civilian sociability.

The participants experienced significant national-collective events during various historical periods and at different life stages. The generation associated most strongly with the Israeli notion of *re'ut* is the "1948 generation" of the *sabra*. I therefore interviewed Haim Guri, who is probably the most prominent "cultural copywriter" of *re'ut* in Israel (see chapter 2). Guri and the associated cultural products of his generation formed the "baseline" of my group, as creators of the songs, poems, and other public images that form the collective memory related to *re'ut*. For the most part, I skipped the subsequent generation, commonly known as the "state generation," except for one interview with Judd Ne'eman, a scholar, film director, and former military commander who received the badge of honor for his combat performance. All other interviewees can be rather loosely defined as belonging to the two following generations:

1) Men who reached adulthood between the 1973 Yom Kippur War and the 1982 Lebanon War, with an average age of 45 at the time of the interview.
2) Men who reached adulthood around the period of the first Palestinian *intifada* (1987–1992), with an average age of 28 during the interview.

The interviews were completed just before the outbreak of the second *intifada* in 2000. The extent of the men's involvement in national events was varied, but all of them could recount experiences directly related to them, and often combined them within their stories of friendship.

The first of these two groups consisted of mostly married men; the second, of mostly single men. Both age groups represent a productive stage of men's involvement in society, either at the onset of their career or at its peak. The overall age range of the whole group enabled an adequate perspective on friendship experiences in childhood and adolescence without being too distant. At the same time, the age difference could reveal possible shifts in the quality assigned to male friendships with changes in marriage and career commitments.

The generational distinctions could potentially result in differences in historical attitudes of friendship. However, these did not surface in a significant way. For instance, Judd Ne'eman, the sole representative of the state generation, has argued that since the founding days of 1948 little has changed in the core values and expectations of Israeli men: "Look how similar it is to current times, it looks different, but I think the dividing line is 1948 . . . since 1948 all the standards have been formed, regular service, then backpack traveling and college." In this vein, rather than examining historical changes, I chose to focus primarily on the cultural continuity of friendship in national consciousness and to explore how the formative attitudes of the "founding fathers" of the 1948 generation are reflected in the everyday life practices and ideals of its followers. How do the men of subsequent generations negotiate the cultural-emotional space of male friendship?

Theoretical Research Questions

The cultural-narrative approach underlying my interviewing method mediates between the individual and collective levels of meaning. The interviewees are perceived, first and foremost, as informants of a localized culture. As meaning-generating organisms, people construct their self-narratives from culturally available building blocks. Their motivations, ideals, and interactions are grounded in collective experience (Bilu 1986; Mishler 1986). Narratives are particularly suited to the study of emotions, since emotions are constructed by both personal and cultural experiences (Lutz 1990). Individuals assign meanings to the emotions they experience through processes of socialization at different life stages and in specific sociocultural contexts. Whereas emotional life is often conveyed as a consequence of childhood experience, it is also implicated in adult social and occupational roles (Averill 1986; Hochschild 1983). In addition, whereas in most psychoanalytic as well as social-psychological frameworks emotions are conceived as fundamentally personality-based, intrapsychic processes, a narrative framework is more attuned to a constructionist approach, which views emotions as an experience constituted through discourse and focuses on the analysis of language, rhetoric, and cultural representations (Yanay 1995: 54). For instance, a narrative-constructionist view of emotional life explores the rhetoric that people use to frame dramatic encounters. They take on dramatic roles as "authors" in order to validate their position in formal or informal social structures (Sarbin 1995). Once again, this authorship is located in cultural narratives, or in what Margaret Somers and Gloria Gibson (1994: 62) defined as "public narratives," i.e., local or grand stories and myths attached to institutions, organizations, or societies at large.

The crux of the present study is its emphasis on *ambivalence* as a cornerstone in emotional experience. Throughout the analysis I focus on spaces that suggest ambivalence in the management of homosocial emotions, be it in managing intimacy, love, or desire. In particular, the emotional space of passion between men may take the form of love, of hatred, or of both simultaneously. The deliberate miscommunication of desire suggests a continuum of possibilities, from an outright denial of desire, through various forms of erasure and concealment of passionate emotions enabled by the aggressive-joking relationship, to the endpoint of actually acknowledging homosocial desire. In addressing the ambivalence of emotions, I do not necessarily argue, along the lines of traditional psychoanalysis, that this ambivalence is an essential condition of male (or female) psychology. Nor do I necessarily take the opposite stand, that emotional ambivalence is socially constructed. Indeed, this kind of modernistic dispute is bypassed by adopting a poststructuralist approach. In other words, I use emotional ambivalence as a *methodological* framework, even a procedure, a simplified version, if you will, of Jacques Derrida's method of deconstruction. I unravel cultural perceptions by delineating tensions and paradoxes in human discourse and practice. When the focus is not only on the implicit, but also on what is avoided, disavowed, or silenced in the narrated cultural text, the discontinuities, institutionalized defenses, and ideological constraints of human emotional subjectivity may surface (Rumsey 1995, following Norris 1991).

Based on the above reasoning, I tapped into male relatedness extending across various discursive dimensions, which could be roughly categorized under four separate concepts: collective solidarity, group cohesion, intimacy, and eroticism. However, these are not distinct categories. Their meanings overlap and converge in intricate ways. It is precisely the purpose of my inquiry to examine how these various facets of male relatedness evolve and shift in their expression and meanings, along the following set of issues:

a) What form do men's bonds take in the routines of everyday life, and what form do they take in dramatic, adventurous, and stressful situations?

b) How does the distinction between public and private spheres affect the management of emotions? In particular, following Gilligan (1982), how can one apply emotions that are often associated with the "private-feminine" domain to the "public-masculine" sphere?

c) What are the boundaries between intimacy and eroticism, and what mechanisms maintain the distinction between the two?

d) How do circumstances associated with the national, such as combat situations, death, and commemoration intensify or transform interpersonal emotions?

Interview Design

The interviews were conducted between 1999 and 2000, mostly in the interviewees' homes, and lasted two to three hours each. I conducted most of the interviews; four were held by two trained research assistants. Interview design was initially examined in light of three pilot interviews and then reviewed and refined. It followed the logic of the traditional open-ended ethnographic interview (Fontana 1994: 365) with some additional structuring, combining two kinds of questions: (a) open-ended questions aimed at eliciting and maintaining a lengthy narrated structure (Rosenthal 1993:

60); (b) specific questions aimed to trigger more formal definitions of homosocial emotions.

Narrative researchers have suggested gender differences in the construction of narratives. In her analysis of autobiographies, Mary Gergen (1992) found that men tend to devise clearly defined plots, while women tend to construct narratives along multiple dimensions. Similarly, Rivka Tuval-Mashiach (in Lieblich et al. 1998: 96) compared Israeli men and women's oral narratives and found the prototypical structure of women's narrative to be far more polyphonic than that of men's. The men presented a relatively linear and consistent narrative structure with little reference to family and relationships, whereas women's stories tended to be more elusive, winding their way simultaneously through diverse plot axes. These potential gender-based differences need to be taken into account when designing a male-focused narrative interview. Scott Coltrane (1994) argues that since men tend to avoid lengthy discussions of their emotional lives, researchers could not afford to accept men's superficial characterizations of their own internal states and needed to push them into self-reflection.

Hence, I presented my research a priori as dealing with male friendships and directed the interviewees to discuss their relational life. I probed stories of friendship from childhood, through high school, military service, to the present stage in the interviewees' life-course, enabling each interviewee to chose one or more periods of his life as his main topic of narration, depending on the circumstances of the specific friendship he chose to recount. I began by introducing the research goal in a general way as "a study of friendship between men in Israeli society, and an exploration of how they perceive these friendships through their life story." This was followed by a short questionnaire addressing the interviewee's sociocultural background. Another formal procedure consisted of Josselson's (1992: 251) "relational space map" method, adapted, following Arlette Mintzer (1997: 74), into a three-level diagram of closeness. The interviewee was asked to draw a diagram for each period in life from late childhood to the present. The diagram is drawn like a solar system. The interviewee is to be situated in the center, and the people who were important to him at the time (both family, partners, and friends) are to be placed at three levels of distance from him, according to their relative importance. The aim is to set the basis for the in-depth interview by enabling the interviewee to reflect on specific friends and groups of friends throughout the various periods of his life (Josselson 1992: xi, 251-252). This procedure facilitated the interviewee's subsequent choice in focusing on specific friendships and enabled keeping track of other individuals mentioned in the free narrative.

As the opening question at the heart of the interview I asked each interviewee: "Could you tell me a specific story of a bond with a close friend you had or still have? You may start at any period in your life." The men were encouraged to reflect on how the friendship evolved and unfolded in particular social and organizational settings. Although the main friendship narrations tended to focus on one close friend, they often incorporated accounts of two friends or a group of friends. Five interviewees focused on a group instead of one close friend as their main narration. The opening question was followed by a set of open-ended yet semistructured questions aimed at eliciting and maintaining a lengthy narrated structure, which facilitated unforeseen issues and idiosyncratic perceptions in people's subjective experience, but still ensured that all interviewees were exposed to the same topics thus enabling comparisons between them (Denzin 1970). This included the following questions:

1. Could you tell me of your first encounter?
2. Could you recount important instances or events in the relationship?
3. What did you like in him? What didn't you like?
4. What was important to you in the relationship?
5. What would you talk about?
6. How did you keep the relationship going?
7. How did the relationship express itself in everyday life?
8. Can you see how the relationship evolved over time? (Changes across situations, changes in dramatic events such as a trip, military activity, etc.)
9. What makes him a close friend (*ha-haver ha-tov*)?
10. With which emotions could you color the relationship?
11. How are you similar to one another, how are you different?
12. How is the friendship similar to or different from your relationships with women?
13. How is it similar to or different from family relationships?
14. What did the friendship contribute to that period of your life? How does it affect you today?
15. Could you recount some other friends from that period? What distinguishes these friends from your special friend?
16. Is there a bond with a group of people you could tell me about? You can relate to school peers, military unit, recreational activity, workplace, sports, etc.
17. Could you tell me about special events and customs (*havay*) in the group ?
18. Do you recall jokes, games, physical contact, sexual discourse?
19. Similar questions were posed regarding additional friends noted at other periods in the initial diagram. When available, interviewees were encouraged to use pictures from photo albums to trigger their memory and emotions. At the conclusion of the open-ended part I asked:
20. What was the most significant period in your life in terms of establishing friendships?

21.   Can you recall an Israeli song, film, book etc. that expressed your feelings about these friendships? (If nothing was evoked the interviewee was presented with a short selection of popular songs ranging from 1948 to the present, centering on male friendship, and was asked to comment on them).

The second part of the interview consisted of a more structured list of questions pertaining to general definitions, attitudes and reflections on male friendships.

1.   What is friendship (*haverut*) between men?
2.   What is the meaning of a best friend?
3.   What is the place of passion (*teshuka*) in male relationships?
4.   What does intimacy in friendship mean to you?
5.   What is love (*ahavah*) between two friends?
6.   How is physical closeness involved in friendship?
7.   How do you understand cohesion (*gibush*) between men?
8.   What is male fraternity (*achvat gevarim*)?
9.   What is combat comradeship/fraternity (*re'ut/achvat lochamim*)?
10. Is there an ideological dimension to men's friendship or solidarity?

The interviews concluded with a short questionnaire on the interviewees' sexual history and self-definitions of sexual orientation in order to confirm the men's heterosexuality according to the Kinsey scale (Kinsey et al. 1948). This was given after the interview to avoid a possible effect on their discussion of male relatedness.

Interviews were recorded and transcribed and the data was analyzed to identify recurring themes and enable comparisons between cases (Denzin 1970). The narratives were analyzed according to Giorgi's (1975) proposal for phenomenological research adapted into a five-stage procedure: a free reading of each narrative; dividing it into separate sequences according to natural 'meaning units'; rereading each unit with the specific question of male friendship in mind; collecting nonredundant themes from each narrative; gleaning recurring and dominant themes from the entire selection of narratives in order to derive a theory of nomothetic value. The interviews were conducted in Hebrew. Names and other identifying details have been changed to ensure privacy.

Notes

1.   Robert Connell (1996: 210) himself notes that one of the key reasons why masculinities are not settled is the emotional "layering" that juxtaposes contradictory desires and logics, so that the public enactment of an exemplary masculinity may covertly require actions that undermine it.

Appendix 2

TABLE OF MAIN INTERVIEWEES

First Age Group

	Name	Age	married	ethnic background	combat role (*concrete combat events)	single best friend	Original setting of main friendship narrative	group bond origin
1	Benny	26	no	ashkenazi	yes *	no	Military (two friends)	Military team
2	Ehud	26	no	mixed	mixed	no	Childhood (two friends)	
3	Hezi	32	yes	mizrachi	mixed	no	Diverse	College
4	Nati	26	no	ashkenazi	no	yes	College	
5	Noam	27	no	mizrachi	yes	no	Diverse	School/ diverse
6	Perry	25	no	ashkenazi	no	yes	Elementary sch.	
7	Raviv	31	no	ashkenazi	yes	no	Career-military	
8	Roi	27	no	ashkenazi	mixed	no	Diverse	
9	Ronen	24	no	ashkenazi	yes	yes	Junior high	High school
10	Shuki	29	no	ashkenazi	yes	no	College	
11	Tamir	34	no	ashkenazi	yes*	no	a) Childhood b) Security services	School and beyond
12	Yaron	33	no	mizrachi	no	yes	Childhood	
13	Yehuda	27	no	ashkenazi	no	yes	High school	
14	Yoram	25	no	mizrachi	no	yes	Childhood	

Second Age Group

	Name	Age	married	ethnic background	combat role (*concrete combat events)	single best friend	Original setting of main friendship narrative	group bond origin
15	Avi	38	no	Mizrachi	no	no	Work	
16	Eli	40	yes	Mizrachi	no	no	Neighborhood	Childhood
17	Gadi	48	yes	ashkenazi	yes	no	Neighborhood	Childhood
18	Haim	41	yes	Mizrachi	yes*	yes	a) Military b) Hitchhike	War
19	Amnon	51	yes	ashkenazi	yes*	yes	Military	
20	Meir	39	divorced	Mizrachi	no	yes	Childhood	High school
21	Mody	43	yes	Mizrachi	yes	no	Diverse/ Military	
22	General N.	52	divorced	Mizrachi	yes*	no	Career-military	
23	Nachshon	47	yes	Mixed	no	yes	Childhood	Military
24	Reuven	50	divorced	ashkenazi	yes	no	Work	
25	Roman	39	yes	Mixed	no	no	High school	
26	Shahar	42	no	ashkenazi	yes*	no	Diverse	
27	Uri	43	no	ashkenazi	no	no	Diverse	
28	Yosi	53	yes	Mizrachi	yes*	no	Work	Work

"State Generation"

	Name	Age	married	ethnic background	combat role	single best friend	Original setting	group bond origin
29	Judd Ne'eman	64	yes	ashkenazi	yes*	no	Military	Combat training

"Palmach Generation"

	Name	Age	married	ethnic background	combat role	single best friend	Original setting	group bond origin
30	Haim Guri	73	yes	ashkenazi	yes*	no	Military	War

BIBLIOGRAPHY

Albaum-Dror, Rachel. 1996. " 'There He Comes, from within Us He Comes, the New Hebrew': On the Youth Culture of the First Waves of Immigrations." In Hebrew. *Alpaiim* 12: 104–35.

Almog, Oz. 1997. *The Sabra—a Profile*. In Hebrew. Tel Aviv: Am Oved.

———. 2004. *Farewell to 'Srulik': Changing Values among the Israeli Elite*. In Hebrew. Haifa: Haifa University and Zemora-Bitan.

Alterman, Natan. 1941. *Simchat Anyim*. In Hebrew. Tel Aviv: Machbarot lesifruth.

Althusser, Louis. 1971. "Ideology and Ideological State Apparatuses." In *Lenin and Philosophy, and Other Essays*, Translated by Ben Brewster. New York: Monthly Review.

Altman, Irwin, and Dalmas A. Taylor. 1973. *Social Penetration: The Development of Interpersonal Relationships*. New York: Holt, Rinehart and Winston.

Anderson, Benedict. 1991. *Imagined Communities: Reflections on the Origins and Spread of Nationalism*. London: Verso.

Annan, David. 1967. "Nationalist Secret Societies." In *Secret Societies*, ed. Norman Mackenzie. London: Aldus Books.

Aphek, Edna, and Yishai Tobin. 1988. *Word Systems in Modern Hebrew: Implications and Applications*. Leiden: E.J. Brill.

Apter, Terri, and Ruthellen Josselson. 1998. *Best Friends: The Pleasures and Perils of Girls' and Women's Friendships*. New York: Crown.

Arendt, Hannah. 1958. *The Human Condition*. Chicago: University of Chicago Press.

Aries, Phillipe. 1979. "The Family and the City in the Old World and the New." In *Changing Images of the Family*, ed. Virginia Tufte and Barbara Meyerhoff. New Haven, CT: Yale University Press.

Aristotle. 1962. *Nicomachean Ethics*. Translated by Martin Ostwald. Indianapolis: Bobbs-Merrill.

Auerbach, Erich. 1953. *Mimesis: The Representation of Reality in Western Literature*. Translated by Willard Trask. Princeton, NJ: Princeton University Press.

Averill, James R. 1986. "The Acquisition of Emotions During Adulthood." In *The Social Construction of Emotions*, ed. Rom Harre. Oxford: Basil Blackwell.

Badinter, Elisabeth. 1995. *On Masculine Identity*. New York: Columbia University.

Baker, Wayne, and Rosanna Hertz. 1981. "Communal Diffusion of Friendship: The Structure of Intimate Relations in an Israeli Kibbutz." In *Research in the Interweave of Social Roles: Friendship*, vol. 2, ed. Helena Z. Lopata. Greenwich, CT: JAI Press.

Bar-On, Dan. 1997. "Israeli Society between the Culture of Death and the Culture of Life." *Israel Studies* 2, no. 2: 88–112.

———. 1999. *The 'Others' within Us: A Socio-Psychological Perspective on Changes in Israeli Identity*. In Hebrew. Beer-Sheva: Ben Gurion University of the Negev Press.

Bateson, Gregory. 1972. *Steps toward an Ecology of Mind*. New York: Ballantine.

Beauvoir, Simone de. 1953. *The Second Sex*. Translated by H.M. Parshley. New York: Alfred A. Knopf.

Beckson, Karl. 1998. *The Oscar Wilde Encyclopedia*. New York: AMS Press.

Ben-Ari, Eyal. 1998. *Mastering Soldiers: Conflict, Emotions and the Enemy in an Israeli Military Unit*. Oxford: Berghahn Books.

———. 2001. "Tests of Soldierhood, Trials of Manhood: Military Service and Male Ideals in Israel." In *Military, State and Society in Israel: Theoretical and Comparative Perspectives*, ed. Daniel Maman, Zeev Rosenhek, and Eyal Ben-Ari. New Brunswick: Transaction.

Ben-Naftali, Michal. 2000. *A Chronicle of Separation: On Deconstruction's Disillusioned Love*. In Hebrew. Tel Aviv: Resling.

Berger, John. 1967. *A Fortunate Man*. London: Penguin.

———. 1972. *Ways of Seeing*. Hammondsworth: Penguin.

Berscheid, Ellen, and Harry T. Reis. 1998. "Attraction and Close Relationships." In *Handbook of Social Psychology*, vol. 2, ed. Daniel T. Gilbert, Susan T. Fiske, and Gardner Lindzey. New York: McGraw-Hill.

Biale, David. 1992. "Zionism as an Erotic Revolution." In *People of the Body: Jews and Judaism from an Embodied Perspective*, ed. Howard Eilberg-Schwartz. New York: State University of New York Press.

Bilu, Yoram. 1986. "Life-History as Text." In Hebrew. . *Megamot* 29, no. 4: 349–71.

Bordo, Suzan. 1994. "Reading the Male Body." In *The Male Body: Features, Destinations, Exposures*, ed. Laurence Goldstein. Ann Arbor: University of Michigan Press.

Boswell, John. 1994. *Same-Sex Unions in Premodern Europe*. New York: Villard Books.

Boyarin, Daniel. 1997a. "Masada or Yavneh? Gender and the Arts of Jewish Resistance." In *Jews and Other Differences: The New Jewish Cultural Studies*, ed. Jonathan Boyarin and Daniel Boyarin. Berkeley: University of California Press.

Boyarin, Daniel. 1997b. *Unheroic Conduct: The Rise of Heterosexuality and the Invention of the Jewish Man*. Berkeley: University of California Press.

Brain, Robert. 1976. *Friends and Lovers*. New York: Basic Books.

Brandes, Stanley. 1980. *Metaphors of Masculinity: Sex and Status in Andalusian Folklore*. Philadelphia: University of Pennsylvania Press.

Bray, Alan, and Michel Rey. 1999. "The Body of the Friend: Continuity and Change in Masculine Friendship in the Seventeenth Century." In *English Masculinities, 1660–1800*, ed. Tim Hitchcock and Michéle Cohen. London: Longman.

Brod, Harry. 1987. "A Case for Men's Studies." In *Changing Men: New Directions in Research on Men and Masculinity*, ed. Michael S. Kimmel. Newbury Park, CA: Sage.

Bunzl, Matti. 1997. "Theodor Herzl's Zionism as Gendered Discourse." In *Theodor Herzl and the Origins of Zionism. Austrian Studies 8*, ed. Edward Timms and Ritchie Robertson. Edinburgh: Edinburgh University Press.

Butler, Judith. 1990. *Gender Trouble: Feminism and the Subversion of Identity*. New York: Routledge.

———. 1993. *Bodies That Matter: On the Discursive Limits of "Sex."* New York: Routledge.

———. 1997. *The Psychic Life of Power: Theories in Subjection*. Stanford, CA: Stanford University Press.

Caplan, Gregory A. 2003. "Militarism and Masculinity as Keys to the 'Jewish Question' in Germany." In *Military Masculinities: Identity and the State*, ed. Paul R. Higate. Westport, CT: Praeger.

Case, Sue-Ellen. 1989. "Toward a Butch-Femme Aesthetic." In *Making a Spectacle: Feminist Essays on Contemporary Women's Theater*, ed. Lynda Hart. Ann Arbor: University of Michigan Press.

Collinson, David L. 1988. "Engineering Humor: Masculinity, Joking and Conflict in Shop-Floor Relations." *Organization Studies* 9, no. 2: 181–199.

Coltrane, Scott. 1994. "Theorizing Masculinities in Contemporary Social Science." In *Theorizing Masculinities*, ed. Harry Brod and Michael Kaufman. Thousand Oaks, CA: Sage.

Connell, Robert W. 1987. *Gender and Power*. Berkeley: University of California Press.

———. 1995. *Masculinities*. Cambridge: Polity Press.

———. 1996. "Teaching the Boys: New Research on Masculinity, and Gender Strategies for Schools." *Teachers College Record* 98, no. 2: 206–235.

D'Andrade, Roy. 1987. "A Folk Model of the Mind." In *Cultural Models in Language and Thought*, ed. Dorothy Holland and Naomi Quinn. Cambridge: Cambridge University Press.

Deitcher, David. 2001. "Dear Friends: American Photographs of Men Together, 1840–1918." New York: Harry N. Abrams.

Dekel, Irit. 2001. "Nationality Enclaved: Peace and Democracy Watch at Rabin Square." Unpublished manuscript. Tel Aviv: Tel Aviv University.

Denzin, Norman K. 1970. "The Sociological Interview." In *The Research Act in Sociology: A Theoretical Introduction to Sociological Methods*, ed. Norman K. Denzin. London: Butterworths.

Denzin, Norman K. and Yvonna S. Lincoln, ed. 1994. *Handbook of Qualitative Research*. Thousand Oaks, CA: Sage.

Derrida, Jacques. 1997. *Politics of Friendship*. Translated by George Collins. London: Verso.

Du Bois, Cora. 1974. "The Gratuitous Act: An Introduction to the Comparative Study of Friendship Patterns." In *The Compact: Selected Dimensions of Friendship*, ed. Elliot Leyton. Toronto: University of Toronto Press.

Durkheim, Emile. 1915. *The Elementary Forms of the Religious Life*. Translated by Joseph Ward Swain. London: Allen and Unwin.

Eisenstadt, Shmuel N. 1974. "Friendship and the Structure of Trust and Solidarity in Society." In *The Compact: Selected Dimensions of Friendship*, ed. Elliot Leyton. Toronto: University of Toronto Press.

Elon, Amos. 1975. *Herzl*. New York: Holt Rinehart and Winston.

Emerson, Joan P. 1969. "Negotiating the Serious Import of Humor." *Sociometry* 32, no. 2: 169–181.

Enloe, Cynthia. 1989. *Bananas, Beaches and Bases: Making Feminist Sense of International Politics*. Berkeley: University of California Press.

Epstein, Isidore, ed. 1935. *The Babylonian Talmud: Seder Nezikin*. London: Soncino Press.

Erikson, Erik H. 1980. "Themes of Adulthood in the Freud-Jung Correspondence." In *Themes of Work and Love in Adulthood*, ed. Neil J. Smelser and Erik H. Erikson. Cambridge, MA: Harvard University Press.

Erlich, Shmuel H. 1998. "Adolescents' Reactions to Rabin's Assassination: A Case of Patricide?" *Adolescent Psychiatry* 22: 189–205.

Eshel, Yohanan, Ruth Sharabany, and Udi Friedman. 1998. "Friends, Lovers and Spouses: Intimacy in Young Adults." *British Journal of Social Psychology* 37, no. 1: 41–57.

Feige, Michael. 2000. "Yitzhak Rabin, His Commemoration and the Commemoration of His Commemoration." In *Contested Memory-Myth, Nation and Democracy: Thoughts after Rabin's Assassination*, ed. Lev Grinberg. In Hebrew. Beer-Sheva: Ben Gurion University.

Fine, Gary A. 1984. "Humorous Interaction and the Social Construction of Meaning: Making Sense in a Jocular Vein." *Studies in Symbolic Interaction* 5: 83–101.

———. 1988. "Good Children and Dirty Play." *Play and Culture* 1, no. 1: 43–56.

Fine, Gary, A. and Kent Sandstrom. 1993. "Ideology in Action: A Pragmatic Approach to a Contested Concept." *Sociological Theory* 11, no. 1: 21–38.

Fishbane, Michael. 1994. *The Kiss of God: Spiritual and Mystical Death in Judaism*. Seattle: University of Washington Press.

Fontana, Andrea, and James H. Frey. 1994. "Interviewing: The Art of Science." In *Handbook of Qualitative Research*, ed. Norman K. Denzin and Yvonna S. Lincoln. Thousand Oaks, CA: Sage.

Foucault, Michel. 1997. *Ethics: Subjectivity and Truth. The Essential Works of Michel Foucault, Vol. 1*. New York: New Press.

Freud, Sigmund. 1953/1974. *Standard Edition of the Complete Psychological Works of Sigmund Freud*. Vol. 12. Translated by James Strachey. London: Hogarth.

Fromm, Erich. 1973. *The Anatomy of Human Destructiveness*. London: Jonathan Cape.

Fussell, Paul. 1975. *The Great War and Modern Memory*. Oxford: Oxford University Press.

Gal, Reuven. 1986. *A Portrait of the Israeli Soldier*. New York: Greenwood Press.

Gay, Peter, ed. 1989. *The Freud Reader*. New York: Norton and Company.

Geertz, Clifford. 1983. *Local Knowledge: Further Essays in Interpretive Anthropology*. New York: Basic Books.

Geffen, Aviv. 1995. "Crying for You." in *Shalom Haver: The collection*. In Hebrew. Tel Aviv: Helicon/Hed Artzi/NMC.

Gellner, Ernst. 1983. *Nations and Nationalism*. Oxford: Blackwell.

Gergen, Kenneth J. 1991. *The Saturated Self: Dilemmas of Identity in Contemporary Life*. New York: Basic Books.

Gergen, Mary M. 1992. "Life Stories: Pieces of a Dream." In *Storied Lives: The Cultural Politics of Self-Understanding*, ed. George C. Rosenwald and Richard L. Ochberg. New Haven, CT: Yale University Press.

Gergen, Mary M., and Kenneth J. Gergen. 1995. "What Is This Thing Called Love: Emotional Scenarios in Historical Perspective." *Journal of Narrative and Life History* 5, no. 3: 221–237.

Giddens, Anthony. 1987. *The Nation-State and Violence*. Berkeley: University of California Press.

———. 1991. *Modernity and Self-Identity: Self and Society in the Late Modern Age*. Stanford, CA: Stanford University Press.

Gilligan, Carol. 1982. *In a Different Voice: Psychological Theory and Women's Development*. Cambridge, MA: Harvard University Press.

Gilligan, Carol, and Eve Stern. 1988. "The Riddle of Femininity and the Psychology of Love." In *Passionate Attachments*, ed. Willard Gaylin and Ethel Person. New York: Free Press.

Gilmore, David D. 1990. *Manhood in the Making: Cultural Concepts of Masculinity*. New Haven, CT: Yale University.

Giorgi, Amedeo. 1975. "An Application of Phenomenological Method in Psychology." In *Duquesne Studies in Phenomenological Psychology, Vol. 2*, ed. Amedeo Giorgi, Constance T. Fisher, and Edward L. Murray. Pittsburgh, PA: Duquesne University Press.

Gluzman, Michael. 1997. "Craving for Heterosexuality: Zionism and Sexuality in Alt-Neu Land." In Hebrew. *Theoria Ve-Bikoret* 11 (winter): 145–62. Greenfeld, Liah. 1992. *Nationalism: Five Roads to Modernity*. Cambridge, MA: Harvard University Press.

Greenfield, Liah. 1992. *Nationalism: Five Roads to Modernity*. Cambridge, MA: Harvard University Press.

Griffith, Mark. 1995. "Brilliant Dynasts: Power and Politics in the Oresteia." *Classical Antiquity* 14, no. 1: 62–129.

Gurdin, Barry J. 1996. *Amitie/Friendship: An Investigation into Cross-Cultural Styles in Canada and the United States*. San Fransisco: Austin and Winfield.

Guri, Haim. 1949. *Flowers of Flame*. In Hebrew. Tel Aviv: Sifriat Poalim.

———. 1950/2000. *Until the Breaking of Day*. In Hebrew. Tel Aviv: Ha-Kibbutz Ha-Meuchad.

———. 1981. *The Crazy Book*. In Hebrew. Tel Aviv: Am Oved.

Gutmann, Matthew C. 1997. "Trafficking in Men: The Anthropology of Masculinity." *Annual Review of Anthropology* 26: 385–409.

Ha'aretz. 2001. "Alternatives to the 'Love of the Country' on Their Way to the Code of Ethics." In Hebrew. 24 January.

Halperin, David. 1990. *One Hundred Years of Homosexuality, and Other Essays on Greek Love*. New York: Routledge.

———. 2002. *How to Do the History of Male Homosexuality*. Chicago: University of Chicago Press.

Hammond, Dorothy, and Alta Jablow. 1987. "Gilgamesh and the Sun-Dance Kid: The Myth of Male Friendship." In *The Making of Masculinities: The New Men's Studies*, ed. Harry Brod. Boston: Allen and Unwin.

Handelman, Don, and Lea Shamgar-Handelman. 1997. "The Presence of Absence: The Memorialism of National Death in Israel." In *Grasping Land: Space and Place in Contemporary Israeli Discourse and Experience*, ed. Eyal Ben-Ari and Yoram Bilu. Albany: State University of New York Press.

Hansen, Karen, V. 1992. "'Our Eyes Behold Each Other': Masculinity and Intimate Friendship in Antebellum New England." In *Men's Friendships*, ed. Peter M. Nardi. Newbury Park, CA: Sage.

Hatt, Michael. 1993. "The Male Body in Another Frame: Thomas Eakins' "the Swimming Hole" as a Homoerotic Image." In *Journal of Philosophy and the Visual Arts: The Body*, ed. Andrew Benjamin. London: Ernst and Sohn, Academy Group.

Hazan, Haim. 2001. *Simulated Dreams: Israeli Youth and Virtual Zionism.* New York: Berghahn Books.

Helman, Sarit. 1999. "Militarism in the Construction of the Life-World of Israeli Males: The Case of the Reserves System." In *The Military and Militarism in Israeli Society*, ed. Edna Lomsky-Feder and Eyal Ben-Ari. Albany: State University of New York Press.

Henderson, Darryl W. 1985. *Cohesion, the Human Element in Battle.* Washington, D.C.: National Defencs University Press.

Hentig, H. von. 1964. *Der Nekrotope Mensch.* In German. Stuttgart: F. Enke.

Herdt, Gilbert, and Robert Stoller, J. 1990. *Intimate Communications: Erotics and the Study of Culture.* New York: Columbia University Press.

Herman, Gabriel. 1987. *Ritualized Friendship and the Greek City.* Cambridge: Cambridge University Press.

Herzfeld, Michael. 1985. *Poetics of Manhood: Contest and Identity in a Cretan Mountain Village.* Princeton, NJ: Princeton University Press.

Herzog, Chaim. 1991. *Heroes of Israel: Profiles of Jewish Courage.* In Hebrew. Tel Aviv: Edanim.

Hever, Hannan. 1986. "Alive Is the Living and Dead Is the Dead." In Hebrew. *Siman Kri'a: A Literary Critique* 19: 188–195.

Hobsbawm, Eric J. 1982. *Invention of Tradition.* Cambridge: Cambridge University Press.

Hochschild, Arlie. 1983. *The Managed Hearts.* Berkeley: University of California Press.

Holstein, James A. and Jaber F. Gubrium. 1998. "Phenomenology, Ethnomethodology, and Interpretive Practice." In *Strategies of Qualitative Inquiry*, ed. Norman K. Denzin and Yvonna S. Lincoln. Thousand Oaks, CA: Sage.

Hornblower, Simon, and Antony Spawforth, ed. 1999. *Oxford Classical Dictionary. Third Edition.* Oxford: Oxford University Press.

Horowitz, Dan. 1993. *The Heavens and the Earth: A Self-Portrait of the 1948 Generation.* In Hebrew. Jerusalem: Keter.

Housman, Michael. 2001. "Is This Play? Hazing in French Preparatory Schools." *Focaal: European Journal of Anthropology* 37: 39–47.

Israel Ministry of Foreign Affairs. 2003. "Capt. Hagai Bibi." http://www.israel-mfa.gov.il/MFA/Terrorism-+Obstacle+to+Peace/Memorial/2003/Capt+Hagai+Bibi.htm, accessed 5 December 2005.

Irrigray, Luce. 1985a. *Speculum of the Other Woman.* Translated by C. Giligan Gill. Ithaca, NY: Cornell University Press.

———. 1985b. *This Sex Which Is Not One.* Translated by Catherine Porter and Carolyn Burke. Ithaca, NY: Cornell University Press.

Josselson, Ruthellen. 1992. *The Space between Us: Exploring the Dimensions of Human Relationships.* San Francisco: Jossy-Bass.

Kaplan, Danny. 2000. "The Military as a Second Bar Mitzvah: Combat Service as an Initiation-Rite to Zionist Masculinity." In *Imagined Masculinities: Male Identity and Culture in the Modern Middle East*, ed. Mai Ghoussoub and Emma Sinclair-Webb. London: Saqi Books.

———. 2003a. *Brothers and Others in Arms: The Making of Love and War in Israeli Combat Units.* New York: Haworth.

———. 2003b."The Construction of Combat Emotions as a Central Site of "Sexonality."'" In Hebrew. *Israeli Sociology* 5, no. 1: 49–73.

Kaplan, Harold I., Benjamin J. Sadock, and Jack A. Grebb. 1994. *Kaplan and Sadock's Synopsis of Psychiatry.* Baltimore: Williams and Wilking.

Kasher, Asa. 1996. *Military Ethics.* In Hebrew. Israel: Ministry of Security.

Katriel, Tamar. 1991. *Communal Webs: Communication and Culture in Contemporary Israel.* Albany: State University of New York.

———. 2004. *Dialogic Moments: From Soul Talks to Talk Radio in Israeli Culture.* Detroit, MI: Wayne State University Press.

Katz, Jonathan, N. 1992. *Gay American History: Lesbians and Gay Men in the U.S.A.* New York: Meridian.

Kellet, Anthony. 1982. *Combat Motivation: The Behavior of Soldiers in Battle.* Boston: Kluwer.

Kern, Stephan. 1996. *Eyes of Love: The Gaze in English and French Paintings and Novels 1840–1900*. London: Reaktion Books.

Kimmel, Michael. 1994. "Masculinity as Homophobia: Fear, Shame and Silence in the Construction of Gender Identity." In *Theorizing Masculinities*, ed. Harry Brod and Michael Kaufman. Thousand Oaks, CA: Sage.

———. 1996. *Manhood in America: A Cultural History*. New York: Free Press.

———. 2000. *Gendered Society*. New York: Oxford University Press.

Kimmerling, Baruch. 1993. "Patterns of Militarism in Israel." *European Journal of Sociology* 34 no. 2: 196–223.

Kinsey, Alfred, Wardell Pomeroy, and Clyde Martin. 1948. *Sexual Behavior in the Human Male*. Philadelphia: Saunders.

Klein, Uta. 1999. "'Our Best Boys': The Gendered Nature of Civil-Military Relations in Israel." *Men and Masculinities* 2, no. 1: 47–65.

Kotes-Bar, Chen. 2004. "How to Go On." In Hebrew. http://www.fresh.co.il/dcforum/Army/9602.html, accessed 5 December 2005.

Kumar, Krishan. 1997. "Home: The Promise and Predicament of Private Life at the End of the Twentieth Century." In *Public and Private in Thought and Practice*, ed. Jeff Weintraub and Krishan Kumar. Chicago: University of Chicago Press.

Lévi-Strauss, Claude. 1963. "The Structural Study of Myth." In *Structural Anthropology*, ed. Claude Levi-Strauss. New York: Basic Books.

———. 1969. *The Elementary Structures of Kinship*. Boston: Beacon Press.

Lieblich, Amia. 1983. "Between Strength and Toughness." In *Stress in Israel*, ed. Shlomo Breznitz. New York: Nostrand Reinhold.

———. 1989. *Transition to Adulthood During Military Service: The Israeli Case*. Albany: State University of New York Press.

Lieblich, Amia, Rivka Tuval-Mashiach, and Tamar Zilber. 1998. *Narrative Research: Reading, Analysis and Interpretation*. Thousand Oaks, CA: Sage.

Liebman, Charles S. and Eliezer Don-Yehiya. 1983. *Civil Religion in Israel: Traditional Judaism and Political Culture in the Jewish State*. Berkeley: University of California press.

Lomsky-Feder, Edna. 1992. "Youth in the Shadow of War—War in the Light of Youth: Life Stories of Israeli Veterans." In *Adolescence, Careers and Culture*, ed. Wim Meeus, Martijn de Goede, Willem Kox, and Klaus Hurrelmann. The Hague: De Gruyter.

———. 1998. *As If There Was No War: Life Stories of Israeli Men*. In Hebrew. Jerusalem: Magnes.

Lomsky-Feder, Edna, and Tamar Rapoport. 2000. "Juggling Models of Masculinity: Russian-Jewish Immigrants in the Israeli Army." *Israeli Sociology* 3, no. 1: 31–51.

Lopata, Helena Z. 1981. "Friendship: Historical and Theoretical Introduction." In *Research in the Interweave of Social Roles: Friendship*, vol. 2, ed. Helena Z. Lopata. Greenwich, CT: JAI Press.

Lutz, Catherine. 1986. "Emotion, Thought, and Estrangement: Emotion as a Cultural Category." *Cultural Anthropology* 1, no. 3: 287–305.

———. 1990. "Engendered Emotion: Gender, Power and the Rhetoric of Emotional Control in American Discourse." In *Language and the Politics of Emotions*, ed. Catherine Lutz and Lila Abu-Lughod. Cambridge: Cambridge University Press.

Lyman, Peter. 1987. "The Fraternal Bond as a Joking Relationship." In *Changing Men: New Directions in Research on Men and Masculinity*, ed. Michael S. Kimmel. Newbury Park, CA: Sage.

Maghen, Zeev. 1999. "Imagine: On Love and Lennon." *Azure: Ideas for the Jewish Nation* 7 (spring).

Mannheim, Karl. 1928. "Das Problem Der Generationen." In German. *Kölner vierteljahrshefte* 2–3: 157–185, 309–330.

Maor, Haim. 2001. "The Disappearing Male." In Hebrew. *Muza* 3: 20–28.

Maoz, Rivka. 1988. "The Transformations of the Forelock in Israeli Literature." In Hebrew. *Moznaim* 62: 50–56.

Marias, Javier. 1999. *Corazon Tan Blanco*. In Hebrew. Tel Aviv: Babel.

May, Herbert G., and Bruce M. Metzger, ed. 1973. *The New Oxford Annotated Bible with the Apocrypha*. New York: Oxford University Press.

Melman, Billie. 2001. "Death of an Agent: Gender, Remembrance, and Commemoration." In *Jewish Women in the Yishuv and Zionism: A Gender Perspective*, ed. Margalit Shilo, Ruth Kark, and Galit Hasan-Rokem. In Hebrew. Jerusalem: Yad Ben-Zvi.

Miller, Stuart. 1983. *Men and Friendship*. Boston: Houghton Mifflin.

Milshtein, Uri, and Dov Doron. 1994. *Sayeret Shaked*. In Hebrew. Tel Aviv: Yediot Achronot.

Mintzer, Arlette. 1997. "Stability and Satisfaction in Close Relationships and Associated Factors: Relationship Style, Homosexual Identity and Social Support in Male Homosexuals in Israel." In Hebrew. Unpublished PhD dissertation. Jerusalem: Hebrew University.

Miron, Dan. 1992. *Facing the Silent Brother: Essays on the Poetry of the War of Independence*. In Hebrew. Tel Aviv: Keter and Open University.

Mishler, E. G. 1986. "The Analysis of Interview-Narratives." In *Narrative Psychology: The Storied Nature of Human Conduct*, ed. Theodore R. Sarbin. New York: Praeger.

Mitchell, Juliet. 1975. *Psycho-Analysis and Feminism*. New York: Vintage.

Monterescu, Daniel. 2003. "'Stranger Masculinities': Cultural Construction of Arab Maleness in Jaffa." In Hebrew. *Israeli Sociology* 5, no. 1: 121–59.

Morgan, David. 1994. "Theater of War: Combat, the Military and Masulinities." In *Theorizing Masculinities*, ed. Harry Brod and Michael Kauffman. Thousand Oaks, CA: Sage.

Moskos, Charles. 1993. "From Citizens' Army to Social Laboratory." *The Wilson Quarterly* (winter): 83–95.

Mosse, L. George. 1975. *Nationalization of the Masses: Political Symbolism and Mass Movements in Germany from the Napoleonic Wars through the Third Reich*. New York: Meridian.

———. 1985 *Nationalism and sexuality: Respectability and abnormal sexuality in modern Europe*. New York: Howard Fertig.

———. 1990. *Fallen Soldiers: Reshaping the Memory of World Wars*. Oxford: Oxford University Press.

———. 1993. *Confronting the Nation: Jewish and Western Nationalism*. Hanover, NH: Brandeis University Press.

———. 1996. *The Image of Man: The Creation of Modern Masculinity*. New York: Oxford University Press.

Mulvey, Laura. 1975. "Visual Pleasure and Narrative Cinema." *Screen* 16, no. 3: 6–18.

Nardi, Chen, and Rivka Nardi. 1992. *Men in Change*. In Hebrew. Tel Aviv: Modan.

Nardi, Peter, ed. 1999. *Gay Men's Friendships: Invincible Communities*. Chicago: University of Chicago Press.

Naveh, Hannah. 1998. "On Loss, Bereavement and Mourning in the Israeli Experience." In Hebrew. *Alpayim* 16: 85–118.

Neale, Steve. 1983. "Masculinity as Spectacle." *Screen* 24, no. 6: 2–19.

Ne'eman, Judd. 1999. "The Death Mask of the Moderns: A Genealogy of New Sensibility Cinema in Israel." *Israel Studies* 4, no. 1: 100–128.

Norris, C. 1991. *Deconstruction: Theory and Practice*. London: Routledge.

Oliker, Stacey J. 1998. "The Modernization of Friendship: Individualism, Intimacy, and Gender in the Nineteenth Century." In *Placing Friendship in Context*, ed. Rebecca G. Adams and Graham Allan. Cambridge: Cambridge University Press.

Oosterhuis, Harry, and Hubert Kennedy, ed. 1991. *Homosexuality and Male Bonding in Pre-Nazi Germany*. New York: Haworth.

Ortner, Sherry. 1973. "On Key Symbols." *American Anthropologist* 75, no. 5: 1338–1345.

Pateman, Carol. 1989. *The Disorder of Women: Democracy, Feminism and Political Theory*. Stanford, CA: Stanford University Press.

Pessachson, Rafi, and Talma Eligon, ed. 1981. *The Israeli Sing-Along: 200 Best Loved Israeli Songs*. In Hebrew. Tel Aviv: Kinneret.

Plath, David W. 1980. *Long Engagements: Maturity in Modern Japan*. Stanford, CA: Stanford University Press.

Plato. 1951. *The Symposium*. London: Penguin.

Pleck, Elisabeth, and Joseph H. Pleck. 1980. *The American Man*. Engelwood Cliffs, NJ: Prentice-Hall.

Pleck, Joseph. 1975. "Man to Man: Is Brotherhood Possible?" In *Old Family-New Family*, ed. Nona Glazer-Malbin. New York: Van Nostrand.

Pogrebin, Letty Cottin. 1987. *Among Friends: Who We Like, Why We Like Them, and What We Do with Them*. New York: McGraw-Hill.

Real, Terence. 1997. *I Don't Want to Talk About It: Overcoming the Secret Legacy of Male Depression*. New York: Fireside.

Rich, Adrienne. 1980. "Compulsory Heterosexuality and Lesbian Existence." *Signs* 5, no. 4: 631–660.

Rogers, Mary F. 1981. "Ideology, Perspective, and Praxis." *Human Studies* 4, no. 2: 145–164.

Rosaldo, Michelle Z. 1974. "Woman, Culture and Society: A Theoretical Overview." In *Woman, Culture and Society*, ed. Michelle Z. Rosaldo and Louise Lamphere. Stanford, CA: Stanford University Press.

Rosch, Eleanor. 1978. "Principles of Categorization." In *Cognition and Categorization*, ed. Eleanor Rosch and Barbara Lloyd. Hillsdale, NJ: Erlbaum.

Rosenthal, Gabriele. 1993. "Reconstruction of Life Stories: Principles of Selection in Generating Stories for Narrative Biographies Interviews." In *The Narrative Study of Lives*, ed. Ruthellen Josselson and Amia Lieblich. Newbury Park, CA: Sage.

Rosenthal, Ruvik. 2001. *The Language Arena: A Portrait of Israeli Hebrew*. In Hebrew. Tel Aviv: Am Oved.

Rosen-Zvi, Yishai. 1999. "*Yetzer Ha-Ra*, Sexuality and *Ychud* Prohibitions: A Chapter in Talmudic Anthropology." In Hebrew. *Teorya Vebikoret* 14 (summer): 55–84.

Rosner, Menahem. 1979. "Changes in Leisure Culture in the Kibbutz." *Loisir et société: Society and leisure* 2, no. 2: 451–481.

Rotblit, Yaakov. 1973. "Song for Peace." In *"Hanachal" band—the big hits*. In Hebrew. Tel Aviv: Hed Artzi.

Rotundo, A. E. 1989. "Romantic Friendships: Male Intimacy and Middle-Class Youth in the Northern United States, 1800–1900." *Journal of Social History* 23, no. 1: 1–15.

Rougemont, Denis de. 1940/1974. *Love in the Western World*. Translated by Montgomery Belgion. New York: Harper and Row.

Rubin, Lillian B. 1985. *Just Friends: The Role of Relationships in Our Lives*. New York: Harper and Row.

———. 1986. "On Men and Friendship." *Psychoanalytic Review* 73, no. 2: 165–181.

Rubin, Zick. 1975. "Disclosing Oneself to a Stranger: Reciprocity and Its Limits." *Journal of Experimental Social Psychology* 11, no. 3: 233–260.

Rubinshtein, Amnon. 1977. *To Be a Free People*. In Hebrew. Jerusalem: Schocken.

Rumsey, Burt. 1995. *The Male Dancer: Bodies, Spectacles, Sexualities*. London: Routledge.

Sarbin, Theodore. 1995. "Emotional Life, Rhetoric and Roles." *Journal of Narrative and Life History* 5, no. 3: 213–220.

Sasson-Levy, Orna. 2000. *The Construction of Gender Identity in the Israeli Military*. Unpublished PhD dissertation. In Hebrew. Jerusalem: Hebrew University.

———. 2002. "Constructing Identities at the Margins: Masculinities and Citizenship in the Israeli Army." *Sociological Quarterly* 43, no. 3: 357–383.

Scheff, Thomas J. 1977. "The Distancing of Emotion in Ritual." *Current Anthropology* 18, no. 3: 483–505.

———. 1994. "Emotions and Identity: A Theory of Ethnic Nationalism." In *Social Theory and Politics of Identity*, ed. Craig Cahous. Oxford: Basil Blackwell.

Scholem, Gershom. 1981. *Walter Benjamin: The Story of a Friendship*. Translated by Harry Zohn. Philadelphia: Jewish Publication Society of America.

Schwarzenbach, Sibyl. 1996. "On Civic Friendship." *Ethics* 107, no. 1: 97–128.

Scollmeier, Paul. 1994. *Other Selves: Aristotle on Personal and Political Friendship*. Albany: State University of New York Press.

Sedgwick, Eve-Kosofsky. 1985. *Between Men: English Literature and Male Homosocial Desire*. New York: Columbia University Press.

Shafir, Gershon, and Peled Yoav. 1998. "Citizenship and Stratification in an Ethnic Democracy." *Ethnic and Racial Studies* 21, no. 3: 408–428.

Shalev, Yitzhak. 1951. *Holding an Almond Branch: Songs [Ochezet Anaf Shaked]*. In Hebrew. Tel Aviv: Devir.

Shamir, Moshe, Haim Guri, and Natan Shacham. 1994. *The Palmach Generation in Literature and Poetry: 50th Anniversary of the Palmach Generation*. In Hebrew. Tel Aviv: Tag Publishing.

Shamir, Moshe, and Shlomo Tanai, ed. 1943/1992. *Yalqut Ha'reim: Young Hebrew Writers in the Mid Forties*. In Hebrew. Jerusalem: Bialik Institute.

Shavit, Ari. 2002. "A Leader Waiting for a Sign." In Hebrew. *Ha'aretz*, 22 March, 14–20.

Shemer, Naomi. 1967. *All My Songs*. In Hebrew. Tel Aviv: Yediot Achronot.

Sherrod, Drury. 1987. "The Bonds of Men: Problems and Possibilities in Close Male Relationships." In *The Making of Masculinities: The New Men's Studies*, ed. Harry Brod. Boston: Allen and Unwin.

Silver, Allan. 1990. "Friendship in Commercial Society: Eighteenth-Century Social Theory and Modern Sociology." *American Journal of Sociology* 95, no. 6: 1474–1504.

———. 1997. "Two Different Sorts of Commerce: Friendship and Strangership in Civil Society." In *Public and Private in Thought and Practice*, ed. Jeff Weintraub and Krishan Kumar. Chicago: University of Chicago Press.

Silverman, Hugh J., ed. 1999. *Continental Philosophy VII: Philosophy and Desire*. New York: Routledge.

Simmel, George. 1915/1950. *The Sociology of George Simmel*. Translated by K. Wolff. Glencoe: Free Press.

———. 1911/1971. "The Adventurer." In *George Simmel on Individuality and Social Forms*, ed. Donald N. Levine. Chicago: Chicago University Press.

Singer, Brian. 1996. "Cultural Versus Contractual Nations: Rethinking Their Opposition." *History and Theory* 35, no. 3: 309–337.

Sion, Liora. 1997. "Images of Manhood among Combat Soldiers: Military Service in the Israeli Infantry as a Rite of Initiation from Youth to Adulthood." In Hebrew. Jerusalem: Shaine Working Papers, no. 3, Hebrew University.

Sion, Liora, and Eyal Ben-Ari. 2005. "'Hungry, Weary and Horny': Joking and Jesting among Israel's Combat Reserves." *Israel Affairs* 11, no. 4: 656–672.

Sivan, Emmanuel. 1991. *The 1948 Generation: Myth, Profile and Memory*. In Hebrew. Tel Aviv: Maarachot, Ministry of Security.

Smith, Anthony. 1998. *Nationalism and Modernity*. London: Routledge.

Sokolowski, Robert. 2002. "Phenomenology of Friendship." *Review of Metaphysics* 55, no. 3: 451–470.

Somers, Margaret R., and Gloria D. Gibson. 1994. "Reclaiming the Epistemological 'Other': Narrative and the Social Constitution of Identity." In *Social Theory and Politics of Identity*, ed. Craig Cahous. Oxford: Basil Blackwell.

Spence, D. P. 1982. *Narrative Truth and Historical Truth: Meaning and Interpretation in Psychoanalysis*. New York: Norton.

Stern-Gillet, Suzanne. 1995. *Aristotle's Philosohpy of Friendship*. Albany: State University of New York Press.

Stone, Lawrence. 1977. *The Family, Sex and Marriage in England, 1500–1800*. New York: Harper and Row.

Swidler, Ann. 1980. "Love and Adulthood in American Culture." In *Themes of Work and Love in Adulthood*, ed. Neil J. Smelser and Erik H. Erikson. Cambridge, MA: Harvard University Press.

Taharlev, Yoram (1993). *The big book of Yoram Taharlev*. In Hebrew. Tel Aviv: Am Oved.

Turner, Victor. 1974. *The Ritual Process: Structure and Anti-Structure*. New York: Cornell.

———. 1980. "Social Dramas and Stories About Them." *Critical Inquiry* 7, no. 1: 141–168.

———. 1992. *Blazing the Trail*. Tucson: University of Arizona Press.

Val de Almeida, Miguel. 1996. *The Hegemonic Male: Masculinity in a Portuguese Town*. Providence, RI: Berghahn Books.

Vinitzky-Seroussi, Vered. 2001. "Commemorating Narratives of Violence: The Yitzhak Rabin Memorial Day in Israeli Schools." *Qualitative Sociology* 24, no. 2: 245–268.

———. 2002. "Commemorating a Difficult Past: Yitzhak Rabin's Memorials." *American Sociological Review* 67, no. 1: 30–51.

Walker, Karen. 1994. "Men, Women and Friendship: What They Say; What They Do." *Gender and Society* 8, no. 2: 246–265.

Weiner, Eugene C. 1990. "The Threat to the Legitimacy of War Posed by the Fallen Soldier: The Case of Israel." In *Legitimacy and Commitment in the Military*, ed. Thomas C. Wyatt and Reuven Gal. Westport, CT: Greenwood Press.

Weintraub, Jeff. 1997. "The Theory and Politics of the Public/Private Distinction." In *Public and Private in Thought and Practice*, ed. Jeff Weintraub and Krishan Kumar. Chicago: University of Chicago Press.

Weiss, Meira. 1997. "Bereavement, Commemoration, and Collective Identity in Contemporary Israeli Society." *Anthropological Quarterly* 70, no. 2: 91–101.

Wilken, Robert L. 1994. "Procrustean Marriage Bed." *Commonwealth*, 9 September, 24–26.

Winnicott, Donald W. 1971. *Playing and Reality*. New York: Basic Books.

Wiztum, Eli, and Ruth Malkinson. 1993. "Grief and Immortalization: The Double Face of the National Myth." In *Loss and Grief in Israeli Society*, ed. Ruth Malkinson, Shimshon Rubin, and Eli Wiztum. In Hebrew. Jerusalem: Ministry of Defense.

Wohl, Robert. 1979. *The Generation of 1914*. Cambridge, MA: Harvard University Press.

Wright, Paul. 1982. "Men's Friendships, Women's Friendships, and the Alleged Inferiority of the Latter." *Sex Roles* 8, no. 1: 1–20.

Yanay, Niza. 1995. "The Meaning of Hatred as Narrative: Two Versions of an Experience." *Journal of Narrative and Life History* 5, no. 4: 353–368.

———. 1996. "National Hatred, Female Subjectivity, and the Boundaries of Cultural Discourse." *Symbolic Interaction* 19, no. 1: 21–36.

Yosef, Raz. 2001. "The Military Body: Male Masochism and Homoerotic Relations in Israeli Cinema." In Hebrew. *Teorya Vebikoret* 18 (spring): 11–46.

Yuval-Davis, Nira. 1997. *Gender and Nation*. London: Sage.

Yuval-Davis, Nira, and Floya Anthias, ed. 1989. *Woman-Nation-State*. London: Macmillan.

INDEX